SOCIAL TRANSFORMATIONS IN SCANDINAVIAN CITIES

Social Transformations in Scandinavian Cities

Nordic Perspectives on Urban Marginalization and Social Sustainability

Erica Righard, Magnus Johansson & Tapio Salonen (eds.)

NORDIC ACADEMIC PRESS

Nordic Academic Press
P.O. Box 1206
S-221 05 Lund, Sweden
www.nordicacademicpress.com

© Nordic Academic Press and the authors 2015
Typesetting: Stilbildarna i Mölle, Frederic Täckström
Cover design: Lönegård & Co
Cover image: *Something rotten in Oslo*.
Painting by Ingrid Forfang, www.askart.se
Print: ScandBook AB, Falun 2015
ISBN 978-91-87675-73-7

Contents

Social transformations in Scandinavian cities   7
An introduction
Erica Righard, Magnus Johansson & Tapio Salonen

I
THEORETICAL PERSPECTIVES
AND THE SCANDINAVIAN WELFARE STATE CONTEXT

1. The great transformation of our time   21
   Towards just and socially sustainable Scandinavian cities
   Hans Abrahamsson

2. International migration and the social-democratic welfare regime   41
   Erica Righard & Pieter Bevelander

3. Discourses of employment and inclusion in Sweden   61
   Governing citizens, governing suburban peripheries
   Magnus Dahlstedt

II
URBAN MARGINALITY
IN THE SCANDINAVIAN WELFARE STATES

4. The necessity of socio-dynamic analyses of the city   83
   The case of Malmö
   Tapio Salonen

5. Trust and distrust in Oslo   107
   Examining the relationship between the ideals of urban policy and the (re)actions of citizens
   Bengt Andersen, Per Gunnar Røe & Oddrun Sæter

6. 'Ghettoization' and 'parallel societies' in Denmark   125
   Public rhetoric and lived lives
   Tina Gudrun Jensen

7. Invading our homelands 143
   New beggars on the streets of Oslo
   Ada I. Engebrigtsen

8. The production of deportability 161
   Klara Öberg

9. Inclusion and exclusion in a residential narrative of 'us' and 'them' 181
   Anne Harju

III
INEQUALITY MANAGEMENT IN SCANDINAVIAN CITIES

10. The whole city or the city as a whole? 199
    Questioning the conceptual assumptions of social sustainability in urban governance
    Randi Gressgård

11. Segregation of living conditions in Nørrebro 217
    Iver Hornemann Møller & Jørgen Elm Larsen

12. Conflicts and meaning-making in sustainable urban development 233
    Magnus Johansson

13. Reflections on the right to health 251
    Anna Lundberg & Emma Söderman

14. Behind the line of disintegration 265
    Practices of transborder citizenship among diasporan Kurds in Sweden
    Khalid Khayati

Urban marginalization in Scandinavian cities 281
    Conclusions and ways forward
    Magnus Johansson, Tapio Salonen & Erica Righard

Acknowledgements 289

About the authors 291

Social transformations in Scandinavian cities
An introduction

Erica Righard, Magnus Johansson & Tapio Salonen

Globalization processes have been raising new questions, even new *kinds* of questions, about social inequality, international migration, and urbanization. As globalization intensified in the 1980s and 1990s, with unprecedented flows of capital and labour across national boundaries, cities have emerged as pivotal centres of social transformation. Political and academic debates have since increasingly considered the role and function of cities in the dynamic of social transformation. The consequences of growing inequalities between groups and places, the lack of political representation, and, not least, how this intersects with cross-border mobilities and ethnic diversification, are felt keenly in city life; in the everyday practices and experiences of a city's inhabitants and its particular neighbourhoods (Lefebvre 1984). This is compounded by the fact that today more than half of the world's population live in cities (UNDESA 2014); indeed, it is in cities that many contemporary social conflicts are being played out. This alone is good reason to examine the dynamics and consequences of social inequality in urban centres, which is typically the result of the restructuring of the economy and the labour market, as well as, at least from a western European horizon, the restructuring of the welfare state. This is what we aim to do, with an empirical focus on Scandinavian cities and from a comparative and interdisciplinary perspective, in this book.

Social transformations in cities

A general argument in the literature is that the development of urban polarization must be understood in its specific societal context. Social transformations in cities are complex and multi-scalar. Building on analyses of cities across the globe, the literature on social inequality in cities shows that while the dynamics and consequences of social inequality share certain features, it also unfolds in distinct ways in each locality (for example, Body-Gendrot 2012). In a more limited, Western view, the role of the state and state policies, not least social policies, is usually considered in these processes (for example, Body-Gendrot 1999; Dikeç 2001; Wacquant 2008; Glick Schiller & Simsek-Çaglar 2011; Fainstein 2010)—that is, urban marginality and social conflicts in cities must be understood in the light of the distinct demographic, geographical, and socio-political environment. Hence, it has been argued that just as the development of urban marginality and policy in France must be understood in relation to the republican tradition, so must the development in American cities be understood in terms of its liberal tradition (Dikeç 2007). Likewise, developments in Scandinavian cities should be understood in relation to the hegemonic position of the Danish, Norwegian, and Swedish welfare states.

The Scandinavian countries are generally associated with universal welfare states, high income tax, substantial welfare services, and relatively low levels of inequality. This picture is one painted in the very influential work *The Three Worlds of Welfare Capitalism* by Gøsta Esping-Andersen (1990). In his analysis Esping-Andersen depicts the Scandinavian countries as examples of the most decommodifying type of welfare states, the social-democratic welfare regime type. Today this picture must be questioned. Inequality in Scandinavian countries has been increasing in the last three decades, increasingly so since the 1990s. This is visible in widening gaps in the population when it comes to poverty, employment, education, and health. As regards income inequality, whereas in the mid-1980s Sweden was a top-ranked nation, it now has a mediocre position by international standards. Income inequality has also increased in Denmark and Norway over this period, but at a slower pace, and, while they were never top of the rankings, their level of income inequality is now lower than in Sweden (OECD 2011). Migrants are typically overrepresented in the groups lagging behind, and the patterns of inequality tend to overlap with residential segregation in cities. Moreover, in Scandinavian cities, as in many other countries, we also see social conflict and even violent unrest, as in 2008 in Rosengård in Malmö (Hallin et al. 2010), in 2009 in Landskrona (Salonen 2011), or in 2013 in Husby in Stockholm (de los Reyes et al. 2014).

These developments are intertwined, and require us not to limit discussions about social transformations to the local neighbourhood or to globalization in terms of flow, but rather to reimagine the global, national, regional, and local scales—the place categories themselves—and to chart the ways in which neoliberal globalization and the restructuring of labour, the economy, and state-led social protection and services at different scales intersect and unfold in people's everyday lives in the city (Glick Schiller & Simsek-Çaglar 2011; Smith 2001).

Cities in the Scandinavian welfare state

The Scandinavian countries have much in common when it comes to geography, population, and the historical development of the welfare state, but there are also some profound differences (Arvidsson 2007). These similarities and differences can be seen in for instance national responses to international migration, the extension of social rights to foreign citizens living in the country, and in national and urban policy. Looking at immigration, Sweden is the Scandinavian country that has received the most migrants in the post-war period—in Sweden in 2012 the foreign-born population was 15.5 per cent, in Norway 13.2, and in Denmark 8.2 per cent—meaning that the proportion of foreign-born residents in Sweden and Norway reached the levels in 'old' immigration countries, such as the US (13 per cent) (OECD 2014). The migrants' integration has been a major policy area in all three countries, with each developing in different ways. In a comparative study of national integration policy, Sweden has been depicted as inclusive, focusing on structural constraints on integration; Denmark as restrictionist, blaming the migrants' culture for integration problems; and Norway as somewhere in between, finding its own more moderate way of going about things (Brochmann & Hagelund 2012; see also Guilherme Fernandes, 2015).

In comparison with other European countries, urbanization came rather late to Scandinavia, and its cities are generally small. Each capital metropolitan area has 1–2 million residents. For a long time, the political and academic debates were more obsessed with the depopulation of rural areas than with urbanization. While a national urban policy was established in France and the UK in the 1960s, in the Scandinavian countries this did not happen until the 1990s (Schulman 2000), by which time increasing unemployment and poverty in immigrant concentrations in suburban areas had become a political issue that spurred the emergence of a state-led urban policy. The measures taken in the three countries had much in common with the welfare state approach.

Crucially, there is a distinction to be drawn between the concepts of 'state politics' and 'local politics' (Brenner 1999, 2004). The Scandinavian countries are usually characterized as state-centred societies; societies with strong 'state politics'. This meant that urban policy was long associated with state-led policy implemented by the local authorities, instead of a locally anchored policy (Dannestam 2009); however, this has gradually changed over time. Moreover, while the conditions and driving forces were similar, urban policy as an area of political intervention developed in different directions in Denmark, Norway, and Sweden (Schulman 2000). All three are facing rising inequality married with rapid economic advancement. In spite of the commonalities, they are tackling the situation in different ways; as this volume gives examples of.

The argument and outline of this volume

The essays collected in this volume bring new understanding to the dynamics of urban marginality from a Scandinavian perspective. They highlight that Scandinavian cities share many of the problems and challenges that are well known from other countries, and how these unfold in Scandinavian cities and their social-democratic welfare state context. In this way, they challenge the standard view that Scandinavian countries are equal and peaceful.

The essays are grouped into three parts, bracketed by this general introduction to the scope of the anthology and a concluding essay discussing the main lessons learned. Of the three parts, the first presents the key theoretical perspectives in the field and introduces the reader to the questions of social sustainability and social disintegration in the Scandinavian context. The second part consists of case studies—qualitative and quantitative analyses of urban marginality in Danish, Norwegian and Swedish cities—while the third focuses on responses to inequality, both in public management and in civil society.

In the opening essay, Hans Abrahamsson provides an overview of the profoundly transformative processes of urbanization, international migration, and globalization. Maintaining that society is undergoing a 'great transformation', he argues that we are faced with a restructuring of social relations. The new economic geography and the changing role of the welfare state have together affected the most vulnerable sections of the population, and, in certain places, led to social upheaval and violent outbursts in urban areas. He proposes a model in which social sustainability seeks to strike a balance between security, development, and justice. He also calls for a shift from urban policy towards urban governance, with increased partnership and co-creation on the part of decision makers and citizens on important policy choices. This is what will determine whether cities descend into social conflict or become nodes of global governance. The two other essays in this part of the volume look at the implications of the national context. While there are many similarities in experiences of immigration and how state policy has responded to this, there are also considerable differences, and hence Erica Righard and Pieter Bevelander present figures that illustrate immigration and labour market integration among different groups in the populations of Denmark, Norway and Sweden over the last half-century. They also discuss the sea change in the social-democratic welfare regimes' responses to cross-border mobility and its consequences for access to state-provided social protection and services for different groups, demonstrating that this has led to the inclusion of certain migrants, but equally the exclusion of others. With his specific focus on Sweden, Magnus

Dahlstedt in turn outlines how the basic characteristics of the Swedish welfare state have changed, the early 1990s being the turning point. With a particular focus on labour and urban policy, he shows how the ideal of active citizenship has become a recurrent theme in public discourse, not least in relation to multi-ethnic areas in Sweden's cities. While the policy of activation is libertarian, it is at the same time disciplinary, and largely concentrated on getting the suburban population to solve their own problems. As he argues in his essay, it is against this background, in combination with the lack of opportunities, that we should understand the social movements that are fighting for equal social rights in certain urban areas.

The second part of the volume shifts focus to the immediate context, and a number of case studies of urban marginality in Scandinavian cities. While the essays describe how tensions are manifested and reproduced in cities and neighbourhoods, together they also illustrate how this unfolds differently in different places. Public discourses reproduced in politics and the media are influential, as are the lived experiences in everyday encounters. In his essay, Tapio Salonen demonstrates the need for socio-dynamic analyses of the social transformation of the city that can fully capture its exogenous, and not just its endogenous, dimensions. While the former place the city in its relevant context, the latter contribute to the understanding of relations and tensions between different spaces in the city. Furthermore, these internal and external aspects are intimately intertwined in the socio-dynamic fabric of the city. Salonen's empirical focus is Malmö's socio-dynamic development over the last two decades, linking the city's role as a node in global and regional migration to the city's differentiation—its spatial segregation and social inequality. Bengt Andersen, Per Gunnar Røe, and Oddrun Sæter then analyse socio-economic and ethno-racial residential segregation in Oslo in an essay that combines several empirical materials, showing, firstly, how the contemporary division between the affluent western and disadvantaged eastern parts of the city has historical roots that go back to the fifteenth century. Secondly, they show how the dividing line between the two parts of the city is maintained by media discourses and property developers' strategies. Thirdly, they show how interviewees, though they might aspire to the ideals of an inclusive city, in their everyday practices actually reproduce the city's divisions.

Tina Gudrun Jensen's essay takes the discourses of 'ghettoization' and 'parallel lives' in Denmark's public debate and contrasts them with the narratives and practices encountered during field studies in a mixed neighbourhood in Copenhagen. It explores the ongoing negotiation of identities and relationships in a certain multi-ethnic neighbourhood and how these relate to and interact with those public discourses. Cultural complexity, based on understandings acquired in everyday interactions in the multi-ethnic neighbourhood, presents a different image of multi-ethnic neighbourhoods than that conjured up by essentialist cultures and the polarization envisaged in the assertions of 'ghettoization' and 'parallel lives'. Returning to Oslo, Ada Ingrid Engebrigtsen's essay focuses on poor newcomers to the city. Using conversations with Romanian Roma begging on the city streets and reactions to this, she shows how place is being contested. By turning public spaces into 'mobile homes', the Romanian beggars challenge the production of safe neighbourhoods consisting of reliable social subjects. The public debate is dichotomized between those who want to help the beggars and those who want to ban begging, with the government seeking to maintain its image as a humanitarian state while at the same time controlling and limiting the possibilities to beg. Klara Öberg, in her essay on the dynamics of Sweden's informal labour market, charts the restructuring of the Swedish welfare state and its implications for labour market relations. Describing the everyday experience of asylum-seekers and irregular migrants working in Gothenburg's informal economy, matched with the employers' view of the situation, she pinpoints the vulnerability that deportability involves and the precariousness these workers experience. Anne Harju then examines how the inhabitants of the post-industrial city of Landskrona in southern Sweden respond to the narratives of 'Swedes' and 'immigrants' currently circulating in the city. Drawing on long-term ethnographic fieldwork, she identifies distinct narratives of 'old' (economic) immigrants, 'new' (refugee) immigrants, and persons with a Swedish background, and shows how these stereotypes are reproduced by representatives of all three groups. She maintains that the prevalent figurations and power relations are very much a case of the established and the outsiders, as in Norbert Elias's work—the established having a more favourable position in relation to the newcomers.

The third and final part of the book looks at how local authorities and civil society respond to urban marginality, with three essays on different aspects of urban strategy to manage tensions and achieve social sustainability in Malmö and Copenhagen, and two essays on civil society, focusing on activism in Malmö, and citizenship practices across borders respectively. Thus Randi Gressgård analyses the assumptions behind the concept of social sustainability in Swedish urban governance and Malmö's urban strategy—a strategy in which 'the whole city' seems to drift towards 'the city as whole', invoking a unifying notion of one future for the city as a single entity. Gressgård warns that if diverging representations of the city and conflicting policy goals are neglected, there is a risk that the strategic framing of social sustainability will reproduce the status quo and thus contribute to the further marginalization of targeted populations. Iver Hornemann Møller and Jørgen Elm Larsen then take us to Nørrebro, a historical locus for immigration and today one of the most immigrant-dense districts in Copenhagen. The essay outlines how Copenhagen City Council's integration policy over the last decade has diverged from the national integration policy, becoming more inclusive and less repressive as regards ethnic and religious pluralism in the city. Relying on survey data, they argue that in spite of large income and health discrepancies between Danes and immigrants and their descendants, there is a high degree of interaction and recognition between different groups of inhabitants in Nørrebro. This means that while Nørrebro to some degree is an instance of social sustainability, at the same time it is threatened by several tensions born from inequality and the reproduction of public and media representations of division and conflict. In his essay, Magnus Johansson discusses a case of value conflicts in an urban regeneration project in Rosengård, a disadvantaged, immigrant-dense housing district in Malmö. As part of the regeneration project, the local authorities and property developers met, together with a number of other actors, in a series of structured workshops in order to design an action plan to achieve a sustainable neighbourhood. During the workshops, it became evident that it would not be possible to combine socially guided development projects and market principles. In the end, the property developers walked out and the initiative came to nothing. The lesson to be learned is that where value conflicts exist, they will be too complex to be solved in a finite number of workshops. This also raises the question of the extent to which sustainable urban development should be a consensus- and expert-driven process, or whether it would gain more from being practice-oriented.

The two final essays in this section direct our focus to civil society. Both bring up examples that challenge the national boundaries of belonging: the first by looking at undocumented persons, the second by considering transnational dynamics of belonging. Anna Lundberg and Emma Söderberg start from the experiences of undocumented young men who arrived in Sweden as unaccompanied minors, and ask questions about their right to healthcare in Malmö. The essay outlines the national and local regulation of healthcare rights for undocumented minors, and, using qualitative fieldwork, describes attempts to exercise those rights. While the local regulations in Malmö are more inclusive than the national ones, much remains before these young people feel they have the right to have rights. In the final essay, Khalid Khayati considers the dynamics of transborder citizenship among Swedish Kurds. Transborder citizenship refers to identities and practices of belonging that are simultaneously anchored in the countries of settlement and origin—in this case, Sweden and Kurdistan. Drawing on long-term fieldwork among Kurds in Sweden, in principle people with political and cultural authority in the Kurdish diaspora, Khayati argues that the Swedish welfare state, and not least its system of grants for associations, has contributed to the building of a strong Kurdish diaspora in Sweden. This has brought political and cultural mobilization, for instance through political manifestations and the production of Kurdish-language publications. The essay illustrates how international migration and national contexts intersect, and, in varying ways, sustain globalization processes in the people's everyday lives and in organizations at the local, national, and transnational levels.

The essays in this book together provide a theoretical and empirical analysis of how the lived experience of migration, urban inequality, and residential segregation intersects with official policy, unfolding in urban landscapes in Denmark, Norway, and Sweden. Much of the literature on social transformation in the cities of western welfare states has concentrated on western Europe and North America, and in particular the US and France. Interestingly, the Scandinavian context of social transformation in cities has been less studied—far less in a way that cuts across national, disciplinary, and methodological boundaries, as we do here. In the conclusive discussion we position these Scandinavian experiences in an international context.

References

Arvidsson, H. (2007) 'Skandinavisk modernisering: Särdrag och likheter', in G. Alsmark, T. Kallehave & B. Moldenhawer (eds.) *Migration och tillhörighet: Inklusions- och exklusionsprocesser i Skandinavien* (Gothenburg: Makadam).

Body-Gendrot, S. (1999) *The social control of cities? A comparative perspective* (Malden: Blackwell).

—— (2012) *Globalization, fear and insecurity: The challenges for cities north and south* (Basingstoke: Palgrave Macmillan).

Brenner, N. (1999) 'Beyond State-Centrism? Space, territoriality, and geographical scale in globalization studies', *Theory & Society*, 28/1, 39–78.

—— (2004) *New state spaces: Urban governance and the rescaling of statehood* (Oxford: OUP).

Brochmann, G. & A. Hagelund (2012) *Immigration policy and the Scandinavian welfare state, 1945-2010* (Basingstoke: Palgrave Macmillan).

Dannestam, T. (2009) *Stadspolitik i Malmö: Politikens meningsskapande och materialitet* (Lund Political Studies 155; Lund: Lund University).

de los Reyes, P., M. Hörnqvist, K. Boréus, F. Estrada, J. Flyghed, A. González Arriagada, M. Lundgren & M. Lundström (2014) *'Bilen brinner ... men problemen är kvar': Berättelser om Husbyhändelserna i maj 2013* (Stockholm: Stockholmia).

Dikeç, M. (2001) 'Justice and the spatial imagination', *Environment & Planning A*, 33/10, 1785–1805.

—— (2007) *Badlands of the republic: Space, politics, and urban policy* (Oxford: Blackwell).

Esping-Andersen, G. (1990) *The three worlds of welfare capitalism* (Cambridge: Polity).

Fainstein, S. (2010) *The just city* (Ithaca: Cornell University Press).

Glick Schiller, N. & A. Simsek-Çaglar (2011) (eds.) *Locating migration: Rescaling cities and migrants* (Ithaca: Cornell University Press).

Guilherme Fernandes, A. (2015) '(Dis)empowering new immigrants and refugees through participation in introduction programmes in Sweden, Denmark and Norway', *Journal of Immigrant & Refugee Studies*, 15/3, 245–64.

Hallin, P. O., A. Jashari, C. Listerborn & M. Popoola (2010) *Det är inte stenarna som gör ont: Röster från Herrgården, Rosengård—om konflikter och erkännande* (Malmö Publikationer i Urbana Studier, MAPIUS 5; Malmö: Malmö högskola).

Lefebvre, H. (1984) *Everyday life in the modern world* (New Brunswick: Transaction).

OECD (2011) *Divided we stand: Why inequality keeps rising* (Paris: OECD Publishing) <http://dx.doi.org/10.1787/migr_outlook-2014-en>.

OECD (2014) *International Migration Outlook 2014* (Paris: OECD Publishing) <http://dx.doi.org/10.1787/9789264119536-en>.

Salonen, T. (2011) (ed.) *Hela staden: Social hållbarhet eller desintegration?* (Umeå: Boréa).

Schulman, M. (2000) *Stadspolitik och urbanforskning i Norden* (Stockholm: Nordregio).

Smith, M. P. (2001) *Transnational urbanism: Locating globalization* (Malden: Blackwell).

UNDESA (United Nations Department of Economic and Social Affairs) Population Division (2014) *World urbanization prospects: The 2014 revision, highlights* (ST/ESA/SER.A/352; United Nations).

Wacquant, L. (2008) *Urban outcasts: A comparative sociology of advanced marginality* (Cambridge: Polity).

I

THEORETICAL PERSPECTIVES AND
THE SCANDINAVIAN WELFARE STATE CONTEXT

CHAPTER 1

The great transformation of our time
Towards just and socially sustainable Scandinavian cities

Hans Abrahamsson

Drawing upon studies of two medium-sized Swedish cities, this essay deals with the role of cities in working towards social sustainability. It will be argued that the potentialities are challenged by three related processes, exposing them to considerable societal strain. The uneven course of globalization, the changing nature of migration, and accelerating urbanization have brought several cities to the brink of being torn apart. The essay thus discusses the area in which most cities find themselves in trouble, as well as some of the deciding factors in the direction in which the cities are heading. Socially sustainable development is here understood as a point of balance between the three dominant values that guide the main ideologies, and hence societal development in recent history. By highlighting the relationship between security, development, and justice, it is argued that urban social cohesion demands 'proventive' security (in a Burtonian sense), where acts of prevention are combined with acts of promotion to build on strengthened popular participation in local democracy. The transition from urban politics to a brand of urban governance with increased partnership calls for decision makers and citizens to come together on important policy choices. This co-creation, however, must encompass the whole decision-making process, stretching from the formulation of the problem and analysis of the structures of possibility to the identification of the measures to be taken and their implementation.

Setting the scene

The processes of globalization, migration, and urbanization, interlinked and self-reinforcing as they are, constitute the main driving forces behind the great changes of our day. Globalization, thanks to the rise of information technologies, has compressed time and space and increased people's mobility and connectivity (Scholte 2000). The world's economic epicentre has started to move east and south, strengthening the geopolitical shift towards a multipolar world order, with the result that the Western world's stranglehold on international agenda-setting is starting to slacken. Europe and the US have tried hard to maintain their dominance by becoming knowledge societies, with the catchwords innovation, flexibility, and cognitive skills; nevertheless, the BRICS countries (Brazil, Russia, India, China, and South Africa) are about to overtake them as engines of economic growth. Indeed, economic growth in India and China is expected to bring some 1.6 billion workers into the global labour market in the next decade. If so, it would change production modes and consumption patterns beyond all recognition, which would have the effect of increasing the rivalry for markets and raw materials, let alone increasing environmental stress and climate challenges.

The process has also had a strong impact on the pattern of migration—the flow of people between different places in global times (Castles 2010; Castles et al. 2014). In an era of fluidity and openness, populations have become more mobile and migration less permanent, with new driving forces or push and pull factors. The use of the internet means that cyberspace can connect migrants with their relatives, making it possible for them to lead their everyday lives in two or more different places simultaneously, thus strengthening the transnational dimension of migration (Eastmond & Åkesson 2007; Righard 2008).

New meeting places are created, most frequently in urban areas. People are attracted by the modern lifestyle offered in the cities and the opportunities it provides. It is primarily migration that is driving the rapid pace of urbanization and its astounding duplication, expected only thirty years from now. This is where the social networks are located; this is where people search for job opportunities. The new economic geography (Krugman 2010) has drawn attention to the new role of cities in the sphere of production, a consequence of the transformation of national production systems into global value chains and networks of assembly, for which cities have become important nodal points. The unequal development that accompanies this, not least the result of the global networks' increased need for both high- and low-skilled workers, has changed the geography of global poverty and misery (Kanbur & Sumner 2012). The poor no longer live mainly in rural areas in poor countries; the new geography sees an increasing number of poor people living in urban areas of middle-income and even high-income countries. Subsequently, a Global South is emerging alongside a Global North in one and the same city, and without borders in between. The concepts of the Global South and the Global North do not refer to their geographical location, but principally to economic and political exclusion and economic and political inclusion respectively.

Historical and theoretical framework

Globalization is here taken to be a lengthy historical process. It commenced as soon as people began to move around and spread their different ideas and beliefs thousands of years ago. Globalization came to a temporary halt during the Enlightenment in conjunction with the nation-state project: following the Peace of Westphalia in 1648, the nation-state took over and drove other actors out of the political arena, and what ensued turned out to be a dark time in European history (Hettne 2009), as a succession of bloody wars extended over hundreds of years. In 1944, during the final throes of the Second World War, the Allies came to an understanding. They established the so-called Bretton Woods system, a regulatory framework for the international political economy, in order to reduce armed conflict. The logic behind this was to create greater economic interaction and, through enhanced interdependence, decrease the scope for political tension between nations (Abrahamsson 2003).

In order to become sufficiently competitive (Cerny 1997), the state many countries stopped serving as filters, trying to absorb un-

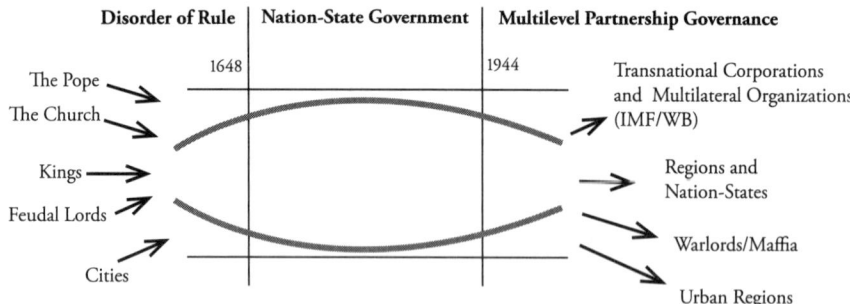

Fig. 1.1. The changing role of the state over the Pre-Westphalian, Westphalian and the Post-Westphalian time periods marked by ruling disorder, the government of Nation-States, and governance through multilevel partnership respectively (after Hettne 2009).

desirable disturbances from the world around them, and went over to functioning as transmission belts that would draw in foreign investment (Cox & Sinclair 1996). Over time, individual nation-states' sovereignty, not to mention their room for political manoeuvre, became increasingly restricted. Economic decision-making became globalized much faster than political decision-making. The state was sidelined in the national political space and gradually replaced by power structures that were more difficult to grasp (Hettne 2009). Among these were international frameworks, transnational companies, supranational regional cooperation, and sub-national regional bodies and local authorities, which, often in partnership with economic actors at the local level, increased their influence at the expense of the state. The state's withdrawal from the political arena has been somewhat equivocal, however. While there are signs of reduced state activity in the welfare sector (some describe this as a transition from the welfare state to the welfare society, others as from welfare to workfare), there is also an evident increase in the state's micromanagement in other areas—particularly those related to surveillance and control (Brown 2010).

In terms of development theory, we can understand this progression with the help of the Hungarian historian and anthropologist Karl Polanyi and his widely cited classic, *The Great Transformation* (2001 [1944]). The era he studied—from 1750 to the outbreak of the Second World War—was characterized by a double movement.

The first consisted of the expansion of the market economy and the integration of the key factors in production, work, and capital. This meant that the economy was 'disembedded' from the social institutions in which it was previously rooted. The second movement, in the form of resistance from below, eventually evolved in response to this initial development. Polanyi pointed out that resistance to the self-regulating market 'may happen in a great variety of ways, democratic and aristocratic, constitutionalist and authoritarian, perhaps even in a fashion yet utterly unforeseen' (ibid. 259). Accordingly, a dysfunctional economy risked giving rise to various countervailing forces, socialist as well as fascist—and the latter 'at the price of the extirpation of all democratic institutions' (ibid. 245).

In line with Polanyian thinking, the British economic geographer and urban researcher David Harvey argues that the market's pursuit of decentralization and privatization, supported and facilitated by the policies of the state, is a natural consequence of the present conditions of capital formation and its process of accumulation based upon the dispossession of the common people (Harvey 2003). Expanded markets and new investments in production and sales that go beyond the traditional production of commodities are required if the economic crisis is to be resolved.

Restructured social relations

The great transformation of our time, with its new economic geography and the changing role of the state, has made it more difficult to meet people's demands for economic security and social welfare. One consequence of this has been a restructuring of social relations. The need for external legitimacy has become prioritized at the expense of internal legitimacy, so gradually transforming state policies from welfare programmes to workfare activities. The social contract, which in modern times and in a Western context has been the basis of internal legitimacy and societal stability (Munck 2005), has started to wither away. Reduced social spending has affected the most vulnerable and exposed in the population. Many of them have seen themselves forced to create an alternative and more informal system for security and social protection, rooted in a more closely defined and immanent basis for identity—so-called primary groups. In the process, the basis of loyalty has shifted from society to such smaller 'we-groups'. In some urban areas, parallel affinity economies with their own legal systems for the exercise of justice have emerged.

When modern institutions cease to function, such 'we-groups' or identity groups are considered to be valuable safety networks. This does not mean the state has lost significance in absolute terms; on the contrary, as we have seen, the state has tried to compensate for its reduced legitimacy and political power by increasing its control and surveillance. In this sense, paradoxically, its impact on the daily lives of ordinary citizens has increased (Brown 2010). These efforts notwithstanding, the erosion of the social contract and the erosion of welfare regimes have led to social upheaval and violent protest in urban areas, as illustrated by recent events all over Europe. The risk of violent social conflict increases with the dissatisfaction of people who lack basic needs in terms of housing and employment, and experience reduced societal belonging. This is particularly the case at a time when identity is based upon what people can afford to consume. Exclusion and alienation create frustration, shame, and outrage (Scheff & Retzinger 2001). Dissatisfied workers used to channel such frustrations collectively and politically. Nowadays, dissatisfied consumers rage individually even if they do swarm together, at times violently.

Cities as nodes for global governance

The processes of change that shape the great transformation of our time are instigated and set in motion by globalization, migration, and urbanization in concert. How they are dealt with politically will be decisive for the sustainability of societal development. Increased connectivity and the compression of time and space mean that different societal problems impinge on one another. An event far away will immediately have consequences somewhere else. This interconnectivity implies that the local has become interwoven with the global. Such an amalgamation—or hybridization—of the global and the local amounts to what is perhaps best termed 'glocalized' societal development (Robertsson 1995). Cities exist in a 'space of flows' (Taylor et al. 2007). Glocalization takes place in those cities capable of attracting these flows—labour, finance, technology, communication—and thereby of embodying and reflecting globalization. The concept of 'glocalization' thus tries to capture the dialectic relationship between global influences and local everyday life (Listerborn 2013).

The process of glocalization has increased the need for a holistic policy and global governance that permit coherence between different policy areas. In order to fully meet the global challenges of our time, global institutions and regulatory frameworks are needed that are capable of dealing with the conflicting goals that may arise from the divergent interests of different actors. The present lack of international institutions and legitimate organizations with the necessary mandate and capabilities to manage global challenges has thus increased the interest in the role that cities and urban settings can play in such an undertaking (Amen et al. 2011): it is where the majority of the world population lives; it is where many of the challenges are created, at the local level (Borja & Castells 1996). Even if a global regulatory framework is required in order to deal with the problems, it is consequently at the local level that pre-emptive action must be taken (Byrne 2005). That is why urban leadership and urban activists have had to deal with issues long before national governments and interstate treaties address them. This strengthens the need for coordinated joint action between the local and the global. Some researchers argue that the growth of cities, their innovative capacity, and global cross-border networks equip them with some of the tools that global governance requires for increased sustainability (Castells 1983; Sassen 2011).

Cities as battlefields for violent social conflict

The possibilities for cities to participate in global governance are, however, constrained by the immense problems and challenges they have to confront, not least due to the rate of urbanization and the subsequent unevenness of development. While cities are attractive centres for migration, the creative arts, innovation, and employment opportunities, they are also centres for acute forms of poverty, substandard housing, and homelessness (Amen et al. 2011). Hence, cities become spaces of contestation, politicizing an economic agenda that fosters social exclusion, marginalization, and uneven development (Harvey 2012). Furthermore, in urban areas people live side by side. They have different cultures, different group identities, and different chances of living decent lives. Consequently, the intensified process of globalization, together with the rate of urbanization, new patterns of migration, and transformed social relations, means that many cities find themselves in danger of being torn apart as they descend into battlefields for social conflict. If the challenges confronting them cannot be managed properly, cities will no longer be able to contribute to sustainable development.

The uneven development of globalization should partly be understood as an unwanted consequence of the emergence of the knowledge city and the distorted income distribution that tends to follow on its heels, not only between countries but above all within countries. In many developed countries, the labour market has started to split between high-income jobs that many workers lack the qualifications for, and low-paid work that they cannot live on. In addition, the strengthened demand for a high-skilled and well-educated workforce frequently results in a process of gentrification, which creates differences between housing areas. Higher levels of income and social status increase demand and push up housing prices in some areas, eventually forcing the existing residents to leave to find new homes in areas with slower price rises. The societal development following the process of gentrification further strengthens the process of segregation (Wacquant 2009). This is one of the reasons why urban divisions and internal conflict dynamics are threatening social stability in so many parts of the world.

Even in European cities, there are strong social tensions between people who find themselves doing well and those who find themselves marginalized and excluded (Dikeç 2007). As the number of 'gated communities' increases, so does the danger of reinforcing xenophobic attitudes and social exclusion (Kazepov 2005). With such urban division and subsequent 'ghettoization', the knowledge city gradually begins to lose its ability to be the innovative and creative site of learning that is required if it is to keep its competitive edge. In this way, the city tends to undermine the very basis upon which it depends for its success.

The two facets of knowledge cities

Malmö and Gothenburg in Sweden are examples of cities that have done surprisingly well in mobilizing the necessary resources in order to become attractive, competitive nodes in the global network. Both cities, with populations of 300,000 and 500,000 respectively, used to be considered too small to act alone in the global context. Greater subnational and regional cooperation has become paramount. The Gothenburg region is one of the fastest-growing in Europe. Through massive investment in transport and communication infrastructure and deliberate capitalization on synergy effects in research, technological development, and innovation that involve Sahlgrenska University Hospital, leading industrial companies such as Volvo, SKF, and Ericsson, and Chalmers University of Technology and the University of Gothenburg, the city has succeeded in placing itself on the map for foreign investors. Gothenburg's varied cultural offerings and reputation in arranging major events are thought to have been crucial in this. The Malmö region is a similar success story. With its impressive investment in IT and advanced technology, the city has managed to reverse the economic stagnation of the 1990s and the 25 per cent unemployment that followed the closure of its factories and all-important shipyard. In its place is an attractive and forward-looking green knowledge city. Its multicultural mix, with over 100 spoken languages and 160 different nationalities, is crucial in the marketing of the city's continental and international atmosphere.

The process of globalization has, however, brought uneven development and hence greater inequality—unwanted consequences that are the downside to the success stories of Malmö and Gothenburg. When aggregated over the city's population, statistics show that rising levels of segregation have left Gothenburg divided into three parts: the more affluent population has moved out to the suburbs in the south-west, leaving the city centre in the hands of the middle class, while accelerating gentrification has forced the lower middle class, workers, and migrants out of the city centre to live in the less expensive suburbs in the north-east. This development manifests itself in strong differences, be it in rates of employment, incomes, life expectancy, or health. In reality, however, the sites where the social consequences of this uneven development are felt are much more complex. In the same neighbourhood, even in the same block of flats, the prerequisites for a decent life vary significantly. The same is true of Malmö. Here too, where every third inhabitant is foreign-born, the multicultural variety of people has brought with it strong segregation (Johansson & Sernhede 2006).

The situation has been aggravated by the changing role of the state and its withdrawal from the political space. The Swedish state has abandoned its metropolitan focus and its tax-funded urban politics for a focus on urban governance. For cities such as Malmö and Gothenburg, this change has manifested itself as local development agreements paid for largely by local public–private partnerships rather than the taxpayer; the cities have tried to find their own financing through a combination of public–private partnerships and increased user fees. This has considerably increased the private sector's leverage, with the result that investment in strengthened economic growth and increased international competitiveness has been prioritized at the expense of social undertakings.

Of special concern for the socio-political development of Malmö and Gothenburg is the urban youth. According to the Swedish National Board for Youth Affairs, which has analysed the living conditions of the suburban population, 35 per cent of young people aged 20–25 in the suburbs of Rosengård (Malmö) and Angered (Gothenburg) neither work nor study. For some residential districts, that figure can reach 50–60 per cent, especially for the foreign-born and less educated. It is alarming that an increasing proportion of young people in some housing estates are the third generation of long-term unemployed. They consider themselves 'unemployable', and have simply stopped looking for jobs. Society is left incapable of harnessing the energy, intelligence, and engagement of the next generation, on which it, and particularly its ageing population, depends. The lack of affordable housing is making things worse. Many young people find themselves having to move in and out of the parental home, 'boomerang kids' who can find neither permanent work nor a permanent home of their own. Both Gothenburg and Malmö at times experience severe social upheavals, fuelled by frustration at what is perceived as discrimination, lack of respect, and lack of opportunities to live a life of dignity. The social tensions have increased as a result of transnational migration and better access to global information about what is going on in other parts of the world. The social exclusion and discrimination that people encounter worldwide rightly give racial and colonial connotations to local experiences, with frustration and alienation the result.

Cities and social sustainability

Many cities are thus torn between the possibility of becoming a node in the global network of production, capable of contributing to sustainable development, and the danger of being transformed into a battlefield for social conflict due to ever-widening gaps in income and health (Abrahamsson 2012; Graham 2010; Lidskog 2006). How cities are to navigate this intact depends on politics: it depends on how citizens and decision makers rate the fundamental values of security, development, and justice that constitute people's basic needs, and on how the resultant demands for social sustainability can be met. These are all essentially contested concepts. The understanding of the conditions that these concepts embody necessarily varies according to the social context that people find themselves in. Nonetheless, given the circumstances that characterize people's living conditions, these three concepts remain the key values that have shaped political ideologies, and have therefore greatly influenced social development in modern history (Hettne 2009).

The effect of globalization, together with the expansion of the market economy and the state's retreat from the political arena, has been to change the conditions that these concepts nominally embody. The dominant understanding or discourse of the concepts' meanings has therefore also changed. Today, security is no longer primarily linked to protection from external military threats; more often it is about people's day-to-day security, about jobs and predictability (Fierke 2007). In the network society, the security of the state has been replaced by human security. The challenges facing development in the era of globalization are less about the creation of the nation-state, the rural problem, and the conditions necessary for the modernization of the countryside. Development issues in the profoundly interconnected, inchoate post-national society are all the more concerned with how to become more inclusive, so that people can increase their participation in the collective process of building society, as well as have a greater say in their everyday lives, regardless of where they or their parents were born. For this reason, development is increasingly about education, quality of life, and public health, and justice is not just about the distribution of material and immaterial resources, but also about cultural recognition and political influence (Fainstein 2010). Justice has increasingly come to mean access to the spaces where the economic and political decisions are taken that affect people's daily lives and livelihoods. Given the uneven development spurred on by globalization and the discussion of sustainable development, the issue of social justice and social inclusion has also recently been adopted as an additional dimension to the concept of justice.

Social sustainability

This brings us to the issue of social sustainability. Here we are also met by a concept whose fundamental significance is debated; a floating signifier that can essentially mean almost anything. Some of the literature on sustainability seeks to give the concept a more definitive meaning by suggesting that social sustainability is a combination of social equity and 'community sustainability', which in turn may be defined as sustainability in a local context or neighbourhood (Dempsey et al. 2011). Others refer to the question of social cohesion—the factors that hold a society together, social cohesion is about people's relationships with one another, or social capital, for which civil society is one of a number of crucial factors (Putnam 1996). Numerous urban researchers therefore argue that cities' ability to manage cultural diversity and to combat social inequality and discrimination will be decisive for their opportunities to develop in an increasingly globalized world; as many define social sustainability as the ability to foster a climate that promotes coexistence between groups from different cultural and social backgrounds, thus encouraging social interaction as well as improved quality of life for all. Social sustainability therefore means that cities must be able to become counterweights, balancing exclusion by being as inclusive as possible (Polèse & Stren 2000; Borja & Castells 1996).

In a globalized world, where the local is increasingly intertwined with the global, I would argue that in any given social context, the way that people relate to the dominant political ideologies and the three basic values—security, development, and justice—on which they are grounded, together form the preconditions for social sustainability. The term social sustainability can therefore only be defined in relation to these three values. The meaning of social sustainability, in other words, is anything but arbitrary or fluid, being comprised of a sort of 'equilibrium' that exists between these three values. If there is a deficit of any one of the values (for example, a deficit of justice in relation to security and development), the system ultimately will not be socially sustainable. The necessity of equilibrium means that the issue of trade-offs and conflicting goals, and how they are dealt with, becomes central to social sustainability (see Fig 1.2).

The vertices of the triangle in the figure represent the values of security, development, and justice. The sides of the triangle may be understood as the axes of interdependence as well as the different types of trade-off and conflicting goals that exist between the values represented by each vertex. The shadowed circle represents the point of equilibrium between the values, which both lays the foundation for these concepts and constitutes the point at which the political balance of power allows social sustainability to be attained. The equilibrium's location within the triangle varies according to the social context and the political balance of power. The closer the equilibrium is to the centre of the triangle, the greater the social sustainability. The further the equilibrium is from the centre of the triangle, in the direction of any one of the vertices, the greater the emphasis on a 'lowest common denominator'. The former may be called 'strong' social sustainability; the latter, 'weak' social sustainability, on the

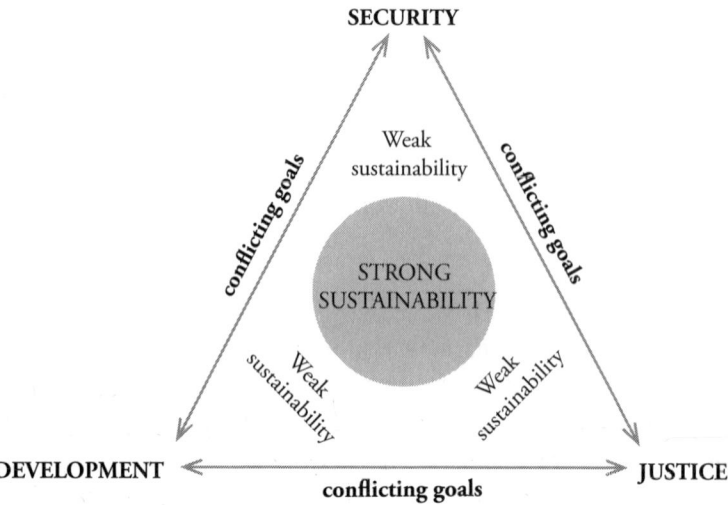

Fig. 1.2. The conflicting goals of security, development and justice, and the equilibrium of social sustainability in the middle.

verge of dissolution. Social sustainability should therefore not be understood as a static state, but rather a dynamic process in constant motion and in need of constant maintenance and reinforcement.

Ultimately, social sustainability entails a non-discriminatory social system that views the individual as a possessor of economic, social, and cultural rights (Dempsey 2011). Social sustainability and cohesion can only be achieved through a social contract and only in the presence of structural conditions that give people a sense of belonging and trust, despite the possibility that different values might exist. Such social identity and affinity strengthen people's self-respect, self-confidence, and self-reliance. This in turn augments people's ability to contribute to the maintenance and reinforcement of social sustainability.

Given this, and given the situation in Malmö and Gothenburg, I would propose the following definition of social sustainability and the socially sustainable city. Social sustainability constitutes a society's ability to deal with complex social issues and, based on this ability, to perpetuate its existence as a functioning social organism. This ability is formed and sustained by the structural relations that open up a space for the individual's participation and opportunity to understand different contexts and to feel self-confident. A socially sustainable city is a just and safe city, with numerous public spaces free from discrimination, and where the people who live and work there have a sense of social trust and fellowship. This requires inhabitants not only to feel that they are involved, but also to truly participate in the city's social development.

From negative to positive security

The pursuit of the greatest possible social sustainability, not to mention the preconditions for this, depends upon how citizens and decision makers relate to the questions of security, development, and justice. The meaning and dynamics of these concepts can be elucidated with the assistance of the founding father of the peace research tradition, the Norwegian scholar Johan Galtung. He made an important distinction between direct and structural violence. By direct violence he meant physical violence, frequently as a result of military intervention, and by structural violence he had in mind the regulatory framework and societal structures that hindered people from fully realizing their potential and at times also taking away their means of subsistence. Galtung talked about the absence of direct violence in terms of negative peace (to be defended from something). In order to achieve a state of positive peace (to have the right to something), constraints in the form of structural violence must be removed—this was what constituted the conditions for sustainable development, and could only be achieved through increased social justice (Galtung 1996) and a more inclusive, territorially based development strategy (Friedmann 1992).

In the same way, I suggest that we can talk about negative and positive security. By creating fences and walls and various technical systems for increased surveillance and social control, people in urban areas are meant to be better defended from crime and violence, and granted increased negative security. However, the measures designed to empower people, increasing their participation in political life and their social recognition, could create legitimate conditions for increased social cohesion and social trust, so strengthening people's rights to safety and the conditions for a more positive security (Lidskog 2006; Sahlin 2010).

In order to create the conditions for positive security, there would need to be acts of prevention and acts of promotion alike. Such 'proventive' measures require financial support and a new mindset (Burton 1990). Social sustainability must be understood as a prerequisite for economic sustainability. Expenditure on increased social cohesion should be recognized not as an operating cost (with demands for an immediate payoff), but as an investment in the future (with more favourable rules for depreciation). The investment is necessary in order to counteract the changing role of the state and to create the social conditions required at the local level in order to attract foreign investments. Hence, a social investment policy with some kind of social investment funds is called for (Morel et al. 2011). Polanyi demonstrated how the expansion of the market in the eighteenth century through its commodification of land, labour, and capital meant that the economy over time became separated from the social institutions in which it was previously embedded; in the same way and for the same reasons three hundred years later, in a post-national global network society, social sustainability requires that the economy is gradually re-embedded in its local social context. Social investment funds may turn out to be an important first step in this direction. However, it is not enough to try to achieve it by adjusting the city's budget in favour of preventive measures. There is also a pressing need for an injection of additional resources for things outside the usual run of activities intended to strengthen social cohesion. Such additional resources would be targeted in order to once again embed the economy in the social conditions that sustainability requires. As will be further highlighted below, this makes the involvement of, and the co-creation by, concerned citizens paramount. It is in this sense that it is impossible to separate the social from the economic, or to see them as two different dimensions of sustainability.

The need for co-creation and citizen dialogue

Important as these measures might be, the conditions for positive security cannot, however, only be created from above by making the financial resources available. They require strong, popular participation and trust-building from below. An increasingly common tool used to strengthen engagement is dialogue. Yet dialogue must not be limited to so-called user dialogue, permitting civil servants, inspired by the new public management, to get inside citizens' heads through first-hand interaction in order to produce services to meet their needs. The challenges that cities face consist of complex issues for which there are no quick fixes and identifiable solutions. Positive security, based upon greater social trust and cohesion, requires urban citizens to participate more fully in political decision-making, whether it concerns the mobilization, allocation, and distribution of various resources or the identification of complex issues and suitable ways to manage them. The same goes for understanding and acting on contested, open-ended concepts such as security, development, and justice, let alone the concept of social sustainability. The transition from urban politics to urban governance, with its increased partnership and important policy choices, demands co-creation by decision makers and citizens; a co-creation, however, that encompasses the whole decision-making process from the formulation of the issues and the analysis of the structures of possibility to the identification of measures and their implementation. The co-creators thus also share responsibility for the output and outcome.

For such an undertaking, an open-ended, inclusive, and empowering citizen dialogue is required. Dialogue is all about making different actors and their perspectives visible, in order that they feel that they are listened to and respected, and that they can influence decisions affecting their everyday lives. Obviously, for some in urban government the very real fear of power sharing is a constraint. However, power should not be thought a zero-sum game. In the network society, power is more a question of *power to do* something than *power over* something. The more people are empowered, and the more they subsequently perceive the power-holders as legitimate, the stronger their capacity to lend their support to such leadership will be. This calls for a transformation-oriented method of citizen dialogue, capable of coping with asymmetric relationships characterized by important conceptual gaps and deep-seated distrust between different stakeholders (Abrahamsson 2003).

In conclusion

The ongoing processes of globalization, migration, and urbanization together constitute the great societal transformation of our time, leaving many cities as little more than battlegrounds for social conflict. Their potential to contribute to sustainable development is in danger. Social sustainability is understood here to be an amalgamation of security, development, and justice—the three values on which dominant political ideologies are built—which, as essentially contested concepts, are open to constant negotiation in the way people understand and relate to them. And that negotiation relies on enhanced co-creation, with the strong participation of concerned citizens. A transformation-oriented method of dialogue is essential, as it is the prerequisite for creating space for dissenting voices and for dealing with asymmetric power relations.

References

Abrahamsson, H. (2003) *Understanding world order and structural change, poverty, conflict and the global arena* (Basingstoke: Macmillan).
—— (2012) *Städer som nav för en globalt hållbar samhällsutveckling eller slagfält för sociala konflikter. Rapport till den Sociala hållbarhetskommissionen i Malmö* [Cities as hubs for a global sustainable development or battlefields for social conflicts. Repport to the Commission for a Socially Sustainable Malmö] (Malmö: City of Malmö).
Amen, M., N. Toly, P. McCarney & K. Segbers (2011) (eds.) *Cities and global governance: New sites for international relations* (Farnham: Ashgate).
Borja, J. & M. Castells (1996) *Local & global: management of cities in the information age* (London: Earthscan).
Brown, W. (2010) *Walled states, waning sovereignty* (New York: Zone Books).
Burton, J. (1990) *Conflict: resolution and prevention* (Basingstoke: Macmillan).
Byrne, D. (2005) *Social Exclusion*. (New York: McGraw-Hill Education).
Castells, M. (1983) *The city and the grassroots: A cross-cultural theory of urban social movements* (London: Edward Arnold).
Castles, S. (2010), 'Understanding global migration: a social transformation perspective', *Journal of Ethnic & Migration Studies*, 36/10, 1565–86.

—— H. de Haas & M. J. Miller (2014) *The age of migration* (Basingstoke: Palgrave Macmillan).
Cerny, P. G. (1997) 'Paradoxes of the competition state: The dynamics of political', *Globalization Government & Opposition*, 32/2, 251–74.
Cox, R. & T. Sinclair (1996) *Approaches to world order* (Cambridge: CUP).
Dempsey, N., G. Bramley, S. Power & C. Brown (2011) 'The social dimension of sustainable development: Defining urban social sustainability', *Sustainable Development*, 19/5, 289–300.
Dikeç, M. (2007) *Badlands of the republic* (Oxford: Blackwell).
Eastmond, M. & L. Åkesson (2007) *Globala familjer: Transnationell migration och släktskap* (Riga: Gidlunds).
Fainstein, S. (2010) *The just city* (London: Cornell University Press).
Fierke, K. (2007) *Critical approaches to international security* (Cambridge: Polity).
Friedman, J. (1992) *Empowerment: The politics of alternative development* (Oxford: Blackwell).
Galtung, J. (1996) *Peace by peaceful means: Peace and conflict development and civilization* (London: Sage).
Graham, S. (2010) *Cities under siege: The new military urbanism* (London: Verso).
Harvey, D. (2003) *The new imperialism* (New York: OUP).
—— (2012) *Rebel cities: From the right to the city to the urban revolution* (London: Verso Books).
Hettne, B. (2009) *Thinking about development* (London: Zed).
Johansson, T. & O. Sernhede (2006) (eds.) *Storstadens omvandlingar: Postindustrialism, globalisering och migration* (Gothenburg: Daidalos).
Kanbur, R. & A. Sumner (2012) 'Poor countries or poor people? Development assistance and the new geography of global poverty', *Journal of International Development*, 24/6, 686–95.
Kazepov, Y. (2005) *Cities of Europe: Changing contexts, local arrangements, and the challenge to urban cohesion* (Oxford: Blackwell).
Kennedy, P. (2010) *Local lives and global transformations: Towards world society* (Basingstoke: Macmillan).
Krugman, P. (2010) 'The new economic geography, now middle-aged', paper given to the Association of American Geographers, 16 April, <http://www.princeton.edu/~pkrugman/aag.pdf>, accessed 26 June 2015.
Lidskog, R. (2006) *Staden: Våldet och tryggheten: Om social ordning i ett mångkulturellt samhälle* (Gothenburg: Daidalos).
Listerborn, . (2013) 'Suburban women and the "glocalisation" of the everyday lives: gender and glocalities in underprivileged areas in Sweden', *Gender, Place & Culture*, 20/3, 290–312.
Morel, N., B. Palier & J. Palme (2011) *Towards a social investment welfare state? Ideas, policies and challenges* (Bristol: Policy).
Mouffe, C. (2009) *Om det politiska* (Hägersten: Tankekraft).
Munck, R. (2005) *Globalization and social exclusion* (Blomfield: Kumarian).

Polanyi, K. (2001) *The great transformation: The political and economic origins of our time* (Boston: Beacon Press) (first pub 1944).
Polèse, M. & R. Stren (2000) *The social sustainability of cities: Diversity and management of change* (Toronto: University of Toronto Press).
Putnam, R. (1996) *Making democracy work: Civic traditions in modern Italy* (Princeton: PUP).
Righard, E. (2008) *The welfare mobility dilemma: Transnational strategies and national structuring at crossroads* (Lund: Lund University).
Robertson, R. (1995) 'Glocalization: Time–space and homogeneity–heterogeneity', in M. Featherstone, S. Lash & R. Robertson (eds.), *Global modernities* (London: SAGE).
Sassen, S. (2006) *Cities in a world economy* (London: Pine Forge).
—— (2011) 'The global city today: Advantages of specialization and costs of financialization', in Amen et al. 2011.
Scheff, T. J. & S. M. Retzinger (2001) *Emotions and violence. Shame and rage in destructive conflicts* (Bloomington: iUniverse).
Scholte, J. A. (2000) *Globalization: A critical introduction* (London: Macmillan).
Taylor, P., B. Derudder, P. Saey & F. Witlox (2007) (eds.) *Cities in globalization: Practices, policies and theories* (London: Routledge).
Wacquant, L. (2009) *Punishing the poor: The neoliberal government of social insecurity* (Durham: Duke University Press).

CHAPTER 2

International migration and the social-democratic welfare regime

Erica Righard & Pieter Bevelander

International migration and state-provided welfare are contentious areas. Both individually, and even more when combined, and this is as true of the Scandinavian welfare states as of many others. The welfare state arrangements built up in Denmark, Norway, and Sweden, starting in the late nineteenth and early twentieth centuries, and which came to fruition in the early post-war period, are usually described as extensive and universal; and, as the influential sociologist Gøsta Esping-Andersen (1990) points out, they are irrevocably linked to the social-democratic welfare regime type. As one of the arguments of this volume is that urban marginalization in Scandinavian cities must be understood in terms of the specific welfare regime, in this essay we set out to situate international migration and migrant social protection in this context.

Drawing on the broader concept of social protection, our focus is state-led migrant social protection in receiving countries, which, in this perspective, consists of access to social rights in the receiving country and the portability of social rights from the country of origin. The theoretical framework also emphasizes the role of labour market participation. As the Scandinavian welfare states have become more market-oriented, and social rights more earnings-related, here too labour market participation has proved decisive for people's access to their social rights. In this essay, we discuss the implications of this move towards earnings-related protection schemes and how the three countries now stand in relation to one another when it comes to labour market participation, particularly by marginalized migrant groups. We also take a broad view of the different trajectories of the

41

social-democratic welfare regimes in the three countries. The essay draws on both primary and secondary sources.

We first provide the reader with a brief background to the tensions between migration and the welfare state, the theoretical framework, and some methodological considerations. In order to set the migration picture in context, we then present an overview of immigration to Denmark, Norway and Sweden in the last three decades. Next we consider the implications of the growing emphasis on earnings-related social protection schemes and on labour market participation among vulnerable migrant groups in a comparative perspective, before pursuing a more general discussion on the different trajectories of migrant rights in the Danish, Norwegian, and Swedish welfare states. The essay shows that while Sweden is typically pictured as the Scandinavian flagship of integration policy, as soon as one widens one's perspective to include labour market participation and welfare redistribution, the picture becomes far more complex, with no obvious flagship in sight.

Background and specification

Welfare states, including the social rights, social security, and social services they provide, are sedentary constructs. Their origins are immanent in the nation-state, to the point that it has been claimed that they constitute the social dimension of the nation-state building project (for example, Clarke 2004). Hence, it is not surprising that international migration—the mobility of workers, entrepreneurs, students, refugees, and their families across state borders—is constructed as an anomaly, and sometimes even a threat (Castles 2010). The sedentary bias is also the reason for the obsession with integration in both political and academic discourses, not least social policy as a field of practice and study. However, about three decades ago the mobility paradigm slowly began to feature in the social sciences, raising new kinds of questions. Thus, instead of focusing entirely on the integration of migrants, an interesting and relevant topic as it may be, we are now also ready to deal with questions such as how welfare states respond to social vulnerability among emigrants and immigrants, and why people for varying reasons continue to cross and recross state borders. While many migrants migrate to escape insecurity and manage risk, migration in itself also involves greater insecurity and risks. Typically, migrants' social vulnerability highlights the need for social protection schemes that span international state borders. For some migrants, this need is most pressing at the time of their migration, compressed into a single, unidirectional movement at a certain point in time. For others, migration might unfold as a life-long and multidirectional process, anchored in two or more countries. Social vulnerability, and the need for social protection and services that span state borders, then becomes an enduring issue for much or all of their lifetimes.

Social protection is a broad concept, and state-provided services are only a limited part of it. Yet, in order to understand the full implications of state-provided welfare, it is important to view it in that wider framework. Social protection comprises both formal and informal systems: formal systems, such as welfare states and to some extent markets, and informal systems, such as NGOs, social movements, markets and market-like systems, family, and household networks (see Brunori & O'Reilly 2011). It is only recently that social protection for migrants as a field of research has begun to expand beyond the integrationist paradigm, and the literature is still limited, in particular with regard to formal social protection. Moreover, while both formal and informal dimensions have a telling impact on social protection in migrants' everyday lives, in research they have typically been approached separately. Informal social protection systems have mainly been dealt with in migration studies, focusing on the social and economic protection systems that transnational families—and various forms of faith-based and hometown associations—establish across national borders (for example, Baldassar et al. 2007; Pries 1999; Chambon et al. 2011). Formal protection, on the other hand, has mainly been treated in comparative social policy studies (for example, Holzmann et al. 2005; Sainsbury 2012). In an attempt to systematize the discussion, Sabates-Wheeler et al. (2011, 93–4) have suggested that social protection has four components: (*i*) access to formal social protection in host and origin countries; (*ii*) portability of vested social rights between host and origin countries; (*iii*) labour market conditions for migrants in host countries and the recruitment process for migrants in the origin countries; and (*iv*) access to informal networks to support migrants and their family members (see also, Sabates-Wheeler & MacAuslan 2007; Brunori & O'Reilly 2011). Obviously, given that in this essay we are concerned with international migration in the Scandinavian welfare states, we focus on the formal aspects of social protection. Yet though we do not have space to dwell on it here, it must be recognized that in order to fully understand all the implications, the informal aspects must also be taken into account.

The formal social protection afforded by different welfare regime types depends to varying degrees on the state and the market; it involves a range of universal and particularistic, flat-rate and earnings-related benefits in varying proportions. Using data from the 1980s, it is apparent that the Scandinavian countries, with Sweden as the prime example, were all state-led, universal, extended welfare states according to Esping-Andersen's typology of welfare state capitalism (Esping-Andersen 1990). However, over time, and after a restructuring driven in particular by the economic crisis of the 1990s, they have become more market-oriented, earnings-based, and particularistic in their composition (for example, Hort 2014). These profound transformations of the Scandinavian welfare states have led to a widening of income gaps between groups in the population, apparently leaving those with a migrant background overrepresented among the groups lagging behind. Evidently, as social protection schemes have become more earnings-related for everyone, this cannot have been due solely to changes in state-provided welfare as such; instead, as highlighted by Sabates-Wheeler et al. (2011), it is closely related to labour market conditions, for the more important one's past work experience and earnings are for one's eligibility for social insurance and services, the more important labour market participation becomes. While it is well known that, as a group, people with migrant background have a weaker position in the labour market than natives, the reasons why that is so are less clear. A lack of education transferability, late-life arrival, or labour market discrimination are all possible explanations.

For the purpose of this essay, three of the dimensions proposed by Sabates-Wheeler et al. (2011) stand out: immigrants' rights in each of the Scandinavian welfare states; the portability of social rights from the emigration to the immigration country; and labour market participation and conditions in the country of immigration. Drawing on a combination of primary research and secondary sources, we discuss these three dimensions. We highlight that although access to social rights is by now less dependent on citizenship, it remains unevenly accessible for different nationalities. For this argument we rely on an analysis of the Swedish old-age pension from its start in 1913 up to the present; a content analysis of government reports and legislative proposals that have preceded new and amended legislation regulating the old-age pension. With such broad material, the analytical focus is on how ideas of state responsibility for national and foreign emigrants and immigrants have changed over time. This case study has been chosen to illustrate how state-led social protection schemes sometimes lead to the reproduction of inequality within populations, including inequality due to (certain) migration backgrounds.

As labour market participation has become more and more crucial for access to social protection, it is discouraging to note from a social justice perspective that people with a migration background have a weaker position in the labour market than do natives. Importantly, those with a migration background are not a homogeneous group: great variation between groups can be identified. In our discussion, we focus on a number of especially vulnerable groups of migrants in the three Scandinavian countries (the migrants' countries of birth are Iran, Iraq, Pakistan, Somalia, Turkey, and Vietnam). The statistical data for this analysis is derived from the national statistics in each country and then modified to be comparable. This means that the figures presented can reflect the actual labour market participation of these groups in each country in a fully comparative perspective.

In then looking at the Danish, Norwegian, and Swedish welfare states and how they respond to migrant social vulnerability, we rely largely on secondary sources, including the comparative work on migration and welfare in Denmark, Norway, and Sweden led by Grete Brochmann and Anniken Hagelund (2012) and on immigrant rights in six countries conducted by Diane Sainsbury (2012). While the findings of these two studies are highly relevant, it is still startling to realize just how limited the Scandinavian literature is. Overall, the literature is more focussed on welfare state aspirations, as stated in national integration policies, than on how they actually respond to migrant social vulnerability in their social policies.

Post-war immigration to the Scandinavian countries

International migration to the Scandinavian countries since the Second World War has been substantial and increasingly diverse, accelerating in the last three decades (Bevelander et al. 2013). The migration flows to the three countries were broadly similar, being linked to societal phenomena such as a growing demand for labour, family reunification, and the acceptance of refugees fleeing war and political conflict. A common Nordic labour market, instituted in 1954, enabled citizens of the Nordic countries to move freely between the countries (see Fisher & Straubhaar 1996 for an evaluation of its economic effects), which in the 1950s brought migration from Denmark and Norway to Sweden. This means that the three countries share a history of exchanging labour. Alongside the Nordic agreement, all three countries also recruited labour from primarily other European countries until the 1970s, when the oil crisis hit the industrial world. In order to cope with the crisis, which slashed employment, all three introduced restrictions on labour migration: Sweden in 1972, Denmark in 1973, and Norway in 1975. These restrictions left migration to all three countries after the 1970s increasingly dominated by refugees and family reunion migrants from non-European countries.

Looking at immigration to Scandinavia in the 1970s by country of birth, the dominant non-European immigrant groups in Sweden were from Chile and Turkey; in Norway, from Pakistan, Turkey, and Chile; and in Denmark, Turkey and Pakistan. Since the 1980s, those arriving in Sweden have predominantly come from Iran, Iraq, and Somalia; in Norway and Denmark, from Pakistan, the Middle East in general, and Somalia. Migration between the Scandinavian countries continued, but at a lower level and, when both Norway and Denmark overtook Sweden economically in a different direction, consisting largely of Swedish emigration. Finally, Denmark's and

INTERNATIONAL MIGRATION AND THE SOCIAL-DEMOCRATIC WELFARE REGIME

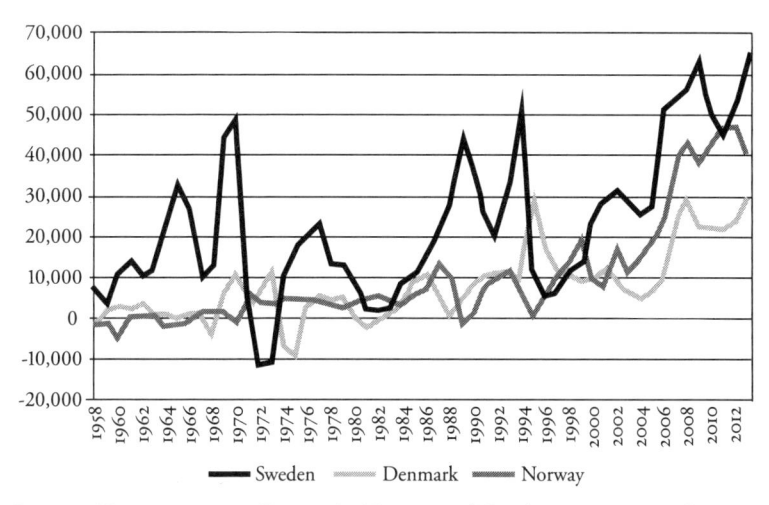

Fig. 2.1. Net migration to Denmark, Norway and Sweden, 1958–2012. Sources: Statistics Denmark, Statistics Norway, and Statistics Sweden.

Sweden's accession to the European Economic Community (EEC) and the European Union (EU) in 1973 and 1995 respectively, along with the European Economic Area (EEA) agreement of 1994, which all three countries joined, led to increased immigration, especially since 2005 from new member states. Indeed, all three Scandinavian countries have experienced increased migration, especially from Poland and Romania.

Looking at the figures in detail, it is immediately apparent that Denmark and Norway had low net migration[1] during the 1960s and 1970s, whereas Sweden had substantial net migration in the same period (see Fig. 2.1). Since the early 1980s, all three countries show substantial and increasing net migration over time. In absolute numbers, Sweden outperformed both the other countries, but, since Norway has a smaller population, the substantial net migration to Norway in the last decade means that immigration per capita to Norway is larger than to Sweden. Meanwhile, the differences in immigrant population between the Scandinavian countries become visible when we measure the size and proportion of their populations. In Sweden, the immigrant population had reached almost 15 per cent of the total by the end of 2012, in Denmark 8 per cent, and in Norway 11 per cent (Bevelander et al. 2013).

As the 1970s saw all three countries close their doors to labour migration from non-Nordic countries, it should be seen as the establishment phase of their current immigration policies. While there were already differences in migration policies between the countries, they become far more pronounced after 2000, with Sweden's and Denmark's being the most apparent opposites (Brochmann & Hagelund 2012; Guilherme Fernandes 2015; see also Sainsbury 2012). In 2002, Denmark introduced an immigration policy that tightened immigration regulations, including limitations on family reunions and more stringent rules on permanent residency and citizenship. These rules are stricter than Sweden's, and have contributed to a fall in the number of refugees and family reunion migrants arriving in Denmark. The Swedish government in the same period has liberalized its rules for citizenship (2001) and labour migration from non-EU/EEA countries (2008). As a result, more economic migrants are now arriving in Sweden, gravitating towards the low-skilled jobs in the private service sector (Emilsson et al. 2014).

Towards a migration—welfare regime, at least for some

International migration in post-war Scandinavia has typically been associated with immigration; still, emigration has always been prevalent too. In fact, looking at the evolution of the Swedish old-age pension, the portability of social rights for Swedish emigrants was an issue before access for foreign immigrants. In the 1960s and 1970s, the government introduced particularistic legislation, at first to compensate for Swedes who left the country, and later for foreigners who immigrated. This legislation was duly abolished in the 1990s; however, in spite of the fact that citizens and non-citizens today have equal rights, there is still a steadily rising proportion of elderly people with a migration background among poor elderly in Sweden.

The national old-age pension was first established in Sweden in 1913. Since then it has undergone a large number of technically complicated revisions (Swärd et al. 2013). A distinction is usually drawn between the national old-age pension before and after its fundamental restructuring in the 1990s. When the national old-age pension reached its full extent in 1959, it consisted of two parts:

the 'people's pension' (*folkpension*) and the 'supplementary pension' (*allmän tilläggspension*). From 1998 onwards, the old-age pension was often called the 'reformed retirement pension', and consisted of three parts: the 'guaranteed pension' (*garantipension*), the 'income pension' (*inkomstpension*), and the 'premium pension' (*premiumpension*). Together, the national old-age pension consists of two kinds of social insurance: the basic-level pension, which is designed to protect pensioners from poverty and ensure they never need poor relief; and the supplementary pension, which is designed to ensure pensioners can enjoy the same standard of living as they did before retirement. Both of these were constructed differently before and after 1998 (see Righard 2014; Righard forthcoming).

Taking the basic-level pension, the rules on portability for emigrants and access for immigrants have changed seven times since 1913. This development of portability and access can be grouped into three phases or periods (see Righard 2014; Righard forthcoming). When the first universal old-age pension was issued in 1913, it only covered Swedish citizens who were registered as residents in Sweden. Foreign citizens had no access, and portability was not an option. This ideology of sedentarism persisted until the 1960s, when Sweden saw the establishment and expansion of social rights for migrants at a time of radical social solidarity. The idea was that anyone with reasonable ties to Sweden should have access to the basic-level of protection of the retirement pension and portability for Swedish citizens who moved away from Sweden was introduced in 1962.

During the 1960s, the principle of equal treatment for foreign nationals living in Sweden gained ground. It was also an international issue, pursued by the International Labour Organization (ILO) among others. Yet, access for foreign nationals residing in Sweden was not introduced until 1979, when those who had lived in Sweden for a period of at least ten years became eligible for the flat-rate 'people's pension', i.e. the basic-level old-age protection. At the same time, Swedish emigrants' eligibility was limited to correspond to the proportion of working years in Sweden (it was calculated in relation to the individual's supplementary pension).

However, as the ideals of social solidarity began to lose their hold and the principle of earnings-based social protection grew stronger, citizenship lost its role as a signifier. While the restructuring was introduced by degrees, new legislation in 1998 marked a definite shift. The regulation of the old-age pension was divided into two, with one part based on income (in the law on income-based pensions, SFS 1998:674) and one on residency (in the law on guaranteed pensions, SFS 1998:702). While this legislation operates independently of citizenship, it has led to widening gaps between the native and foreign-born pensioners in Sweden. This is due to the growing importance of portability of social entitlements as regulated in bi- and multilateral agreements between states.

Today, pensionable incomes are only portable across certain borders. In principle, pensioners who had moved to Sweden from countries with no international agreement on social security will lag behind, as is the case for many elderly people from non-EU countries (SOU 2010:105). Hence, what is at stake is not only the extent to which an individual has earned pension eligibility, but also whether that eligibility is portable between countries. Those who cannot take their eligibility with them will have to start all over again. Consequently, we see a reinforced segmentation between groups of nationals. Moreover, for those who have had a limited or no pensionable income, forty years of residence in Sweden before the age of sixty-five is required for full eligibility for the guaranteed pension, thus excluding many migrants. This highlights two things: the long-term effects of uneven labour-market participation and the effects of the non-portability of pensionable income across certain borders (SOU 2010:105). While this discussion draws on the particular case of the Swedish old-age pension, labour market participation and international agreements for the transferability of social entitlements stand out as essential for access to the state's social protection in an earnings-based welfare system.

Migrant labour market participation

Denmark, Norway, and Sweden have a number of common features when it comes to the labour market. They all have relatively high levels of unionization, high minimum wages, a narrow wage distribution, and a large public sector. In addition, all have gone through the transition from an industrial economy to a service economy in which women's labour market integration has reached the same level as men's (Rosholm et al. 2006).

Economic integration is a key element in the overall integration of newcomers. Many factors have been given in the literature to explain immigrants' varying labour market integration. One is the official introductory programmes for newcomers. The shift in these programmes towards 'workfare' has become more and more pronounced, and has made immigrants' employment and livelihoods increasingly important (Djuve & Kavli 2007). Although intended to lead to faster labour market integration, in Sweden, unlike Denmark and Norway, the programmes are not compulsory, and passing the programmes, or even participating in the first place, has no bearing on applications for permanent residence. Other important factors for labour market integration are the state of the labour market, the immigrants' education and skills, the reasons for migration, and the attitudes towards immigrants on the part of the settled population.

Few studies have compared immigrants' labour market integration in the Scandinavian countries. Blume et al. (2007) studied the determinants of relative poverty among immigrants and natives in Denmark and Sweden in the 1980s and 1990s, and found substantially higher levels of poverty among immigrants, which increased over time. Rosholm et al. (2006), also studying Denmark and Sweden, found that the shift to a service economy, in which greater stress is placed on communicative and social skills, indicated that immigrants had greater problems obtaining work, and even when employed it depressed their annual earnings.

Since the majority of immigrants in all three countries have come from developing countries outside Europe—Iran, Iraq, Pakistan, Somalia, Turkey, and Vietnam—a comparison of employment rates in Denmark, Norway, and Sweden of the six largest population groups originating from developing countries is revealing (Bevelander et al. 2013). The comparison covers both men and women aged 25–54. The lower age category was chosen since most people nowadays go on to tertiary education after school; the upper, because individuals gradually leave the workforce due to early retirement.

The employment rate for men in all three countries in 2008, by

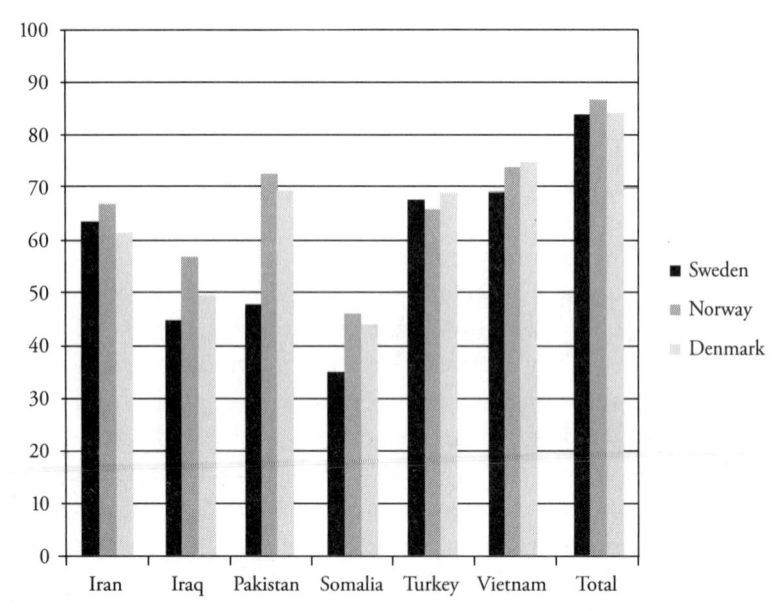

Fig. 2.2. The employment rate in per cent for the male population aged 25–54 by country of birth, 2008. Sources: Statistics Denmark, Statistics Norway, and Statistics Sweden.

country of birth and by total population, is revealing (see Fig. 2.2). The total male employment rate in all three countries was well over 80 per cent in 2008, but most immigrant groups in Sweden show lower employment levels compared to Denmark and Norway. Three countries of birth display the same pattern in all three Scandinavian countries: Iran, Turkey, and Vietnam. Thus the employment rates of the Iranian group ranged from 62 to 67 per cent in all three countries; for the Turkish group, 66 to 69 per cent; and for the Vietnamese group, 69 to 76 per cent. The Iraqi immigrant group had the highest employment rate in Norway (57 per cent) compared to Denmark (50 per cent) and Sweden (45 per cent). Pakistani immigrants were doing better in both Norway and Denmark (70 per cent and 73 per cent, respectively) than in Sweden, where their employment rate was a mere 48 per cent. Similarly, the Somali men had higher employment levels in Norway and Denmark than in Sweden (47 per cent and 44 per cent, compared to 35 per cent).

The women were broadly speaking less likely to be in work than the men (see Fig. 2.3). Total female employment in the three Scandi-

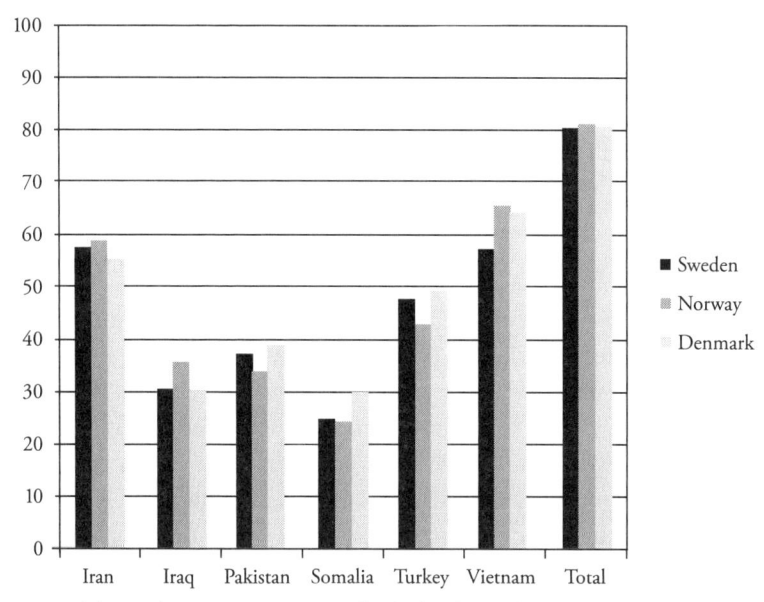

INTERNATIONAL MIGRATION AND THE SOCIAL-DEMOCRATIC WELFARE REGIME

Fig. 2.3. The employment rate in per cent for the female population aged 25–54 by country of birth, 2008. Sources: Statistics Denmark, Statistics Norway, and Statistics Sweden.

navian countries was just above the 80 per cent mark, or two or three percentage points lower than male employment rates. In general, no common patterns can be discerned in the female employment rates. Iranian women have about the same rates in all three countries (59 per cent, 58 per cent, and 55 per cent) and the same is true of the Pakistani group. Iraqis have lower rates in Denmark and Sweden and higher in Norway (30 per cent and 31 per cent, as opposed to 36 per cent). The Somali group had a 25 per cent employment rate in Norway and Sweden, but 30 per cent in Denmark. The Turkish women had about the same employment rate in Denmark and Sweden, but slightly lower in Norway. Finally, the Vietnamese women had the highest levels of employment in all three countries.

Immigrants' labour market participation in the Scandinavian countries is substantially lower than for the total population, which is dominated by the native population. Some of the groups have been in the Scandinavian countries for a number of decades, including the Turkish populations in all three countries and the Pakistani population in Denmark and Norway. In earlier cohorts these groups consisted of labour migrants; subsequently, family reunion migrants and refugees have become more prominent in the Turkish and Pakistani populations. The other groups studied consisted mainly of refugees and their families, most of whom have moved to the Scandinavian countries in the last two or three decades.

The trajectories of state-provided social protection

The interaction between migration, migration policies, and social protection varies considerably between countries (Carmel et al. 2012), even when they belong to the same type of welfare regime, whether liberal, conservative, or social-democratic (Sainsbury 2012). The Danish, Norwegian, and Swedish welfare states are all categorized as belonging to the social-democratic regime type, but here too we find considerable differences in migrant access to welfare rights (Brochmann & Hagelund 2012; for Sweden and Denmark, see Sainsbury 2012); indeed, the dissimilarities are sometimes blatant. While the three countries initially took a similar line on migrants' access to state-provided welfare, developments in each country began to diverge about two decades ago. In fact, Grete Brochmann and Anniken Hagelund (2012) have even described the Scandinavian welfare regime type as 'a model with three exceptions'.

Among the shared features are regime-defining attributes such as universalism, in the shape of unitary programmes applying to the entire population and entitlements based on citizenship or residence. Taxation is the main source of revenue, funding benefits and services, and the state is the main service provider, often channelled through local governments and private companies (Sainsbury 2012). When it comes to dissimilarities in migrants' access to state-provided social protection and services, Denmark is described as the least inclusive country and Sweden as the most, with Norway somewhere between the two (Brochmann & Hagelund 2012; see also Guilherme Fernandes 2015).

As Sweden experienced immigration earlier than Norway and Denmark, it became something of a role model for the other two. Social democracy was hegemonic, and up until the 1970s in all three countries there was a strong belief in integration through immigrants' access to rights, and not least social rights. Brochmann and Hagelund (2012) conclude that the strong divergence that we see between Denmark and Sweden, in particular in the 2000s, can actually be identified as early as the 1980s, when Sweden seems to have begun to place special emphasis on *demos*, while Denmark instead put it on *ethnos*.

The system of state-provided protection and services is complex in itself, and the development of migrants' access is likewise; depending on the social protection scheme its trajectory can vary enormously, and it is beyond the scope of this essay to summarize it here. Instead, we shall present a few illustrative examples that refer to the comparative analysis by Diane Sainsbury (2012) of migrants' access to social rights in six countries, two from each welfare regime type as outlined by Esping-Andersen. Denmark and Sweden offer contrasting examples of the social-democratic welfare regime type. Like Brochmann and Hagelund, Sainsbury (2012) points out that while the differences became acute in the 2000s, they could already be seen in the 1980s. In both countries, entitlements have become increasingly based on residence instead of citizenship. Denmark, however, has been more reluctant and slower than Sweden in extending entitlements based on citizenship to non-citizens.

Sweden's strong claims to universal protection schemes led it to implement a child benefit, including immigrant children, as early as 1948. In Denmark, the first family support schemes introduced in the 1950s onwards involved means testing, and a universal child benefit was not introduced until 1967. As regards parental leave, in Sweden this consists of a combination of flat-rate and earnings-related benefits, while in Denmark it is solely earnings-related. As a result, proportionally many more immigrant parents have access to this protection scheme in Sweden than in Denmark, due in no small part to low labour market participation among immigrant women. However, by the mid-1980s the main family benefits were available on more or less the same basis in the two countries (Sainsbury 2012).

Another difference between Denmark and Sweden is means-tested social assistance. In Denmark, social assistance is limited to

Danish, Nordic, and EU citizens, citizens covered by international agreements, and refugees. Others are not eligible, although if they intend to settle permanently in Denmark they cannot be excluded. In Sweden, by contrast, all residents are eligible to apply for social assistance (Sainsbury 2012).

Returning to the case of the old-age pension, Sweden and Denmark opted for different solutions from the start. While Denmark prioritized entry into international agreements with an increasing number of countries, Sweden initially chose a general solution that would make immigrants eligible for old-age pensions after ten years of residence in the country. When Denmark became a member of the EEC in 1973, it introduced a hefty residence requirement to safeguard its universal pensions. However, since the reform of the Swedish pension system in the 1990s, the two countries have become more alike, and when Sweden became a member of the EU in 1995 it applied a solution much like the Danes'. While both countries have also established minimum income schemes for the elderly (*äldreförsörjningsstöd*), the old-age pensions in both countries stratify the population according to residence and pensionable income.

The existence of formal social rights says little about how they are actually accessed, of course. The challenge in Sainsbury's study is that she does not limit it to policy, but also considers policy outcomes. Interestingly, she finds that, compared to Sweden, a larger proportion of immigrants in Denmark are poor (as a percentage of the immigrant population in each country). This outcome is the combined result of market income and social benefits. She also finds that social transfers generally have a greater effect for natives than for immigrants—and a greater effect for migrants in Sweden than in Denmark. Sainsbury also considers the effect of social transfers, depending on the main source of income (earnings or transfers), finding that among those reliant on transfers as their main source of income, the poverty rate is relatively lower among both natives and immigrants in Sweden than in Denmark, whereas for those whose earnings are their main income, the poverty rate is relatively lower among natives in Denmark and among migrants in Sweden. In sum, while at the policy level Sweden has a more inclusive welfare regime, this also seems to have an effect on poverty reduction among both native and migrant dependents. However, natives with earnings as their main income have lower poverty rates in Denmark than in Sweden.

Conclusion

This essay has discussed international migration and migrant social protection in the Scandinavian countries. We argue that migrant social protection in the host country should be considered not only in terms of access to social rights, but also labour market participation and the portability of social rights from the country of origin to the receiving context. The Scandinavian welfare regime's move towards earnings- and residence-based social protection has led to increasing social and income gaps, with those with a migration background typically being overrepresented in the groups that are lagging behind. This underscores the pivotal role of labour market participation and of the portability of rights between countries. In this essay, the example of the Swedish old-age pension is used to illustrate this. Since 1954, Denmark, Norway and Sweden have granted one another's citizens special privileges when it comes to residence, work permits and access to social protection. Denmark became a member of the EEC in 1973, Sweden and Norway became affiliated with the EEA in 1994, and the following year Sweden also became a member of the EU. Besides these multilateral agreements, the three countries have entered into a large number of bilateral agreements on social security schemes. However, far from all nationalities are covered by such agreements, and these are needed in order to transfer existing social rights to a new country. The upshot is that some immigrants can transfer their social rights, while the rest cannot and have to start again from scratch. This inevitably leads to gaps in provision.

Patterns of social stratification in social protection and labour market participation intersect not only with migration backgrounds, but also with access to housing, healthcare facilities, schools, and services such as childcare and eldercare. They are visible not only as abstract entities in the population—they are tangible, experienced in everyday urban life. Moreover, while welfare states and social policy were built on assumptions of sedentary populations, today 'circular migration' is a catchword in political and academic debate. The movement of labour, capital, and goods must be understood in terms of the societal processes of globalization. Given this, it is crucial to consider state-led social responsibility for the global labour market and the mobility of people—what has been called the 'transnational social question'.

Notes

1 Net migration refers to immigration minus emigration. When immigration is higher than emigration, net migration is positive, otherwise it is negative.

References

Baldassar, L., C. V. Baldock & R. Wilding (2007) *Families caring across borders: Migration, ageing and transnational caregiving* (Basingstoke: Palgrave Macmillan).
Bevelander, P., R. H. Bilde, I. Dahlstedt, M. Eskelund, L. Møller Hansen, M. Macura, K. G. Pedersen & L. Østby (2013) *Scandinavia's population groups originating from developing countries: Change and integration* (TemaNord 2013:561; Copenhagen: Nordic Council of Ministers).
Blume, K., B. Gustafsson, P. J. Pedersen & M. Verner (2007) 'At the lower end of the table: Determinants of poverty among immigrants to Denmark and Sweden', *Journal of Ethnic & Migration Studies* 33/3, 373–96.
Brochmann, G. & A. Hagelund (2012) *Immigration policy and the Scandinavian welfare state, 1945–2010* (Basingstoke: Palgrave Macmillan).
Brunori, P. & M. O'Reilly (2011) 'Social protection for development: A review of definitions' (Munich: Munich Personal RePEc Archive, MPRA Paper No 29495, available at http://mpra.ub.uni-muenchen.de/29495/ as of 10 March 2011).
Carmel, E., A. Cerami & T. Papadopoulos (2012) (eds.) *Migration and welfare in the new Europe: Social protection and the challenges of integration* (Bristol: Policy).
Castles, S. (2010) 'Understanding global migration: A social transformation perspective', *Journal of Ethnic and Migration Studies* 36/10, 1565–86.
Chambon, A. S., W. Schröer & C. Schweppe (2011) (eds.) *Transnational social support* (London: Routledge).
Clarke, J. (2004) *Changing welfare, changing states: New directions in social policy* (London: SAGE).
Djuve, A. B. & H. C. Kavli (2007) *Integrering i Danmark, Sverige och Norge. Felles utfordringer—Like løsninger?* (TemaNord 2007:575; Copenhagen: Nordic Council of Ministers).
Emilsson, H., K. Magnusson, S. Osanami Törngren & P. Bevelander (2014) *The*

world's most open country: Labour migration to Sweden after the 2008 law (Malmö: MIM, Malmö University).

Esping-Andersen, G. (1990) *The three worlds of welfare capitalism* (Cambridge: Polity).

Fisher, P. A. & T. Straubhaar (1996) *Migration and economic integration in the Nordic common labour market* (Nord 1996:2; Copenhagen: Nordic Council of Ministers).

Guilherme Fernandes, A. (2015) '(Dis)Empowering new immigrants and refugees through participation in introduction programmes in Sweden, Denmark and Norway', *Journal of Immigrant & Refugee Studies* 15/3.

Holzmann, R., J. Koettl & T. Chernetsky (2005) 'Portability regimes of pension and health care benefits for international migrants: An analysis of issues and good practices' (Social Protection Discussion Paper No. 0519; Washington, DC: World Bank).

Hort, S. (2014) *Social policy, welfare state, and civil society in Sweden*, ii: *The lost world of social democracy, 1988–2015* (Lund: Arkiv).

MIPEX (2015) *Migrant integration policy index: Key findings* (Brussels: Migrant Policy Group, available at http://www.mipex.eu/key-findings).

Pries, L. (1999) (ed.) *Migration and transnational social spaces* (Aldershot: Ashgate).

Righard, E. (2014) 'Internationell migration och social trygghet: Det svenska pensionssystemet i historiskt perspektiv', in P. Lalander & B. Svensson (eds.) *Perspektiv på social utsatthet* (Lund: Studentlitteratur).

Righard, E. (forthcoming) 'Transnational social responsibility. The case of Swedish retirement pension 1913–2013', in L. G. Gingrich & S. Köngeter (eds.) *Transnational social policy: Social support in a world on the move* (London: Routledge).

Rosholm, M., K. Scott & L. Husted (2006) '"The times they are a-changin'": Declining immigrant employment opportunities in Scandinavia', *International Migration Review* 40/2, 318–47.

Sabates-Wheeler, R., J. Koettl & J. Avato (2011) 'Social security for migrants: A global overview of portability arrangements', in R. Sabates-Wheeler & R. Feldman (ed.) *Migration and social protection: Claiming rights beyond borders* (Basingstoke: Palgrave Macmillan).

Sabates-Wheeler, R. & I. MacAuslan (2007) 'Migration and Social Protection: Exposing Problems of Access', *Development* 50/4, 26–32.

Sainsbury, D. (2012) *Welfare states and immigrant rights: The politics of inclusion and exclusion* (Oxford: OUP).

SOU (2010:105) *Ålderspension för invandrare från länder utanför OECD-området* (Stockholm: Fritze).

Swärd, H., P. G. Edebalk & E. Wadensjö (2013) (eds.) *Vägar till välfärd: Idéer, kontroverser, perspektiv* (Stockholm: Liber).

CHAPTER 3

Discourses of employment and inclusion in Sweden
Governing citizens, governing suburban peripheries

Magnus Dahlstedt

In the 1990s, there was a lively debate in Sweden about the state of its suburban areas. The focus was, yet again, the suburban areas built in the 1970s as part of the ambitious housing project known as the Million Programme. Right from the start these housing estates figured large as a political problem in public debate, defined in terms of social and/or ethno-cultural otherness (Ristilammi 1994; Molina 1997). In the 1970s, the Million Programme had been described as different primarily in social terms: different because residents were somehow socially different, whether working class, less educated, or in some cases drug abusers. In time the discourse gradually changed, and many of the conflicts and problems, previously interpreted in social terms, were now put down to ethnicity or migration. There was much talk of the Million Programme areas developing into parallel societies, with their own rules, norms, and social codes, more or less decoupled from the rest of Swedish society.

In the past decade, the Million Programme estates have once again been constructed as a problem. This time, however, they have been referred to as 'areas of exclusion', inhabited by people who are represented as somehow different in relation to current ideals of citizenship. This period has seen rapid changes to welfare policy across Europe and indeed in other parts of the world. The European political landscape has seen the formation of a certain kind of citizenship; a particular conception of what rights and responsibilities the citizen should have, and how the citizen should think and act. Not least, the discourses of 'employability' within the European Union characterized the citizen as active, as taking responsibility for developing his or her own life. This ideal of citizenship, centred on availability and a willingness to enter the labour market (increasingly under inferior terms and conditions of employment) as described in European policy documents, is encapsulated in 'active citizenship' (Fejes 2009): 'Active citizenship focuses on whether and how people participate in all spheres of social and economic life, the chances and risks they face in trying to do so, and the extent to which they therefore feel that they belong to and have a fair say in the society in which they live' (European Commission 2000, 5).

The notion of active citizenship has become more and more mainstream, and as a policy narrative is now widely accepted, not least in labour and urban policy, where there is a strong focus on making citizens take social responsibility, whether for themselves or others. Taking as a theoretical starting point the work of Michel Foucault and his concept of governmentality, this essay analyses the main developments in Swedish labour and urban policy, with a particular focus on the formation of an ideal active citizenship and correspondingly active citizens. It draws in particular on an analysis of the central ideas and arguments in employment and urban policy documents from the 1990s onwards. The current challenges of the Swedish welfare state are situated in the broader context of changes to welfare policy in the last two decades, looking at two discourses in particular—labour market activation and the exclusion/inclusion of multi-ethnic suburbs.

In Swedish urban policy in recent years, multi-ethnic 'areas of exclusion' have been represented as embodying everything that active citizenship is not. The analysis indicates that these areas, together with their inhabitants, have increasingly been identified as a serious political problem that needs to be 'dealt with'. The issue repeatedly raised in Swedish urban policy is how to get the suburban population to abandon its morality of impotence, dependence, and passivity for the supposed diligence, confidence, employability, and enterprise of Swedish society as a whole. In the urban policy discourse, exclusion is first and foremost something to be resolved from inside the 'areas of exclusion'. This type of argument has prompted a large number of activating measures designed to motivate, provide opportunities, remove obstacles, and stimulate self-sufficiency, all directed specifically at multi-ethnic suburbs.

Governing citizens in an advanced liberal society

The theoretical starting point here is an understanding of citizenship informed by Michel Foucault (1991) and his notion of governmentality. The concept of governmentality focuses on 'different mentalities of government' (Dean 1999, 16), drawing attention to the complex ways in which thought is linked to a wide range of procedures and techniques. Seen in this way, citizenship is not a 'given', but rather something constantly produced and imagined in certain ways (Cruikshank 1999; Hindess 2002). Citizenship could be seen as an ongoing process of forming citizens as a certain kind of subjects, where the construction of the norm (the ideal citizen) as well as the others (those lacking the virtues and competences of the ideal citizen) is inextricably entwined (Nicoll et al. 2013).

The classic formula for the governing of citizens in the welfare state, according to Nikolas Rose (1996), is state-centric. It consists of making the state the primary agent that forms, guides, and controls events and people, based on uniform policies. However, as Rose points out, we are living in an 'advanced liberal society', which 'does not seek to govern through "society", but through the regulated choices of individual citizens, now constructed as subjects of choices and aspirations to self-actualization and self-fulfilment' (1996, 41). The exercise of power involves constant 'responsibilization'—the creation of active and responsible citizens who take charge of the entire course of their own lives (from education and work, politics, and housing to family and leisure activities) according to their own ideals, circumstances, ambitions and, of course, efforts. Thus the object of these interventions is 'implanting in citizens the aspiration to pursue their own civility, wellbeing and advancement' (Rose 1996, 40), with the creation of individuals who are motivated, willing, and able to be active and take the initiative. The creation of such citizens demands a broad repertoire of technologies, operating in different fields, forming subjectivities in ways that spur individuals to *want* to take the initiative and not be 'a burden on society'.

The politics of welfare change

The Swedish welfare model, as it evolved in the early post-war period, was based on the pillars of centralism and universalism, social intervention, and consensus (Rothstein 1998). Starting in the late 1980s, several of the cardinal principles underpinning the Swedish model came under increasing attack. The model was criticized, among other things, for its alleged inefficiency and highly centralized micro-management, which was said to stand in the way of individual initiative, hampering people's will to participate and have their say (Boréus 1994). In recent decades, the Swedish model has thus undergone a radical transformation, starting back in the 1970s and 1980s, but accelerating after the deep economic crisis of the early 1990s (Lindvall 2004). As in many other countries in Europe and across the world, the Swedish welfare model has witnessed a gradual shift in emphasis towards individual autonomy, initiative, and freedom of choice vis-à-vis governmental control, endeavours to achieve equality, and the redistribution of societal resources (Ryner 2002)—in other words, a shift towards active citizenship.

The Swedish model, widely recognized as the paradigm for a national welfare regime in the social-democratic tradition (Esping-Andersen 1990), has thus moved step by step towards becoming a post-national workfare regime (Jessop 2002). Flexibility, innovation, and international competitiveness constitute its overriding goals in all essential respects. In order to force the labour market to be more flexible and competitive, economic policy is given precedence over social policy. Social welfare expenditure is thus viewed more in terms of a cost of production than as a means of redistributing resources. Both social and labour market policy are primarily focused on the supply side of the labour market, on the workforce, in an endeavour to create a more competitive 'knowledge economy'. The system of transfer payments is made more cost-effective in order to promote a 'climate of enterprise'. State intervention in the shape of social policy measures is viewed less and less as a means of protecting citizens from the destructive forces of an unregulated market economy.

Although it is not a question of a total regime shift in the sense of the traditional 'Swedish model' being replaced by a completely new model, it is nonetheless evident that Sweden in a number of respects is moving towards a new welfare regime (Schierup 2006). These developments have not least taken place in labour market policy over the past two decades (Ryner 2002).

The right to work is usually accounted one of the fundamental rights of social citizenship (Marshall 1950). Work was also a cornerstone of the traditional Swedish model. The Swedish welfare state as it evolved in the post-war period was based on the doctrine known as *arbetslinjen* or workfare ('work, not welfare'), which was predicated on full employment, in the sense that everyone who was able to work should as far as possible be in work, and a solidarity-based wages policy, whose objective was to level out wage differentials. This in turn was founded on a strong, centralized collective bargaining system involving all parties to the labour market, both employers and trades unions (Esping-Andersen 1990). However, beginning in the 1980s and accelerating in the 1990s, the traditional Swedish model's labour market policies underwent a series of dramatic changes.

From full employment to full employability

When we look more closely at Sweden's 1990s' labour market policies, a number of central, interwoven themes emerge. In the discourse of the day, the main challenge was said to be finding the measures that could lift the unemployed from a 'passive' dependency on benefits to an 'active' occupation. In order to succeed, a broad repertoire of 'activation' measures would be required in order to improve the 'employability' not only of the unemployed, but also of those already in work. At the same time, there was concern at the increasingly marked social polarization and 'exclusion', particularly in suburban areas, with those who were excluded thought to be at risk of developing a distinct mentality, separating them from the rest of society (see Junestav 2004; Hörnqvist 2007). We will return to the issue of exclusion and urban policy later.

The idea that the main point of labour market policy should be to stimulate activity (either employment or measures to promote employment), rather than relying on passive dependency on benefits, has dominated Swedish labour market policy throughout the post-war period, but it was particularly pronounced in the climate created by the deep economic crisis of the early 1990s, with its growing inequality, record levels of inflation, and mass unemployment at a level not witnessed since the Great Depression of the 1930s. The crisis of the 1990s seriously challenged the Swedish model and had a lasting effect on Swedish politics—not least in the area of labour market policy.

How then were greater numbers of citizens to be 'activated' through work? The main answer to this question, in both Sweden and the EU, was employability. In the 1990s, there was a growing sense that an individual's employment was dependent on his or her power of initiative (Garsten & Jacobsson 2004; Hörnqvist 2007): individuals themselves should be responsible for their own successes and failures. In order to get a job, the individual would need to have the 'right' qualities. Those seeking work had to be employable, or become so. In order to increase employment levels, a broad repertoire of measures were therefore required to improve the employability not only of the unemployed, but also of those already in work.

With the focus increasingly directed at formulating measures to generate employability, the character of labour market policy gradually shifted. The problem was redefined. Having been a question of a lack of job opportunities, labour market policy was now defined in terms of a shortfall in employability. Initiatives to produce full employment were retargeted to create full employability. In Sweden, however, this shift had already been initiated prior to the crisis of the 1990s as a result of the Social Democratic government's prioritization of the battle against inflation over the goal of full employment, something which subsequently continued as part of Sweden's intensified collaboration with the EU (Jacobsson 2004).

With the shift from full employment to full employability, state responsibility for labour market policy has clearly been circumscribed. More is left to private interests. The focus is wholly on the supply side of the labour market, 'to "flexibilize" and "motivate" the unemployed' (Peck & Theodore 2000, 729). Activating measures are developed in order to cultivate the unemployed, getting them to want to become more employable. This process is described in terms of lifelong learning: those who want to find work and those who want to keep their jobs are to continuously work on themselves, improve their competitiveness, update their qualifications, undergo additional education, and develop the 'right' attitude in terms of initiative, enterprise, and flexibility (Fogde 2007; Vesterberg 2013).

Restoring workfare

The focus on activation has remained the dominant theme in the labour market policy of the 2000s. Indeed, activation was high on the political agenda in the general election of 2006. Prior to the election, the centre–right parliamentary political parties—Moderaterna (lit. moderates, or conservatives), the Liberals, the Centre Party, and the Christian Democrats—declared their intention to challenge the ruling Social Democrats by forming, for the first time in the history of Swedish politics, an alternative government of the centre–right, the 'Alliance for Sweden'. The centre–right parliamentary parties had never previously joined forces in this way prior to a general election in order to offer voters the possibility of a united alternative government.

During the election campaign, the Alliance succeeded in taking command of the political debate by defining the political dilemma as a series of choices between two alternatives: work or exclusion, enterprise or benefits, bottom up or top down. According to the Alliance, who went on to win the election, the fault line in modern society was no longer between labour and capital—the interpretation on which the Swedish Model had been built—but rather between work and exclusion. The Alliance's central definition of the problem was concisely formulated in its Declaration of Government in 2006:

> The progress of society is dependent on people's will to work, their capacity to assume responsibility, their inventiveness, enterprise, and courage to invest in the future. Over a million people are outside the labour market. Despite strong economic growth, there is mass unemployment. (Government 2006, 2)

The most important political challenge was to take those who found themselves in 'the Sweden of the excluded'—those who made no contribution to the economy through work, the unemployed, those who were dependent on benefits—and bring them into the community by making them provide for themselves.

> Sweden needs a vigorous programme for more jobs throughout Sweden that make it more rewarding to work and easier to provide employment. The thresholds to entry to the labour market must be lowered, and working more or taking on more responsibility must be rewarded. ... High taxes, complicated regulations, and far-reaching commitments mean that employers are afraid to employ people. (Government 2006, 2)

By successfully exerting pressure on public opinion prior to the election, the Alliance managed to divide Swedish politics into two opposing camps: those advocating work and activity (and who thus supported the Alliance) and those advocating exclusion and passivity (and who thus supported the ruling Social Democrats). It appeared quite impossible to even imagine that there might be any additional alternatives other than these two. The language had a moral undertone, with work being assigned a superior moral status. 'Workfare and the value of work shall be restored'. Work was viewed as a fundamental precondition of human existence: 'Having a meaningful occupation is important for individual self-determination, quality of life, and participation. Feeling needed produces networks of security between individuals and makes people dare to assume responsibility and to grow in line with the tasks that face them' (ibid. 13–14). For the Alliance, work—contributing to the economy rather than receiving benefits—was the most important element in responsible, active citizenship.

The moral–political narrative of the Alliance openly combined 'new' elements with 'old'. Yet at the same time as it was careful to distance itself from social democracy and its 'passivizing' benefits policy, its emphasis on workfare contained clear continuities from the ideals of the earlier labour movement—discipline, conscientiousness, and a sense of duty. During the election campaign, Moderaterna, the largest of the centre–right parliamentary parties, proclaimed themselves to be *new* Moderaterna, 'the new workers' party', the party that was taking on the task of restoring 'the value of work', which had been lost through unwieldy welfare edifices built by the social-democratic movement.

For the Alliance, however, employment was not only a fundamental precondition of human existence. The Declaration of Government states forcefully that increased employment is necessary if Sweden is to maintain its position in a seemingly harsher climate of global competition. The theme of work as a means of improving Swedish competitiveness was repeatedly emphasized by the Alliance: 'Tougher global competition means an increased risk of jobs moving abroad' (Government 2006, 2); 'Entrepreneurship and the spirit of enterprise are critical to increasing employment, laying the foundations for continued progress across the whole of Sweden and strengthening Sweden's position in the world' (Government 2006, 1). In order to assert Sweden's position in the face of global competition, the Alliance stressed that the Swedish labour market needed to be made more adaptable to the demands of an increasingly globalized economy: 'Sweden needs a well-functioning and flexible labour market' (Skr. 2006/07:23, 6). For the Alliance, such an understanding of work, and the importance of work, is intimately related to another concept—that of exclusion.

The multi-ethnic suburb and the threat of exclusion

The concept of exclusion has been crucial in the political vocabulary of the Alliance, who have referred to it as the problematic opposite to their ideal of active citizenship, legitimating the various proposed activating measures. They do not have a monopoly on it, however, as the concept of exclusion has been used in Swedish labour market policy ever since the 1990s, particularly in relation to ethnicity and the challenges of multi-ethnic suburbs throughout the country. These areas, as well as their inhabitants, have been seen as one of the most urgent challenges for Swedish labour market policy, and welfare policy more generally (Urban 2005).

With their 1998 Bill *Progress and justice—an urban policy for the first decade of the twenty-first century* (Government Bill 1997/98, 165), the ruling Social Democrats introduced an integrated urban policy for the first time (Tedros 2008). The Bill offered an alarming description of the situation in Sweden's larger cities. During the 1990s, the cost of income support payments in the three largest cities, Stockholm, Gothenburg, and Malmö, had almost tripled. Towards the end of the 1990s, levels of employment in what the government referred to as the 'most disadvantaged city districts' fluctuated between 30 and 40 per cent. Against this background, the government concluded that 'One of the most important goals for urban policy is to improve the level of employment in disadvantaged neighbourhoods' (Government Bill 1998, 82). The critical challenge for urban policy was how to turn passivity and exclusion into activity and participation. When it came to developing a policy intended to activate, the importance of a job of one's own naturally assumed a central position.

> Since participation in the life of the community and the possibilities for a good financial, social, and cultural life are strongly associated with having a job and being able to provide for oneself, this is critical to continued social progress. (Government Bill 1998, 82–3)

Once again, the emphasis was on the fundamental importance of paid work to both the individual citizen and to society at large. It was first and foremost through waged work that the citizen would become part of the community in a meaningful way. The opposite, being out of work and 'dependent on benefits', left the citizen at risk of being drawn into a vicious spiral that in time could lead to permanent exclusion.

> Unemployment is most serious for those people who are excluded from the job market for long periods. They experience greater risks to their health than many other groups, their long-term income increases more slowly, they lose competence and therefore run the risk of becoming permanently cut off from the job market. ... In practice, they become trapped in unemployment and dependency on benefits. (Government Bill 1998, 83)

As before, the Social Democrats stressed the necessity of reacting to the threat of being trapped in exclusion and dependency on benefits by being active and eschewing passive measures. According to the government, 'extended periods of nothing but benefits can lead to people becoming passive and losing confidence in themselves'. In order to avoid this kind of passivity, measures were needed to produce employability, which 'both maintains and improves the competence of those seeking work' (Government Bill 1998, 83).

The government pointed out that its policy was based on an 'explicit reciprocity, in which the individual has both rights and obligations'. The obligations of society were focused on the unemployed individual. Society had a duty to offer various measures and programmes to improve the unemployed individual's employability. 'On the one hand, society is prepared to support those who have a hard time finding work, both financially and by means of active measures' (Government Bill 1998, 83–4). At the same time, the unemployed individual had an obligation to actively participate in these measures and programmes—'On the other hand, society expects unemployed individuals to actively utilize their own resources and opportunities, and to be prepared to take any suitable job' (Government Bill 1998, 84). There was particularly strong emphasis on the individual's obligations to society—'The right to receive payments from the various benefit systems is linked to some form of condition or requirement for the individual to do something in return'—and the Bill noted that what was required of benefit recipients in return could take different forms, with the unemployed individual being required to 'seek and accept a new job even outside the occupation or profession in which he or she has previously worked' or 'to accept a different wage, to move, or to commute to work, to retrain, or to participate in job training measures' (Government Bill 1998, 88–9).

At the time, the centre–right opposition parties were strongly critical of several aspects of what they regarded to be too much of a traditional, state-managed, top-down policy. 'It is not enough to make people employable', the Liberals noted in an Opposition Bill on integration policy (Mot. 1997/98:Sf8); a policy to produce real employability 'needs fresh ideas', requiring amongst other things 'that labour market policy is not viewed as a storage system and that people are viewed as being capable'. The party emphasized that the system of state benefits needed to be overhauled in order to promote employment and free enterprise, or, as they put it, 'The benefits systems have to become opportunities for life, not prisons'. They argued that in residential districts with high levels of unemployment, and where a large proportion of residents were forced to live outside the regular labour market for long periods of time, a distinctive attitude tended to develop over time, not least among the younger generation:

> The children and young people who grow up in an environment where there is no relationship between work and income do not learn this relationship for themselves, of course. Instead they grow up in an environment that is no doubt poisoned by discontent and frustration at this situation. It is not strange that this becomes transformed into aggression and even hatred. (Mot. 1997/98:Sf8)

With time, emotional currents of this kind could produce major challenges to the provision of welfare and security. Similar ideas were also expressed by the other opposition parties.

The emergence of cultures of exclusion

In 1999, Moderaterna appointed a special Working Group against Social Segregation and Exclusion. One of the central figures in this working group was Mauricio Rojas, an economic historian, public figure, and at the time the vice-executive director of a business-oriented think-tank called Timbro. In a report entitled *Renewal and citizen power*, the Working Group stated that Sweden's integration policy had been a large-scale failure as a result of 'counterproductive social engineering' (Moderaterna 1999, 3). The Swedish welfare system as a whole was described as 'a social project based on social planning ideals, centralization, doing everything on a large scale, and uniformity' (ibid. 4).

This social project was said to have led over time to the establishment of a countrywide 'benefit-financed exclusion and a devastating benefit culture', not least in increasingly marginalized suburban environments where life 'does not revolve around work and enterprise, but around the art of maximizing benefits and living on the margins of society' (Moderaterna 1999, 20). These ideas are largely the same as the Liberals', even if the presentation is rather more direct: exclusion is defined in terms of both unemployment and morals. To combat passivation from above the Working Group proposed citizen power from below, the only reasonable alternative being to 'create more competition, openness, and flexibility in our societal economy' (ibid. 22) and to 'give the citizens the simple but very important power to behave as customers and not as clients' (ibid. 26).

Shortly after the Working Group had completed its work, Rojas left Moderaterna to join the Liberals—not without fuss—whereupon he became the latter party's new spokesman on integration policy. He soon left his mark on the party's work in relation to 'suburban Sweden'. Largely thanks to the strategic development of a strong profile on the 'integration question', the Liberals had a very good election in 2002, in which they almost tripled their level of electoral support compared with the preceding election, going from 4.6 to 13.3 per cent of the popular vote (see Dahlstedt 2014).

In December 2004, the party leader, Lars Leijonborg, together with Rojas, who was now a newly elected MP, presented a new report on the 'development of exclusion' in multi-ethnic suburbs across Sweden (Folkpartiet 2004). The picture of suburban life presented in the report was a dismal one. Leijonborg and Rojas (2004) concluded that:

> A new social landscape has emerged in Sweden, a landscape characterized by exclusion from the labour market, by residential segregation, dependency on benefits, powerlessness, and vulnerability. It is about tens of thousands of people among whom the vital processes of social mobility have ceased to function, and residential neighbourhoods whose life is almost completely lived under socio-economic conditions that are strikingly different from those of the rest of society. (Leijonborg & Rojas 2004)

The report emphasized that 'islands of profound exclusion' were now to be found 'in almost all large- and medium-sized Swedish cities' (Folkpartiet 2004, 8). Sweden was said to be 'dangerously close to the point where ethnic and social conflicts may degenerate into open riots and other extremely tragic events' (ibid. 6). In the definition of the problem that informed not only the report, but also all the other statements and documents in which the party focused on 'the suburban problem', the morals of the residents were ascribed a central role (for example, Mot. 2004/05:Sf288). One particularly serious problem was identified as the 'cultural framework of reference', which was said to be developing in 'the neighbourhoods of exclusion' as a consequence not only of immigration and 'significant cultural differences' between 'immigrant' and 'native-born groups', but also the fact that residents were living in the shadow of central social arenas or completely outside them (Folkpartiet 2004, 8).

As the Social Democrats had done in the 1998 urban policy Bill, the report published by the Liberals emphasized that the central problem was the high levels of unemployment found in the 'neighbourhoods of exclusion'. In spite of this, the report argued that once it had taken shape, the specific morality generated by such conditions had its own, independent dynamic. 'When life for a majority of those living in a given area is entirely pervaded by socio-economic conditions and cultural frames of reference that are radically different from those of the rest of society, individual disadvantage is transformed into collective processes with a dynamic of their own', a description that divorces the 'culture of exclusion' from its social context. Instead, the report described a downward spiral in which 'exclusion generates more exclusion and where the culture of exclusion is passed on to subsequent generations', and where 'that which started as an effect—exclusion—becomes transformed into a cause' (Folkpartiet 2004, 9).

Another important element in the party's view on the 'neighbourhoods of exclusion' was recognizable from Moderaterna's Working Group, namely the idea that the 'culture of exclusion' had been promoted by the state's 'overprotective and overindulgent policies'. The implementation of such policies throughout the post-war period had in practice stripped people of their creativity and initiative in favour of solutions formulated from above. According to the Liberals, the benefits systems had itself created a 'dependency' from which it was very difficult to recover. 'There is a fast habit-forming effect', the party argued in an Opposition Bill; 'Those who become used to being provided for by others will after a time come to see this as a natural condition' (Mot. 2004/05:Sf288, 33). In line with this, Leijonborg and Rojas (2004) argued that it was high time for a 'change of perspective that opens the way for an inclusive policy for progress based on individual empowerment instead of indulgence, on work instead of benefits'. They continued with a clear reference to a successful slogan in the 2002 election, 'Making demands is caring':

> A new ability is needed to dare to insist that all individuals should do as much as they are capable of—to make demands is to care. Because exclusion cannot be broken from the outside. It is only from the inside, when those affected themselves take things into their own hands, that anything positive can happen. (Leijonborg & Rojas 2004)

As their argument was based on a strong normative assumption about independence constituting the ideal, the party proposed a series of activating measures, where the obligation to work was advocated as an alternative to the passivizing (right to) welfare. The idea of activation ran as a central theme through the battery of proposed measures designed to bring renewal to the 'neighbourhoods of exclusion'.

This use of the integration issue by the Liberals as a means of attracting political attention has had a major effect on the integration policy debate over the last decade, in which the party was able to take command of the political debate by focussing on 'increased demands', among other things in relation to migrants' Swedish language skills (Dahlstedt 2014). Following the change in government after the 2006 election, the party's urban and integration policy has had considerable impact at the governmental level, while the Liberal MPs Nyamko Sabuni and later Erik Ullenhag were made minister for integration.

This brings us back to the general election of 2006 and the Alliance's endeavours to 'restore workfare'. The government's position in its urban and integration policy was stated openly in 2006 in the Declaration of Government: 'One consistent element in the government's integration policy will be the removal of obstacles and the opening up of opportunities' (Government 2006, 7). In line with the drive to 'restore workfare', the government stressed that employment and enterprise were the route out of the state of exclusion that many 'immigrants' were forced to live in. It was therefore essential that 'people who have migrated to Sweden are respected as individuals and not regarded as a homogeneous collective' (ibid. 7). In contrast to previous initiatives, which had comprised too many measures specifically focused on 'immigrants', a more general 'emancipatory' policy was proposed: 'Beyond the initial period in Sweden, no separate policy is required for immigrants, but rather a policy that frees people's inherent power and breaks down the exclusion that has become established in Sweden' (ibid. 7).

Concluding remarks

For the last two decades, active citizenship has been a recurrent theme in public discourses about the challenges facing multi-ethnic cities in Sweden. The focus of this essay has been the formation of the ideal 'active citizen' in Swedish labour market and urban policy from the 1990s onwards. Active citizenship has been an ideal since the early 1990s, a notion of citizenship as something that safeguards and promotes the autonomy, initiative, and freedom of the individual vis-à-vis the state's efforts to exert control, redistribute resources, and promote equality. Here, both centre–right and social-democratic governments have increasingly emphasized work as a duty, rather than a right, of citizenship. This is part of a more general change in the way welfare provision is organized in many countries in and beyond Europe. Even though there have been differences between the social-democratic and centre–right governments regarding their view of welfare and state intervention, there are still a number of similarities, not least in the way both underline the importance of activating measures, the desire to improve the individual's employability, and the ever present threat of growing exclusion.

The activation policies developed since the 1990s amount to a complex, neo-liberal form of governing. On the one hand, they are libertarian, in the sense that they strive to motivate and release the creativity of the individual. On the other hand, they are disciplinary, in the sense that they emphasize work as an obligation and require something in return (Hörnqvist 2007). In the traditional Swedish model, there was also a strong emphasis on work as the citizen's obligation—all who were able to work were expected to do so. The obligation to work was balanced, however, both by a collective wage policy that was designed to ensure reasonable levels of pay and by a public benefits system for those who were unable to get a job (Junestav 2004). Meanwhile, the labour market policy that evolved in the 1990s individualized the question of the citizen's right to work. Following Rose (1996), we could talk of a change in governing rationality from a state-oriented form to one more oriented towards the individual. Work became a question of the individual's own qualifications and characteristics, ambitions and abilities. 'Passivizing' benefits were replaced by 'activating' interventions, making the unemployed more employable. Increased levels of responsibility and more demands were placed on the individual, while the state increasingly disclaimed responsibility for the outcome of its labour market policy.

The central welfare policy issue of resource redistribution has been more or less removed from the political agenda, and as a result, society's responsibility for guaranteeing citizens a reasonable level of welfare has gradually been undermined. The welfare of citizens, which in the golden age of the Swedish Model was guaranteed by the social insurance systems of the welfare state, was once again increasingly determined by the value of their work (Esping-Andersen 1990; Johansson 2001). The contours of a new Swedish Model began to emerge, with this new model emphasizing citizens' obligations, duties, and morality over their rights (Junestav 2004; Schierup 2006).

This transformation is plain to see in Swedish urban policy. In a way, the multi-ethnic suburb has come to represent the other which gives the ideal of 'active citizenship' its meaning (Tesfahuney & Dahlstedt 2008). The issue that has repeatedly been raised in the context of the urban policy debate since the late 1990s is how to get the suburban population to abandon its impotence, dependence, and passivity for the supposed diligence, confidence, employability, and enterprise of the rest of Swedish society. Everything seemed to hang on the ambition of the suburban residents themselves. Exclusion could only be resolved from the inside. Suburban residents might well find themselves completely excluded, suffering as a result of a lack of knowledge of the Swedish language or of Swedish society, but the solution to their problems was to be found among the very people categorized as the problem. Even the most excluded citizens could 'take control over their own lives' and find their way into the community—if they were given the opportunity. On the basis of this type of argument, a large number of activating measures intended to motivate, provide opportunities, and remove obstacles have been targeted specifically at multi-ethnic suburbs.

As the obligation to work has been given increasing weight, the conditions for combating socio-economic and ethnic hierarchies in the Swedish urban landscape and in society as a whole have become worse. This kind of policy has far-reaching consequences in terms of social rights—the right to a reasonable income, security of employment, reasonable housing, and educational equality—but it also risks gradually undermining civil and political rights. When social rights are increasingly circumscribed, suburban residents may also find it increasingly difficult to exercise their civil and political rights, voicing their needs and interests. Thus, at least in the longer term, the ongoing changes to the Swedish welfare state have important consequences for the ideal of a vital, functioning democracy.

However, as shown by recent developments in peripheral suburban areas across Europe, such seismic shifts of welfare policy can also transform multi-ethnic suburbs into contested sites, where it is possible for residents to articulate alternative ways of becoming a citizen and to pursue a citizenship beyond prescribed models, beyond hierarchies and unequivocal distinctions. These suburban contestations can actively involve the young, whose lives have been hugely affected by ongoing welfare changes, privatization and cuts in public spending, increased poverty, long-term unemployment, stigmatization, problems at school, and police surveillance. In the last decade, Sweden has also witnessed sporadic urban unrest, even violent disturbances, with cars and schools set on fire and local confrontations with the police—witness Ronna, Södertälje, and Rosengård in Malmö in 2005, or Husby in Stockholm in 2013. Suburban Sweden has also seen the rise of new social movements, campaigning for equal social rights, claiming citizens' rights to the city, and challenging current notions of citizenship in contemporary multi-ethnic Sweden (de los Reyes et al. 2014; Schierup et al. 2014). And the outcome of these struggles is anything but predictable.

References

Bonoli, G. & D. Natali (2011) *The politics of welfare states in Western Europe* (EUI Working Paper RSCAS 2011/17).

Boréus, K. (1994) *Högervåg* (Stockholm: Tiden).

Cruikshank, B. (1999) *The will to empower* (Ithaca: Cornell University Press).

Dahlstedt, M. (2014) 'The politics of making demands: Discourses of urban exclusion and medialized politics in Sweden', *International Journal of Politics, Culture & Society*, 28/2, 101–117.

Dean, M. (1999) *Governmentality* (Thousand Oaks: SAGE).

de los Reyes, P., M. Hörnqvist, K. Boréus, F. Estrada, J. Flyghed, A. González Arriagada, M. Lundgren & M. Lundström (2014) *'Bilen brinner… men problemen är kvar': Berättelser om Husbyhändelserna i maj 2013* (Stockholm: Stockholmia).

Esping-Andersen, G. (1990) *The three worlds of welfare capitalism* (Oxford: Polity).

European Commission (2000) *A memorandum on lifelong learning* (Brussels: European Commission).

Fejes, A. (2009) 'Active democratic citizenship and lifelong learning', in M. Bron, P. Guimarães & R. Vieira de Castro (eds.) *The state, civil society and the citizen*, 79–95 (Frankfurt am main: Peter Lang).

Fogde, M. (2007) 'The making of an employable individual', in B. Höijer (ed.) *Ideological horizons in media and citizen discourse* (Gothenburg: Nordicom).

Folkpartiet (2004) *Utanförskapets karta* (Stockholm).

Foucault, M. (1991) 'On governmentality', in G. Burchell, C. Gordon & P. Miller (eds.) *The Foucault effect* (Brighton: Harvester).

Garsten, C. & K. Jacobsson (2004) (eds.) *Learning to be employable* (Houndsmills: Palgrave Macmillan).

Government (2003) *Sveriges handlingsplan mot fattigdom och social utestängning 2003–2005* (Stockholm: Socialdepartementet, Regeringskansliet).

Government (2006) *Regeringsförklaringen 6 oktober 2006*, <http://www.regeringen.se/sb/d/6316/a/70232>, accessed 26 June 2015.

Government Bill (1996) *Regeringens proposition 1995/96:222, Vissa åtgärder för att halvera arbetslösheten till år 2000, ändrade anslag för budgetåret 1995/96, finansiering m.m* (Stockholm: Fritze).

Government Bill (1998) Regeringens proposition 1997/98:165, *Utveckling och rättvisa: En politik för storstaden på 2000-talet* (Stockholm: Fritze).

Hindess, B. (2002) 'Neo-liberal citizenship', *Citizenship Studies*, 6/2, 127–43.

Hörnqvist, M. (2007) *The organised nature of power: On productive and repressive interventions based on considerations of risk* (Stockholm: Stockholm University).

Jacobsson, K. (2004) 'A European politics for employability', in C. Garsten & K. Jacobsson (eds.) *Learning to be employable* (Houndsmills: Palgrave Macmillan).

Jessop, B. (2002) *The future of the capitalist state* (Cambridge: Polity).

Johansson, H. (2001) 'Activation policies in the Nordic countries', *Journal of European Area Studies* 9/1, 63–77.

Junestav, M. (2004) *Arbetslinjer i svensk socialpolitisk debatt och lagstiftning, 1930–2001* (Uppsala: Uppsala University).

Köhler, P. A., K. H. Thorén & R. Ulmestig (2008) 'Activation policies in Sweden', in W. Eichhorst, O. Kaufmann & R. Konle-Seidl (eds.) *Bringing the jobless into work?* (Berlin: Springer).
Leijonborg, L. & M. Rojas (2004) 'Explosiv ökning av antalet utsatta bostadsområden', *Dagens Nyheter*, 5 December.
Lindvall, J. (2004) *The politics of purpose* (Gothenburg: Gothenburg University).
Marshall, T. H. (1950) *Citizenship and social class* (Cambridge: CUP).
Moderaterna (1999) *Förnyelse och medborgarmakt* (Working Group against Segregation and Exclusion).
Molina, I. (1997) *Stadens rasifiering* (Department of Cultural Geography; Uppsala: Uppsala University).
Mot. (1997/98:Sf8) 'Med anledning av Prop 1997/98:16 Sverige, framtiden och mångfalden—från invandrarpolitik till integrationspolitik' (Folkpartiet).
Mot. (2004/05:Sf288) 'Egenmakt och arbete—den liberala vägen till integration' (Folkpartiet).
Nicoll, K., A. Fejes, M. Olson, M. Dahlstedt & G. Biesta (2013) 'Opening discourses of citizenship and citizenship education', *Journal of Education Policy*, 28/6, 828–46.
Peck, J. & N. Theodore (2000) 'Beyond "employability"', *Cambridge Journal of Economics*, 24/6, 729–49.
Ristilammi, P.-M. (1994) *Rosengård och den svarta poesin* (Stockholm/Stehag: Brutus Östlings Bokförlag Symposion).
Rose, N. (1996) 'Governing "advanced" liberal democracies', in A. Barry, T. Osborne & N. Rose (eds.) *Foucault and political reason* (London: Routledge).
Rothstein, B. (1998) *Just institutions matter* (Cambridge: CUP).
Ryner, M. J. (2002) *Capitalist restructuring, globalisation, and the third way* (London: Routledge).
Schierup, C.-U. (2006) 'Den sociala exkluderingen i Sverige. Migration, arbetsmarknad och välfärdsstat i förändring', in P. de los Reyes (ed.) *Arbetets (o)synliga murar. Rapport av Utredningen om makt, integration och strukturell diskriminering* [The Commission on Power, Integration and Structural Discrimination] (SOU 2006:59; Stockholm: Fritze).
Schierup, C.-U., P. Hansen & S. Castles (2006) *Migration, citizenship and the european welfare state* (Oxford: OUP).
Schierup, C.-U., A. Ålund & Kings, L. (2014) 'Reading the Stockholm riots', *Race & Class*, 55 [3]; 1–21.
Skr 2006/07:23, *Sveriges handlingsprogram för tillväxt och sysselsättning 2006–2008* (Stockholm, 23 November 2006).
Tedros, A. (2008) *Utanför storstaden* (School of Public Administration; Gothenburg: Gothenburg University).
Tesfahuney, M. & M. Dahlstedt (2008) 'Tärningen är kastad', in eid. (eds.) *Den bästa av världar?* (Stockholm: Tankekraft).
Urban, S. (2005) *Att ordna staden* (Lund: Arkiv).
Vesterberg, V. (2013) 'Ethnicized un/employability', *Ephemera* 13/4, 737–57.

II

URBAN MARGINALITY IN THE SCANDINAVIAN WELFARE STATES

CHAPTER 4

The necessity of socio-dynamic analyses of the city
The case of Malmö

Tapio Salonen

A city can be considered from an immense range of perspectives. It may be in the nature of urban life for it to be in a constant state of flux, but there is also a considerable measure of continuity about it. Depending on the observer, any given community can appear in a very different light, for where some might home in on the signs of stability, the dominant impression for others might be change and instability. Writ large, the shifts in the city's existence reflect the vagaries of collective human life, whether changes that are cyclical and demographic in character, or those which are ultimately driven by structural, economic, and social shifts. The physical environment is frequently more resilient than the social environment. Buildings often last longer than people, after all. The built environment can change its social complexion—it can become run down, for example, or it might be gentrified—yet while residential and commercial property may survive, albeit many times with a change of purpose, where and how people choose to live and work varies far more, to the point of impermanence.

Studies of the city usually adopt specific, and thus limited, vantage points. Frequently they are concerned with a specific aspect of the city: the physical environment, say, or the situation of one population group. The focus of urban planning and public policy tends to be smaller city districts earmarked for new-build or urban renewal measures. Needless to say, detailed planning is essential when setting out the city's future development, but the risk remains that an overall perspective on the city is lacking. Such wholesale approaches as there are usually rely on mass data, which is used to describe changes in the city's progress. The problem with such comparisons over time is that they fail to take into account the social changes undergone by different population groups, which are then collectively summarized in statistical overviews of the city's development.

This essay thus discusses the city's development using a broad socio-dynamic approach, which provides an accurate overview of the demographic and social changes that are always underway in the city. Perhaps the commonest metaphor for such socio-dynamic change is the 'melting pot', which in the international literature is invariably used to describe the successive mixing of groups of Americans from different backgrounds and cultures. Hence, 'The ethnic diversity, multicultural neighbourhoods, and the close proximity to these neighbourhoods make Chicago a true melting pot and define the feeling of ease and comfort' (Arrival Guides 2015).

As Abrahamsson points out in the second essay in this volume, Scandinavian society has been increasingly caught up in a transformation that has seen its cities change in terms of globalization, migration, and urbanization. In this essay, these broad, contemporary trends are matched by examples taken from a single urban perspective—Malmö. Sweden's third largest city, Malmö has changed rapidly, for where it was once an industrial city dominated by a relatively homogeneous Swedish population in the mid twentieth century, it is now one of Europe's most cosmopolitan cities.

This essay demonstrates the need for socio-dynamic analyses of the social transformation of the city that manage to capture both its exogenous and endogenous dimensions, the former by viewing the city in its relevant context, the latter by contributing a proper understanding of the relations—and tensions—between different city districts. These internal and external aspects are enmeshed in the socio-dynamic fabric of the city. Instead of concentrating on a specific aspect of social development, as is customary, such a study offers a more consistent analysis of demographic and employment dynamics in Sweden's third largest city. It consists of three interconnecting sections that together illustrate a city in flux, whether in terms of population movement, people's relationships to employment opportunities, or city districts as the anchor points of social cohesion.

Understanding the city's changeability

Studies of the changeability of post-industrial cities present a challenge to many of the generally accepted theories and empirical methods (Kazepov 2005). As Abrahamsson insightfully puts it elsewhere in this volume, a city such as Malmö is part of an ongoing globalization, whereby all-pervasive processes of globalization, migration, and urbanization leave an indelible mark on the city's development. Interwoven and complex as they are, these are processes that do not lend themselves to being studied separately. Questions about social sustainability and cohesion in a city such as Malmö can only be fully answered by linking different perspectives. Pinpoint the structural macro-issues that determine the course of everyday life, a more complete and credible analysis of city development emerges. Traditionally, different areas of an urban analysis are kept separate, because in many cases it is necessary in order to retain both precision and focus in the transition from the specific to the general; however, in order to offer a credible summary of the city's development, especially if focusing on its social dimensions, one must cast the net wider to include the dynamic processes intrinsic to individual lives, groups, city districts, and urban structures.

This essay takes its lead from a socio-ecological research tradition that can be traced back to the interwar Chicago School (Andersson 2003; Sampson 2012). It is a tradition that considers marginal phenomena or the situation of vulnerable groups, with an eye on the interaction of structural framing with organizational or human behaviour, taking a pluralistic approach to the causes and effects of various social phenomena—an approach which means the differences in a given neighbourhood cannot be reduced to a narrowly defined set of individual effects, but must also be understood in a relational and structural perspective. Some neighbourhoods or groups are ascribed specific functions and roles to play in the wider urban environment. Inequalities in living conditions, whether between households or city districts, are taken to be a social dynamic, with causal processes at different levels.

Like Sampson (2012), I would argue for the necessity of a broad, contextual understanding of urban inequality and social differentiation. Changes in one city district or a group's circumstances necessarily include a diversity of both macro and micro perspectives and, ranged between them, institutional and political influences. The different levels of analysis are intertwined and, when seen relative to one another, can provide a richer, more complex analysis of social change in an urban setting. People's circumstances need to be understood in terms of the ways things work in their environment. Neighbourhood development cannot be understood without placing it in context, whether that context is the city or society as a whole. At the same time, each individual city district often displays in its built structures a high degree of spatial continuity—in other words, it retains its position in the city's and the region's socio-economic hierarchy. With this contextual approach, each city district is understood as both a cause and a consequence of social change. In this socio-ecological tradition, Sampson (2012) argues convincingly for the importance of studying the external, contextual factors in the development of a city and its districts, but without objectifying or losing sight of people's everyday lives.

> Neighborhoods are both chosen and allocated; defined by outsiders and insiders alike, often in contradiction to each other, they are both symbolically and structurally determined; large and small; overlapping or blurred in perceptual boundaries; relational; and ever changing in composition. (Sampson 2012, 55)

Elias and Scotson's classic sociological study (1999/1965) of what happened when a new group set about establishing itself in a British industrial city in the 1950s revealed the universal patterns of relationships between long-standing residents and newcomers. One of the lessons taken away from the study was the importance of how negative group characteristics were ascribed to the new arrivals and the role of rumour in the exercise of the locals' power. Elias and Scotson's point was that people's standard responses to an unestablished group of outsiders help to create distance and even antipathy between the groups, sometimes extending to alienation and oppression.

Ramberg (2012) uses the term 'urbanity' to capture the ideas and values of both the physical environment, the city-dwellers, and the constant dialectical interplay of built environment and social conditions. Some districts occupy a stable position in a city's social stratification, while others may find themselves on an upwards or downwards trajectory. Using studies of architectural competitions held for Swedish cities, Ramberg charts the absence not only of a critical analysis of the real problems facing urban development, but also of any vision of how the future of the city might best be framed.

The analysis in the present essay begins with a brief summary of a comprehensive analysis of one city's development. The emphasis is on statistical results and on temporal and spatial comparisons. Obviously, this is then supplemented by detailed, qualitative narratives to flesh out the analysis with examples taken from the steady stream of urban life stories, encounters, and events.

The city and the wider world

When it comes to exogenous change, there are a range of factors that affect a city from outside. In an age of accelerating migration and urbanization, particular account must be taken of the wider context. At the moment, every year sees an average of one in eight people in Sweden move house. Swedes move on average eleven times in a lifetime. Such migrations are largely associated with an age-related pattern, with the vast majority of moves occurring among the 20–29 age group of young people making a start in life. Most people who move do so within their local area (two-thirds). The vast majority remain in the county where they were born, or return there in later life (SCB 2012).

Two clear trends have emerged in recent years. First, there has been a rise in immigration from other countries. Sweden now leads the field in immigration, having overtaken many west European countries traditionally associated with immigration such as France, Germany, and the UK. Between 2001 and 2013, the number of foreign-born people in Sweden increased by half a million, from approximately 1 to 1.5 million, so that by 2013 they numbered 15.9 per cent of the population, compared with 11.5 per cent back in 2001 (SCB's statistical database). Thus nearly one in six people in Sweden was born in another country. In the past few years, immigration to Sweden has been at its highest levels ever, with more than 100,000 immigrants, mainly as a result of the wars in Syria and Somalia (SCB 2014).

Second, there has been a noticeable wave of urbanization in Sweden's major cities, particularly those with universities. This generally correlates with changing patterns of employment and an increased demand for university-educated employees. Whereas the national population grew by 14 per cent between 1990 and 2014, Sweden's three largest urban populations grew much faster: Stockholm by 35 per cent, Gothenburg by 25 per cent, and Malmö by 36 per cent.

How have these demographic trends in migration and urbanization affected a city such as Malmö? Malmö is one of Europe's fastest-growing cities, and should increasingly be seen as a key global node. The city stands out for its population flows, which are strikingly fluid, and its marked regeneration. Malmö has become a magnet for both short- and long-distance migration. In the short range it is dominated by young people in an establishing phase, who move to the city to study, work, and set up home. In the past decade, the level of higher education in Malmö has increased much faster than in the country as a whole. The percentage of residents aged 25–65 with a university education has risen from 41 to 54 per cent in the decade from 2004 to 2014 (SKL database KOLADA). Largely, this can be explained by the expansion of Malmö University and the fact that Malmö has become an increasingly attractive place to live, even for students at Lund University nearby.

The amount of direct immigration from foreign countries has been remarkable in the past two decades, accounting for about one-third of the approximately 20,000 people who move to Malmö each year. Since 2000, the migration surplus has averaged nearly 3,000 people annually, almost all of whom are overseas arrivals. The city's population changes in the past half-century were if anything even

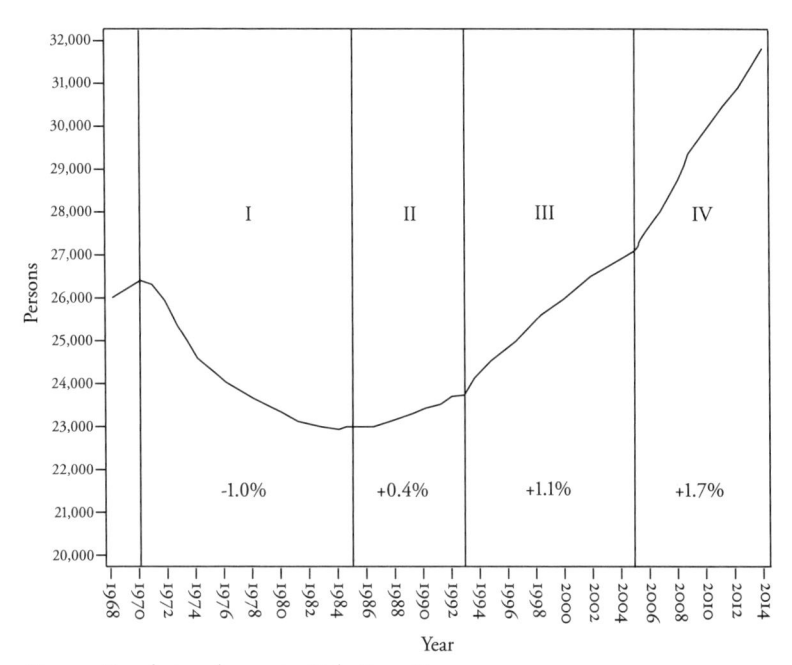

THE NECESSITY OF SOCIO-DYNAMIC ANALYSES OF THE CITY

Fig. 4.1. Population changes in Malmö, 1968–2014.

more dramatic (see Fig. 4.1). Once the industrial era had peaked in the early 1970s, the city lost 35,000 inhabitants by the mid-1980s, mainly families and young people who moved away from Malmö, often to nearby cities in the region. Until 1993, the population increase was only very modest, but it gained momentum once immigration prompted by the Balkan Wars began the following year. Since then, the population increase in Malmö has been steady, and during the 2000s it has risen by about 5,000 people a year. Between 1985 and 2014, Malmö's population increased by 85,000 people or 37 per cent. According to the latest population forecast (Malmö 2015), the city's population will increase over the next 25 years to reach 376,000 in 2025 and about 470,000 by 2040. If so, this would see its population double in the fifty years from 1985 to the mid-2030s. If nothing else, it demonstrates the rapidity of the changes the city has undergone, for where its population was a quarter of a million at the end of the industrial era, it will likely be half a million by the middle of this century.

The increase seems even more pronounced if one applies a sociodynamic perspective that is able to follow population flows over time. A socio-dynamic study (Salonen 2012) illustrates these rapid changes in terms of population movement, people's relationships with the city's various employment arenas, and residential structures as centres of social cohesion. The city's current population is about 300,000 at any given point, but seen over time—between 1990 and 2008—almost 500,000 people have lived in the city for a year or more. There appear to be far more city-dwellers than those who are actually living in the city at any particular time. Only a quarter, 23 per cent, have lived in Malmö for the whole of the period in question. The city functions as a first port of call and transit area for some, a student city for others, and for a number of people a space for future generations. Young people are drawn to the city as a place to start out in life and get an education, while certain regional and transnational streams run in other directions. International commuting into Denmark across the Öresund strait is a fact of life for an increasing number of people, yet there have been problems in adapting social and welfare systems to the new cross-border commuting patterns. Migration channels from distant countries end in Malmö's residential areas, where close relatives and friends already live. Clearly, a socio-dynamic analysis of the city's ongoing changes has much to offer.

A changing population

Malmö's demographic transformation has also seen the composition of its population alter from a largely ageing population to a young one, in which the proportion of foreign-born or first-generation immigrant residents (both parents born abroad) has risen rapidly. The foreign-born proportion of Malmö's population has gone from 5 per cent in 1960 and 16 per cent in 1990 to 31 per cent in 2014 (see Fig. 4.2). Include those both of whose parents were born abroad (the official definition of 'foreign origin' in Sweden) and this figure increases to 43 per cent in 2014. The largest groups have come from Iraq, former Yugoslavia, Denmark, Poland, and Bosnia and Herzegovina. During the 2000s, the number of people of Swedish

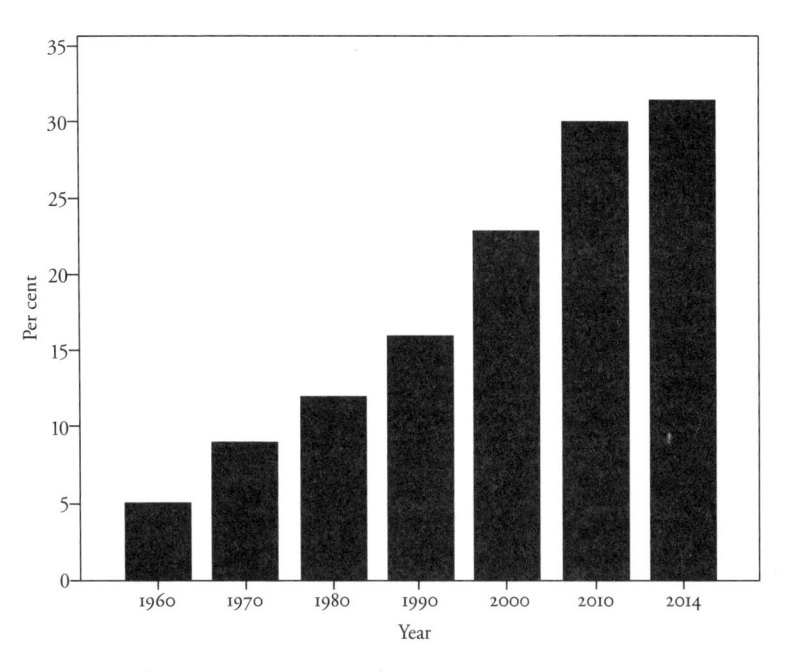

Fig. 4.2. The foreign-born proportion of Malmö's population, 1960–2014.

background (born in Sweden or with at least one Swedish-born parent) has remained essentially unchanged in Malmö. The population increase of over 50,000 since 2000 consisted almost entirely of people of foreign origin—an annual increase of 4,000–5,000 people. If this trend continues, by the early 2020s half the population of Malmö will be of foreign background. In the past few years, foreign immigration to the city has been increasingly dominated by Arabic-speakers from the Middle East and Asia, and especially from war-torn Syria. Malmö has thus strengthened its position as Sweden's most important node in an increasingly global situation, with large flows of refugees and family reunification immigration.

Malmö can thus be taken as perhaps the most obvious Swedish example of the transformation of a former industrial port into a post-industrial, multicultural city that is now a global node in an increasingly globalized world. It is this that presents the existing urban transformation with a new set of shifting challenges and scenarios. A comparative European study, analysed in Salonen (2012), presents a somewhat paradoxical picture of Malmö, alongside 78 other major cities in the European Union. On the basis of the answers provided by 500 respondents selected at random in each city, it appears that Malmö is in the middle on the central question of how people view their satisfaction with life in general (31st out of 79 cities). However, it comes 77th (with only the two Greek cities behind it) on the question of how well integrated its foreign residents are thought to be: fully two-thirds of Malmö respondents felt this was not the case. Another problematic aspect is the degree to which respondents trusted other people in general. Of the eight Nordic cities, Malmö clearly differed. All the other Nordic cities had a confidence level of at least 80 per cent (including Ålborg in Denmark with 92 per cent, Copenhagen with 86 per cent, and Stockholm with 81 per cent), while Malmö mustered a mere 69 per cent. This reinforces the admittedly controversial impression of Malmö as a polarized city, struggling with inter-communal tension.

This general description of Malmö's structural and demographic transformation is essential for understanding, for example, the individual city districts' siting and development in terms of residential segregation, social cohesion, and sustainable urban development, as will be discussed later.

Employment, income, and hidden Malmö

Another exogenous perspective on urban life is the increase in daily commuting across city limits. In a city such as Malmö, commuting to work is immensely important in a regional context, especially given the paradox that the number of jobs in Malmö has increased steadily, while the employment rate for residents continues unchanged at what for Sweden is a relatively low level. In 2013 the number of people commuting from Malmö was about 31,000, while more than twice that number, 63,000, commuted daily into the city from the surrounding region (Statistic Sweden's Database, <www.scb.se>). The number of jobs in the city has grown steadily in recent years, from 151,000 in 2008 to 163,000 in 2013 (ibid.). Yet only about 60 per cent of them are currently held by people who also live in Malmö. Add to that the number who commute in to attend university, and

Malmö appears to be an employment magnet, drawing in people from across the county of Skåne.

Malmö's low employment rate—just over six in ten of working age—thus persists, despite the growing number of jobs and rising levels of education. Almost one-third of Malmö's residents have no job to go to and are not in further education. Of these, about 8 per cent are officially unemployed, while the same percentage are on sickness or unemployment benefits. What the rest are doing is unclear, proof if proof were needed of the shortcomings of the statistics, as well the existence of alternative sources of employment in the informal sector and the parallel market.

The overall employment rate in Malmö in the 2000s remained a steady 11–14 percentage points lower than the country as a whole (Salonen 2012); despite a marked increase in jobs in the city, its employment rate remained under 65 per cent for all those aged 20–64. The difference between Swedish- and foreign-born employees remained unchanged at around 30–35 percentage points (75 per cent of Swedish-born residents are in work, compared with 40–42 per cent of foreign-born residents). Compared with Sweden as a whole or even the two other largest cities, the differences in patterns of employment appear to be even more polarized in a city such as Malmö. The proportion of NEETs (not in employment, education, or training) among all people aged 20–64 was 31 per cent in Malmö in 2010, compared to 18 per cent in Stockholm and 21 per cent in Gothenburg (Statistic Sweden's Database, <www.scb.se>). The difference between those born in Sweden and those born outside the EU was proportionally the same in Malmö as in the other big cities, but at a much higher level—18 per cent for those born in Sweden and 48 per cent for those born outside the EU.

Malmö's distinctive employment pattern reflects both structural and demographic factors. The low employment rate among certain migrant groups cannot be dismissed as a passing trend, the result of it being a slow business to get established, as it is also manifestly the case for foreign-born people who have lived in Sweden—and Malmö—for many years. There are pronounced differences in employment rates among the various immigrant groups too, and the Iraqi-born group, which is the largest among foreign-born residents of the city, has had greater difficulties than most in gaining a foothold on the Swedish labour market (Salonen 2012, 29).

A particular problem that previous studies have drawn attention to (Salonen 2012, 2014) is 'hidden Malmö'—all the people who for various reasons are not included in the official statistics or are otherwise invisible. A growing proportion of the population lives beyond the scope of the standard modes of life. Some 12,000 adults of working age, or 6.5 per cent, had no officially reported income in 2008 (Salonen 2012, 33). They might simply not be registered with the various established arenas such as the official job centres, the education system, or the welfare systems for the unemployed and sick. In addition, there are people living illegally in the city, and indeed Sweden, often referred to as 'undocumented' migrants. Here there are obvious gaps in our knowledge because of the way the authorities function (and gather statistics), but also because the research community has unanswered questions about the increasing proportion of people who are living on the margins of the official systems.

Growing income inequality

Changing employment circumstances are also reflected in an increase in household income inequality in Malmö (Salonen 2012)—differences that have multiplied in recent years, and which again differ considerably from the national trend. The poorest households have become poorer, in absolute as well as relative terms, while the wealthiest households are now much better off than they were in the early 1990s. The richest decile of the city's population has gone from being six times richer than the poorest decile in 1990 to being twelve times richer in 2008. And this is despite the fact that all those with no earnings are automatically excluded from such statistics. Income inequality can largely be explained by the position of households vis-à-vis the labour market, and not along ethnic lines. Taking the official European Union definition of income poverty to be those earning less than 60 per cent of national median income, it is plainly on the rise in Malmö, where it applies to three in ten residents of working age. This in turn explains the high percentage of households

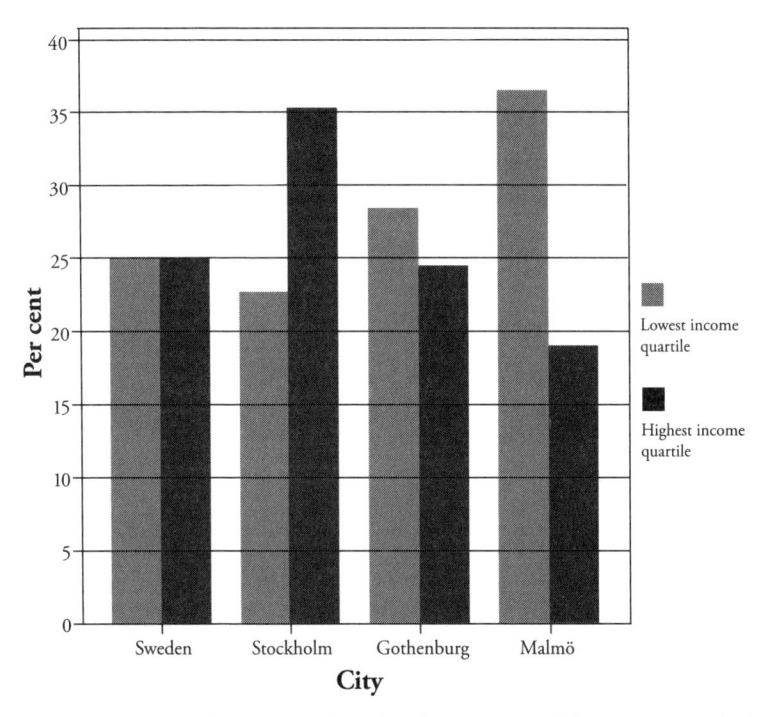

Fig. 4.3. Income distribution in Sweden's three largest cities and the country as a whole in 2012, by percentage of households in the lowest and highest income quartiles. Source: Statistics Sweden's housing profiles, processed by the author.

reliant on municipal means-tested social assistance, with more and more households receiving support for longer periods.

Fig. 4.3 shows the extent of Malmö's divergent income profile. Based on the calculated disposable income per consumption unit (taking into account household size and composition) Malmö's population has a far greater concentration in the lowest income group: more than 36 per cent of households are in the lowest income quartile, compared to 23 per cent in Stockholm and 28 per cent in Gothenburg. Moreover, the lowest income quartile in Malmö has grown, from 31 per cent in 1998.

In brief, average income levels in Malmö lag behind national levels, and the income gaps between various groups and city districts have widened over the last two decades (Salonen 2012). Most households in recent years have become slightly better off in real terms, while the poorest have also become poorer in an absolute sense and the richest decile enjoy considerably better incomes than average households (ibid. 38). This extreme income distribution will be a decisive factor in the challenges Malmö faces in achieving an inclusive and cohesive urban development for the city as whole, as will be seen.

Malmö, the sum of its parts

Spatially, Malmö can be said to be a fairly compact city, with a high population density compared to many other Swedish cities. Unlike Stockholm and Gothenburg, Malmö has expanded into areas that are geographically close to its centre, including the land for the ambitious public housing programmes (the Million Programme) of the 1960s and 1970s, which means that the distances from the suburbs to the city centre are relatively short. Excluding some smaller districts on the outskirts, Malmö has approaching 4,000 inhabitants per square kilometre, compared with the Swedish average of about 1,500 for all urban areas.

There are three principle forms of tenure in Sweden: private ownership, joint ownership (in the shape of tenant-owners' associations), and rented housing (both public and private). Private ownership—generally single-household homes—and tenant-owned housing are generally classified as home ownership. Joint ownership has many similarities with private ownership, but there are also some differences, primarily the fact that tenant-owners in housing cooperatives own the property collectively, but each tenant has an exclusive right to live in their own flat or house. Housing in Malmö is dominated by multi-household dwellings, that is blocks of flats—more than 80 per cent, of which almost a fifth are in private ownership—of which up to 36 per cent are tenant-owned, 29 per cent are private rented housing, and 15 per cent are public rented housing.

As in other Swedish cities, Malmö's residents increasingly live in households that resemble the ones in which they grew up, both socio-economically and geographically (Salonen 2012). People tend to live in districts that are increasingly homogeneous, socio-economically speaking. There are few wealthy areas in Malmö, based on analyses of income, housing, family status, occupation, and education; much of the city is characterized by a high proportion of low incomes and residents who were born outside the Nordic countries or western Europe. Social position and ethnicity often overlap to determine where you live in Malmö. The majority of its population therefore lives in poorer areas. There has been a marked increase in these areas since 1990, leaving only 2 per cent of the city population living in wealthy districts, compared with an average 15 per cent of Sweden's total urban population (Salonen 2012). This is mainly because the better-off areas in the Malmö region are located outside the city boundaries, in smaller, affluent municipalities. There are therefore significant differences in purchasing power, measured as a household's disposable income, between Malmö and the surrounding county of Skåne.

In a national study of the changing role of public housing in Sweden, Malmö's distinctive distribution of low- and high-income households stands out (Salonen 2015). At the national level, the net balance is 1.0 when the number of low-income households is as great as the number of high-income households, based on the household's disposable income per consumption unit. Malmö has far more low-income households, with a net balance of 1.92 in 2012—in other words, the city has almost twice as many low-income households as high-income ones—whereas the figure for Stockholm was 0.65 and for Gothenburg 1.16. In Fig. 4.4, the same net balance is used to illustrate the income distribution across different residential districts in Malmö, using Statistics Sweden's classification of SAMS areas (the Small Area for Market Statistics). Only those districts with at least 100 households have been counted, which for 2013 gave a total of 251 districts, with a district average of some 700 households. Only about a quarter of Malmö's residential districts (66 in 2013) have a net balance of between 0.5 and 2.0, or a reasonably balanced population by household income. More than 70 residential districts are dominated by high-income households (up to 0.49)—about 10 fewer than in 2005. Meanwhile, nearly half the residential districts are dominated by low-income households (113 in 2013), while extremely poor districts (with values over 10.0) have increased in number from 23 in 2005 to 29 in 2013, all of them in the east and south of the city, and all consisting almost entirely of rented housing, both privately and publicly owned. The results

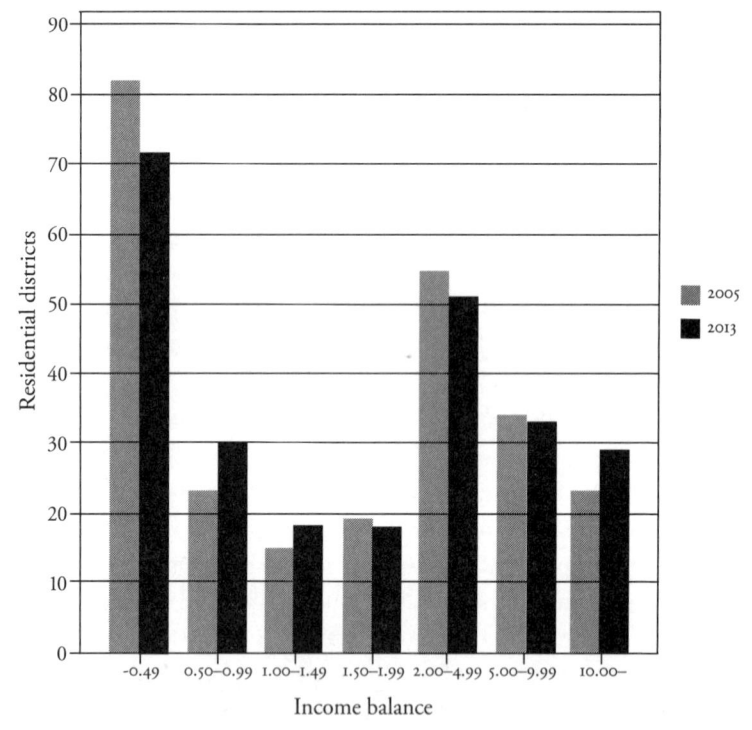

Fig. 4.4. Residential districts in Malmö by household purchasing power in 2005 and 2013. Source: Statistics Sweden's housing profiles, processed by the author.

show not only that Malmö stands out from other major cities in Sweden in socio-economic terms, but also that the socio-economic divisions within the city are significant. Such hierarchical housing patterns clearly follow the distribution of different forms of tenure and geographical locations across the city.

Income inequality and residential segregation

Over the last two decades, as Scarpa (2015) has established, social differentiation between neighbourhoods and communities in cities such as Malmö largely mirrors the broader social changes such as demographic fluctuations, education and employment patterns, greater income inequality, and cuts in state benefits. Scarpa (2015, 41) underlines that although it is characteristic of large Swedish cities to have comparatively low levels of income inequality by international standards, they are as much or even more sharply divided along ethnic lines than the cities in other Western countries that have higher levels of general income inequality. There seems to be a much more pronounced division along ethnic lines in large Swedish cities. This is particularly noticeable in Malmö, where a large proportion of immigrants are concentrated in low-income areas in the east and south of the city, while the west, nearest the coast, is dominated by the more affluent, Swedish-born middle class.

Scarpa (2015) disputes the accepted notion of a correlation between income inequality and residential segregation in large Swedish cities, and especially in Malmö. Instead of studying the consequences of residential segregation, particularly in poorer areas, his results show the importance of focusing on the underlying economic causes behind the spread of residential segregation. In fact, residential segregation can perhaps best be seen as the spatial manifestation of existing disparities in income distribution, because people's choice of residential district ultimately depends on their financial means. In this respect, Sweden is an interesting case: it is still one of the least unequal countries in the world, nevertheless it is also one of a group of countries that has experienced the fastest rise in income inequality in recent decades. With this in mind, there are three results that must be singled out from Scarpa's analysis (2015) of the relationship between income inequality and residential segregation in large Swedish cities: (*i*) immigration has not affected income inequality in Swedish cities much, as is evident from the fact that income inequality has increased among both Swedish-born and foreign-born residents; (*ii*) cuts in the redistribution of taxes and benefits have helped fuel income inequality in Swedish cities; and (*iii*) it is primarily rising income disparity that drives segregation in Swedish citics.

The first result is noteworthy, for it empirically refutes a common belief in Sweden that it is immigration which has driven income inequality over the past two decades. Using sophisticated registry analyses, Scarpa (2015) shows that immigration's contribution to overall inequality is negligible. It is the widening income gap between those in work and those out of it, and not that between existing residents and immigrants, that has the significant impact. After all, 'Residential segregation is the outcome of the combined effect of the prolonged situation of marginalization of immigrants in the labor market and their spatial concentration in neighborhoods with affordable housing' (Scarpa 2015, 43).

This pattern of immigrants, especially non-Western immigrants, being largely excluded from the labour market and their spatial concentration in certain residential districts, and especially in rented housing, has been confirmed by several Swedish studies (Andersson et al. 2007; Biterman & Franzén 2007; Hedin et al. 2012; Salonen 2015). Further, the differences in employment rates between nationals and non-EU citizens are far greater in Sweden than in any other EU country: indeed, the difference is more than 30 percentage points (81 per cent for Swedish-born citizens as opposed to 50 per cent for non-EU citizens), while the EU average is 13 per cent, which suggests that there are greater obstacles to entering the labour market in Sweden than in any other EU country (Eurostat 2014). The corresponding difference in the other Nordic countries is conspicuously lower. Several Swedish studies have drawn attention to the underlying ethnic discrimination in the Swedish labour market (Rydgren 2004; Carlsson & Rooth 2007).

Socio-dynamic changes in residential districts

Although many residential districts appear to have a relatively stable position in the local housing hierarchy, analyses based on longitudinal, individual data—following specific people for a number of years—have nuanced this view. The advantage of such a socio-dynamic approach is that the variables in a district's social conditions can be charted, with a focus on people's daily lives.

What is presented here is an analysis of the two housing estates in Malmö that are very much at the bottom of the local housing market. The Herrgården housing estate in the Rosengård district and Lindängen housing estate both consist of private rented housing, and demonstrate extremely low levels of income, employment, and other standard socio-economic variables.

First, however, it should be noted that the population of both

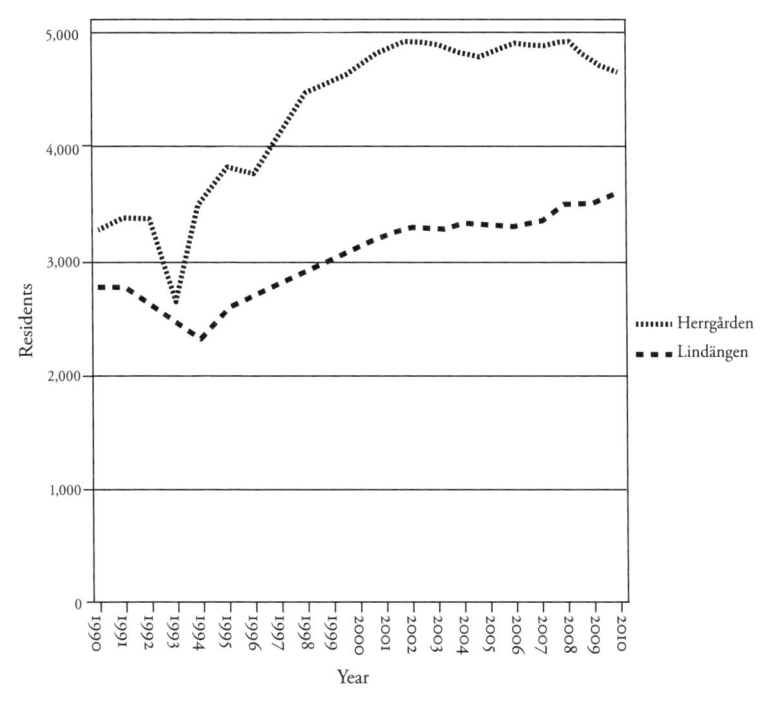

Fig. 4.5. Number of residents in the Herrgården and Lindängen housing estates, 1990–2010.

housing estates has grown rapidly over the last two decades: Herrgården by 75 per cent and Lindängen by 55 per cent (see Fig. 4.5). This in itself is remarkable, given that no new housing has been built there in the same period. Instead, this indicates an increasing densification, and in many cases overcrowding. Given that the figures only include people who are formally registered as residents, it is reasonable to assume that even greater numbers lived in the housing estates without ever being registered. For example, the current landlords have indicated that there is a hidden market in sublets to people who are not registered as residents—illegal or undocumented immigrants, in other words.

By studying data (Statistic Sweden's database LISA) on how long individuals and households have actually lived in the two housing estates in 1990–2010, the sheer scale of the ebb and flow of population becomes apparent. In both housing estates, almost four times as many people have lived there for at least one year in the twenty-year period: 18,389 people in Herrgården and 12,475 in Lindängen. Statistically, then, the population of each housing estate changes completely every five years. Over 40 per cent of the gross population in each housing estate has only lived there for less than two years. This underlines the housing estates' transitional character: they are often the first places where recent arrivals can find somewhere to live, and once on their feet they move on relatively quickly, generally to other areas in Malmö. Despite this constant throughput, nearly 1,000 people in each housing estate have lived there for at least 15 years. At any given time, long-term residents make up a quarter of all residents, while as a proportion of the gross population over the entire twenty-year period they only amount to 5 per cent and 8 per cent. The annual figures for those moving in or out run at about 15–25 per cent. The proportion of immigrants from countries outside western Europe has been stable in Herrgården at around 80 per cent a year, while it has gradually increased in Lindängen to 60 per cent in 2010 (Salonen 2014, 16).

In addition to site-specific knowledge, this kind of socio-dynamic analysis at the district level shows just how strong the case is for the public sector to take the long view, investing in prevention and job creation in residential districts at the bottom of the housing ladder. The results underline the need for long-range community-building work, which coordinates the physical and social measures in individual districts; however, it also places great demands on people's ability to think and act in new ways to generate sustainable social development in such districts all across Malmö.

To sum up, there are four general lessons to be learned from local socio-dynamic analyses of this sort (Salonen 2014, 29–30). First, there is a need for detailed flow analyses of marginalization patterns over time, following young people's or migrants' attempts to get a start in life. Local authorities, housing associations, and other public sector bodies would do best to keep up to date with each district's socio-dynamic development.

Second, the ability to trace individuals' and households' circumstances relative to migration patterns, including cross-border commuting and onward migration, is particularly important for cities that are experiencing far-reaching changes in urbanization and migration. It is not sufficient merely to note that households have moved on; there needs to be a concerted effort to gather more information about what happened to individuals and households during or after the move.

Third, remedial measures targeted on specific urban areas can have an impact far beyond the intended limits—they often lead to changes in circumstances, which in turn drives migration. The lesson to be learned here is that local development in so-called disadvantaged districts must be understood in a broader context, in which the interaction of residential districts and adjoining communities is of central importance. There is also a need for control studies that follow the individuals and households in question, given that they are subject to various measures, whether they live in the district or not.

Fourth, there needs to be a greater acceptance of participation by local households in the district's development. An in-depth participatory approach is called for in order to prevent rafts of measures being imposed on residential districts without consulting those directly affected. This in turn places considerable demands on all those involved in encouraging the democratization of decision-making in local urban development.

In addition, there is always a risk of overemphasizing each individual district's potential for change, ignoring that it is embedded in the structural and institutional systems of a city, a region, a country. As Urban so eloquently puts it:

> Area-based development projects tend to treat certain areas as vulnerable and segregated, instead of seeing geographically concentrated poverty and increased polarization. An exclusive focus on trying to solve the city's problems in the residential districts where many low-income people live, risks placing the blame on those with weak resources, hit by housing patterns and the flight of the rich, as well as by increased unemployment and the polarization of the labour market. (Urban 2014, 39)

Challenges for inclusive urban strategies

This essay seeks to demonstrate that like so many other cities, Scandinavian cities in general, and Malmö in particular, are undergoing a rapid and profound urban change in a markedly more globalized world (Saunders 2010; Glaser 2012). In a multicultural city such as Malmö, with its sharp contrasts between rich and poor, native and outsider, and spatially between supposedly vulnerable and prosperous districts, questions about social cohesion and sustainable urban development come to a head. Malmö's *Comprehensive Plan 2014* announced that it needs to 'knit together' in order to become a fully cohesive city. Physical barriers will need to be torn down and the gaps reduced by generous social investment. This echoes the recommendations of an independent commission that was appointed to study inequalities in health and living conditions, and the central elements in its proposed strategy for a socially cohesive and sustainable city (Commission for a Socially Sustainable Malmö 2013).

The gist of the official rhetoric of urban development in Malmö is that the city will best grow by increasing the density of existing urban structures, thereby achieving a balanced and varied 'mixed city'. The case for a mixed city sits well with the stated ambitions for social cohesion and sustainable urban development, starting as it does 'with a far-reaching objective and a determination to include not only social objectives such as reducing segregation and increasing public health, but also the more specifically local experience of a place as vibrant and safe' (Modin 2002, 8). It has been used as a vision, an attitude, and an urban type, and in order to achieve it, a number of approaches have been formulated that most of those involved seem to agree on: measures designed to increase public safety and security call for a relatively compact city, and the design of the urban environment's public spaces is crucial if they are to be properly inclusive. Diversity of both function and population, together with the element of movement, will provide the sought-after urban ambience for much of the day.

In the light of the results presented here, these political ambitions seem necessary, but difficult to implement. Nylund (2014) had taken Fainstein's theoretical understanding of the just city (2014) and used it to examine the official plans for Malmö. In contrast to the dominance of neo-liberal urban policies and planning of recent decades, Fainstein draws on the work of capability theorists such as Amartya Sen and Martha Nussbaum to identify three criteria for 'a just city': equity, diversity, and democracy. Fainstein's analysis emphasizes both substantive and procedural justice—the what and the wherefore of the just city, if you will. This broadly agrees with the Malmö Commission's two general recommendations to 'establish a social investment policy that can reduce inequities in living conditions and make societal systems more equitable' and 'change processes by creating knowledge alliances and democratised management' (49–52). Nylund (2014) shows that the aims of combatting both substantive and procedural injustice show signs of being realized in general political terms in Malmö, but that it is yet to be seen how far these ambitions will be realized on the ground in the coming years.

As this essay set out to show, detailed socio-dynamic analyses are needed in order to determine whether the far-reaching ambitions for sustainable urban development are capable of breaking the polarization seen in many cities in recent years, both in Scandinavia and across the world.

Translated by Dr Charlotte Merton

References

Andersson, O. (2003) *Chicagoskolan: Institutionaliseringen, idétraditionen och vetenskapen* (Lund Monographs in Social Anthropology, 11; Lund: Lund University).

Andersson, R., Å. Bråmå & J. Hogdal (2007) *Segregationens dynamik och planerings möjligheter: En studie av bostadsmarknad och flyttningar i Malmöregionen* (Malmö: Stadskontoret).

Arrival Guides (2015) 'Chicago', <http://www.arrivalguides.com/sv/Travelguides/North_america/United%20States/Chicago/thecity>, accessed 9 October 2015.

Biterman, D. & E. Franzén (2007) 'Residential segregation', *International Journal of Social Welfare* 16/1, 127–62.

Carlsson, M. & D.-O. Rooth (2007) 'Etnisk diskriminering på svensk arbetsmarknad: Resultat från ett fältexperiment', *Ekonomisk Debatt* 3, 55–68.

Commission for a Socially Sustainable Malmö (2013) *Malmö's path towards a sustainable future: Health, welfare and justice* (Malmö: Malmö stad).

Elias, N. (1999) *Etablerade och outsiders* (Lund: Arkiv).

Eurostat (2014) 'Unemployment rate for Non-EU citizens notably higher than for nationals in the EU28', news release 119/2014, 30 July 2014, 3-30072014-AP.

Fainstein, S. (2010) *The just city* (Ithaca: Cornell University Press).
Glaser, E. (2012) *Stadens triumf* (Stockholm: SNS).
Hedin, K., E. Clark, E. Lundholm & G. Malmberg (2012) 'Neoliberalization of housing in Sweden: Gentrification, filtering and social polarization', *Annals of the Association of American Geographers* 102/2, 443–63.
Kazepov, Y. (ed.) (2005) *Cities of Europe: Changing contexts, local arrangements and the challenge to urban cohesion* (Oxford: Blackwell Publishing).
Malmö (2014) *Översiktsplan för Malmö: Antagen av Kommunfullmäktige 22 maj 2014* (Malmö: Malmö stad).
—— (2015) *Befolkningsprognos 2015–2025* (Malmö: Malmö stad).
Modin, A. (2002) 'Blandstad—en vision med och utan verklighet?', *Plan* 4, 25–6.
Nylund, K. (2014) 'Conceptions of justice in the planning of the new urban landscape: Recent changes in the comprehensive planning discourse in Malmö, Sweden', *Planning Theory & Practice*. DOI: 10.1080/14649357.2013.866263.
Ramberg, K. (2012) *Konstruktionen av framtidens stad: Arkitekttävlingar om bostäder och stadsdelar i Sverige 1989–2003* (Stockholm: Hemmavid).
Rydgren, J. (2004) 'Mechanisms of exclusion: Ethnic discrimination in the Swedish labour market', *Journal of Ethnic & Migration Studies* 30/4, 697–716.
Salonen, T. (2012) *Befolkningsrörelser, försörjningsvillkor och bostadssegregation: En sociodynamisk analys av Malmö* (Rapport för Kommission för ett socialt hållbart Malmö; Malmö: Malmö stad).
—— (2014) *Sysselsättning och försörjningsvillkor i Lindängens hyresrätt—en sociodynamisk analys* (Delrapport i Mil-projektet; Malmö: Malmö stad).
—— (2015) 'Allmännyttans skiftande roll på den lokala bostadsmarknaden', in Salonen, T. (ed.) *Nyttan med allmännyttan* (Stockholm: Liber).
Sampson, R. J. (2012) *Great American city: Chicago and the enduring neighborhood effect* (Chicago: University of Chicago Press).
Saunders, D. (2010) *Arrival city: How the largest migration in history is shaping our world* (New York: Pantheon).
Scarpa, S. (2015) *The spatial manifestation of inequality: Residential segregation in Sweden and its causes* (Linnaeus University Dissertations 201/2015; Växjö: Linnaeus University).
SCB (Statistiska centralbyrån) (2012) *Svensken flyttar i snitt elva gånger* (Statistiska centralbyrån).
—— (2014) *Inrikes flyttning 2013: Var åttonde person flyttade under 2013* (2014:65, 20 November; Statistiska centralbyrån).
Urban, S. (2014) 'Områdesutveckling mot fattigdom', *Plan* 3, 35–9.

CHAPTER 5

Trust and distrust in Oslo
Examining the relationship between the ideals of urban policy and the (re)actions of citizens

Bengt Andersen, Per Gunnar Røe & Oddrun Sæter

Like its Scandinavian neighbours, Norway enjoys a high level of socio-economic equality, but, even so, patterns of socio-economic and ethno-racial residential segregation are visible in the capital.[1] Until about 1970, Norway was relatively homogeneous. Today, however, about 30 per cent of Oslo's population have an immigrant background and about 21 per cent are categorized as having a 'non-Western' immigrant background (Municipality of Oslo 2015).[2] The 'white' upper classes tend to live in the area known as the West End (Vestkanten); the lower classes and non-Westerners, in the East End (Østkanten). These patterns indicate that the ideal of a just or socially sustainable city is far from being realized.

In this essay, we examine the conditions for social sustainability, taking Oslo as our case. Or rather, having just noted that Oslo can hardly be termed a just city, we shed light on why this is so. We interpret urban social sustainability as encompassing strategies for reducing inequality or affording equal opportunities, and it is often associated with the socio-economic and/or ethnic mix at the neighbourhood level (Ley 2012, 64). Connecting analytically the concept of trust to that of social sustainability, we would argue that there is a need to investigate everyday social life, relations, and individuals' notions of other people—that is, we are interested in actions and relations at the micro level, and consider an analysis of these to be key to an understanding of city-wide integration (see Savage et al. 2005, 1).

We have drawn on a qualitative case study that comprises some

250 interviews as well as participant observations in Oslo during the period 2007–2015. While the ethnographic fieldwork lasted for about two years, the interviews were conducted in nine selected neighbourhoods in the Oslo Region in separate phases throughout the period (in this essay we present a few interview excerpts that are representative of the whole material). We begin by discussing the socially sustainable city as an ideal (Tretter 2013, 298) for politicians and urban planners. Rather than present a detailed analysis of urban policy discourse, we instead critically examine the degree to which this political and planning ideal is compatible with the city's material legacy, with the strategies of urban developers, and with the actions and ideals of Oslo's citizens. Having presented the ambitions of urban policymakers, we briefly outline Oslo's historical development—from the city's reconstruction following the fire of 1624, affluent citizens and non-affluent suburbanites were segregated. We then turn to the contemporary city, to discuss how influential actors and institutions, such as the media and property developers, reproduce a fragmented city, while our respondents are concerned with securing their families' comfort and well-being. Finally, we summarize our analyses and reflect on the likelihood of Oslo becoming a socially sustainable city, an 'inclusive and conflict-free city' (Basu 2013, 48).[3]

The socially sustainable city as a policy ideal

In 2010, Oslo signed the Eurocities Integrating Cities Charter, by which signatories are committed 'to integrating migrants and migrant communities in European cities' (Eurocities 2010a). Two key aims for the partner cities are to work towards more cohesive and integrated cities and to secure 'equal opportunities for everyone living in the city' (Eurocities 2010b). To demonstrate its fulfilment of these worthy policy goals—or policy ideals—the City of Oslo refers to its high score on the Council of Europe Intercultural Cities Index (Municipality of Oslo 2011, 120). Among the indicators are 'How intercultural is the education system?' measured for instance by 'the ethnic composition of the student body' and 'The existence of policies to increase ethnic mixing in schools' (Council of Europe

2014b). Also of importance is the question of 'How intercultural are residential neighbourhoods?' measured by 'the existence of policies to increase neighbourhood diversity'. The last indicator of the cities' intercultural achievements to be specified here is 'How intercultural is public space?' (ibid.). According to the figures, in 2012 Oslo scored above the European city average when it came to the status of its education system and neighbourhoods (Council of Europe 2014a). Thus, Oslo claims to be successful in its 'sustainable multicultural policy' (Municipality of Oslo 2011, 120).[4]

The specific content of Oslo's sustainability policy is not obvious. Nevertheless, this local policy corresponds to national policy. In the government report on improving integration (NOU 2011:14) and the subsequent White Paper on integration policy (Stortingsmelding 2012), it was argued that residential segregation should be counteracted.[5] Given that most Norwegian children attend a local school, ethnic residential concentrations will usually result in school segregation as well. It was assumed that such forms of segregation reduce interactions between minority groups and the majority. As a result, it was claimed, the majority and various ethnic minority groups establish their own social networks. Moreover, the formation of more or less ethnically homogeneous networks diminishes the minority residents' prospects of finding a (relevant) job (Stortingsmelding 2012, 89, 92; NOU 2011:14, 20–1, 137). Importantly, the assumption was that minimal actual interethnic interaction equalled 'low levels of social capital', which in turn meant 'low levels of interpersonal trust'. This too could result in social disintegration (NOU 2011:14, 279–80, referring to Putnam and Putnam-inspired Norwegian scholars). As this was not a welcome scenario, the policymakers instead aimed for 'a more inclusive and sustainable society' (NOU 2011:14, 12). While integration was said to be a goal, segregation always has been, and still is, the order of things in Oslo.

A history of socio-spatial fragmentation

The dividing line between the eastern and western parts of the city has a long history going back to the seventeenth century. After the city burned down in 1624, it was ordered that the buildings be made of bricks in order to prevent fires. However, as brick was expensive, many could not afford to settle in the new city. Thus, they had to move outside the city's boundaries. Living in the suburbs—mainly to the east—one lacked the right to trade, and consequently it was difficult to accumulate wealth; the privileges (including trading privileges) were specifically bestowed upon the citizens of the city proper. The king then donated a vast area west of the city for all residents to use. This land was quickly appropriated by the affluent. Myhre argues that more than many other pre-industrial European cities, the city with its suburbs 'was socially divided already from 1624' (1990, 100).

Industrialization in the nineteenth century brought a growing working-class population and deteriorating living conditions in the eastern suburbs. At the same time, the West End was growing and being consolidated under private-led development (Myhre 1990, 221). After the Second World War, there was a major housing shortage in Oslo (Kjeldstadli 1990, 467–470). Blocks of flats became the preferred solution in the Grorud Valley, north-east of the East End. Furthest west, meanwhile, owner-occupied detached housing continued to dominate. The expansion eastwards of the working-class East End came about for several reasons: land to the east was less expensive (Hansen & Sæterdal 1970, 32–34); the eastern valley was thought an appropriate location for the working class, being not too close to middle-, upper-middle, and upper-class districts; and planners wanted to retain 'the traditional pattern' of the West End for the affluent and the East End for the workers (Kjeldstadli & Myhre 1995, 93–4). The same paradigm still structures Oslo's socio-spatial development. Since flats were cheaper in the east of the city, this helps explain why the non-Western immigrants who have moved to Norway since 1967 have mostly settled in the East End. However, other forces were also pushing them eastwards.

Channelling residents

Where people live in a city is not entirely a matter of their own choosing. The affluent can more freely decide where to live, whereas the less fortunate are to a larger degree channelled into certain districts. This was certainly the case in Oslo, where the working class and the poor were expected to steer clear of the upper classes and their haunts, and it continues today, as most public housing units are located in the eastern parts of town. It was still the case that

> during the 1980s the municipality channelled disadvantaged immigrants to social housing in the east and south[east] of the city, while there were restrictions on the allocation of housing to immigrants in the outer west where the city had a quota of housing in new developments. (Blom 2012, 8)

More recently, private actors have continued such practices, albeit by different means. Property developers and construction companies in Oslo have for some time tended to build flats in which the kitchen is not a separate room. Instead, the kitchen is part of the living room. According to a major builder operating in Oslo, potential Norwegian Pakistani customers have approached them asking for separate kitchens. In response, the company has built such flats in an eastern residential district with a pre-existing concentration of Norwegian Pakistanis, where buyers could opt for either a separate or an open-plan kitchen. The project was then marketed in Oslo's Urdu-language press. According to the head of the construction company, these were

> newspapers you have to subscribe to, and you cannot buy them from the newsstands. And we did that as a test to see if we would reach the target group, and that we did. We had very good sales; lots from the target group bought these homes. (Head of the construction company)

When we asked whether they used the same newspapers to market their properties in a middle-class West End neighbourhood, the answer was they did not: 'We used normal marketing there'. Both the marketing strategy and the fact that they had built separate kitchens in the flats in the eastern district contributed to the established pattern of the eastbound movement of non-Westerners. While scholars have found that many Norwegian Pakistanis opt to live close to one another (Moen 2009, 146–8), it is reasonable to argue that the construction company's strategies reinforced or reproduced the established socio-spatial residential pattern. In short, maintaining segregation.

Since East Enders seldom visit the West End and vice versa (Andersen 2014), bridging social capital—social, inter-group, or citywide trust in fellow citizens—can be a policy aim that is difficult to achieve (cf. Putnam 2007). If a residential concentration of minorities can be problematic in itself, equating to neighbourhoods where residents' life chances are less than in majority areas (Wessel 2013, 252), the developer can be said to be working against the ideal of socially sustainable urban development. Inequalities are not reduced, and perhaps even increased. Then, of course, there is the all-important role of the media in reproducing the socio-spatial paradigm, and consequently helping counteract the goals of politicians and planners.

The Oslo-based media are powerful city-makers. Through stigmatization or branding they can influence property values and people's decisions about where to live. As previously documented (Andersen 2014, ch. 5), numerous newspaper articles about the problems of the East End have stigmatized those neighbourhoods and the people who live there for several decades. The East End is described as the city's 'backyard', with bad schools, neighbourhoods, housing, and even bad people or potential rioters. According to Wacquant (2008, 244), such area stigmas can indirectly 'work to decrease interpersonal trust and undercut local social solidarity'. If he is correct, media representations pose yet another challenge to social sustainability. What is certain is that for many ethnic Norwegians the East End is not an environment to be trusted, especially when it comes to where to raise one's children. One of our respondents was an ethnic Norwegian, Heidi. Heidi and her family had moved from an apartment in the Inner East to a house in a suburb outside Oslo. It was out of the question to move to an affordable detached house in the Outer East, because there were too many immigrants there. Consequently, the family feared that the children would suffer academically. Like many others, Heidi had not been to the outer eastern parts of Oslo, but knew how it was from reading newspapers.

As Heidi's case indicates, it is not only structural factors that condition the well-being of citizens—or their search for a place affording well-being or safety and security. From the interviews and observations, it is evident that people's level of everyday comfort was largely influenced by the context of their daily lives. Being employed or not, having the necessary financial resources, and so on, were all significant factors in this respect, but who they lived amongst was of no less importance. In the following section, we elaborate on this argument by discussing three different empirical cases, in the shape of three families in their respective neighbourhoods. First of these is Vinderen in the affluent West End. Second, we move across town to the far less privileged East End neighbourhood of Linderud, located in the outer eastern and stigmatized area of Groruddalen, or the Grorud Valley (Norwegian Ministry of Local Government and Modernisation 2014). Our last and third case is St. Hanshaugen, located in the city centre between the traditional east–west divide.

Comfort in everyday life

Vinderen is a privileged area dominated by villas and other similar houses. One of our respondents, Sondre, was born and raised in Vinderen. He is in his forties, has two Master's degrees in economics, and works as a financial analyst. As his wife Liv also has a high-paid job, his family, which includes three young children, can be categorized as upper middle class. Sondre's family live in a newly renovated terraced house, with a modern and spacious interior. Their home has a floor area of about 200 square metres. Liv and Sondre's local friends in Vinderen are the parents of their children's friends, more acquaintances than anything, who they got to know through kindergarten and school. They know them, but do not socialize much. Liv underlines that 'the people who live here are just ordinary, with completely ordinary jobs and totally ordinary incomes and young children. In this sense, it is a very homogeneous area.' As they are fairly average themselves, according to Liv, Sondre feels that they fit right in among the other Vinderen people. The couple elaborate, explaining that they are on the same wavelength as their neighbours, for they are close to the local political average, and thus share the same values: 'We notice it at school: the parents have the same view on how things should be'. Sondre and Liv's neighbours are similar to them. They stress that it is pleasant to have nice neighbours. Vinderen was the only place they looked at when they wanted to move back to the city. While they like their house, they emphasize that they would never have bought it if it were not in Vinderen. 'We picked this as this was the one available *here*,' Liv said, explaining that Vinderen 'is a very good area. The people who live here are very pleasant.' According to her, the neighbourhood is safe: 'there are no shady people walking around here'. She stresses that their neighbours are similar to them; thus, the probability of conflicts is low. This is a positive thing, she says. Liv also points out that Oslo is a diverse city with people from other cultures. This is a good thing, she explains, since we can learn from them. Sondre challenges his wife's claim, stressing that the ethnically diverse city is not something he experiences, as he only moves about within the non-diverse West End. And so do their children. Liv then says that 'I would have been very sceptical if foreign-speaking children were in the majority at our school.' However, there is no reason to worry, as their school 'is very homogeneous'. Liv concludes that 'It's a good school!' As far as they know, Vinderen is seldom mentioned in the Oslo-based media—it is thus unidentifiable, anonymous, or discrete. Or rather, by not being written about or mentioned by the media, Vinderen can be said to be a secluded area, an area where the residents can retain their privacy or way of life without unwelcome disturbances. In interviews with local estate agents, it was stressed that Vinderen is an exclusive brand, a place that is very attractive to people like Sondre and Liv.

Ceren lives with her husband and two children in a two-bedroom flat in a block of flats in Linderud in the outer eastern Grorud Valley. Their daughters both attend a local kindergarten. Like her husband, Ceren was born in Turkey. The family is lower working class. Like the majority of the approximately 130,000 Valley people, they own their home. However, they paid far less for their flat than Sondre and Liv did in Vinderen. Ceren and her husband selected Linderud as they had close kin living nearby. Although their children had been born there, she wanted to move away, preferably to an area where the schools had a good reputation. One important reason for wanting to move away from Linderud was the presence of certain others. While Ceren did not know her neighbours well and most of them are nice, as she puts it, there was someone who made her uncomfortable:

> A young man had rented the apartment below us. And after some time it started to smell strange in the hallway and inside our apartment. I called the board, but nothing happened at first … When we finally were able to get the police to come they found that he had a cannabis farm inside. (Ceren)

Ceren says that she was frightened after this experience, as she feared that the man would come after her since she had called the police. She adds that compared to the other buildings next to them, few people rent apartments in their building, and she is glad because 'there are more problems where the others live as there is more subletting there'. Ceren also says that many of those renting are foreigners as they prefer to rent, and that they like the fact that the area is close to the metro since many of them do not have cars. By being tenants and not owning cars, they are socio-economically below Ceren. She thinks it is peculiar that there is only one Norwegian family with children living in the neighbourhood. All the other families with children have an ethnic minority background. With the exception of that one family, the Norwegians living in her neighbourhood are all senior citizens. According to Ceren, the media always portray the Grorud Valley as a place where many people are in bad health, where few have studied at the university, and which is plagued with high crime rates. Moreover, as the Grorud Valley is singled out as an area where the government needs to intervene in order to improve residents' quality of life, she says that there must be a reason why the Grorud Valley needs such help. This makes her a bit sceptical about the Valley, as good areas do not need fixing. As opposed to Sondre and Liv's district, the place name Linderud is not considered an exclusive brand by local estate agents. According to the latter, Linderud is attractive to people like Ceren, but not for ethnic Norwegian families and certainly not for the likes of Sondre and Liv.

Just as she is concerned about her former neighbour, Ceren is uncertain about her children's future if they were to attend the local school. She says that they will try sending their oldest child to the school, and are very anxious about how this will work out. She wonders whether or not the girl will enjoy school and learn the things that she is supposed to learn. Part of the reason why Ceren is uncertain about the local school is the fact that the majority of the children (close to 80 per cent) have a foreign background. If more than half of a class consists of foreigners, she says that the children will never learn proper Norwegian, but will instead speak broken Norwegian. Another thing Ceren emphasizes is that it is important to 'know Norwegian culture … I have lived here for almost 30 years and never experienced a Christmas Eve'. Yet, she does not interact much with Norwegians her age in the course of an ordinary day. While her oldest child has a Norwegian friend in kindergarten, most of the children she plays with at home are Turkish, the children of Ceren's friends—some living nearby, albeit not in the same neighbourhood, whereas others live farther away. Ceren meets them regularly at a Turkish organization or club where she is an active member.

Ceren's case is fairly common in the material. Based on fieldwork observations in eastern Oslo and on conversations with numerous residents, Andersen noted that

> The ethnic Norwegian Valley residents … took the metro … went to the mall, and often travelled downtown and walked around surrounded by the [ethnic] others. But instead of [the different groups interacting and thus building trust], diversity … was associated with more or less uneasiness or discomfort. (Andersen 2014, 273)

While Linderud and Vinderen can be said to be typical East and West End residential districts respectively, St. Hanshaugen is located in the middle of the city centre. The mean income level in St. Hanshaugen is between those in the affluent west (for example, Vinderen) and the less affluent east (for example, Linderud). However, St. Hanshaugen is one of the most expensive city districts to buy a flat.[6] Like Vinderen and other Oslo districts dominated by the majority, St. Hanshaugen, according to the local estate agents, is not an area that receives particular attention from the media.

Karen is 32 years old and lives with her husband and their 5-month-old son in an old apartment building, in an architectural style typical of the building boom in the late nineteenth century. Their fifth-floor flat has a ceiling height of three metres, a fireplace, and a balcony overlooking a popular park. Karen describes the location as perfect, adjacent to the city centre and other popular or fashionable districts. She can be characterized as well-educated middle class. Karen is an industrial designer and her husband is an architect. She was raised in Bærum, an affluent suburban municipality west of Oslo (where Sondre and Liv lived briefly). When moving to Oslo, she looked at flats in the western parts of town, and was happy when she came upon this area: 'When I saw this flat, I knew I had to have it!' She describes her childhood in an area consisting of villas and terraced houses, with the local schools only a short way off, and mentions the feeling of safety and freedom as positive aspects of her upbringing in that part of suburban Oslo. She also describes her childhood and adolescence as socially stable: 'I have been lucky to have the same gang of friends. Some of them I met in kindergarten—.' Some of her friends have moved out to Bærum again, after studying or working in the city for a while. She is not certain that she and her family will follow. She likes living in the city, frequenting cafés and exhibitions, and contrasts this with her suburban home tract, where the main recreational activities seem to be biking or skiing. Yet this may change in couple of years, she says; if they have another child, they may want to have a house and a garden.

Karen explains that the neighbourhood has changed. More young couples like them have moved in, replacing senior citizens. She describes them—including herself—as a gang, but they are not close-knit friends: 'At least we say hi and talk in the hallway, and such things; it's a very comfortable milieu. And then I've been on the housing association board. Then we sort of visit one another. But we don't call one another and have dinner together. It's not like that.' As a board member, one important task is to deal with the formal rules concerning the flats and the use of shared spaces. These rules, and their interpretation, regulate social conduct, practices, and relations among the residents. There should be no noise after eleven at night, and the common spaces should be kept tidy and clean. Karen says that there have been no problems with neighbours breaking the rules, 'but we live in the city centre, so if someone's having a party, that's OK'.

Karen expresses her satisfaction with St. Hanshaugen's social composition, describing it as socially, culturally, and geographically a middle ground, between the hustle and bustle of Grünerløkka (a gentrified but socially mixed area further east) and the snobbish atmosphere in Frogner (a wealthy and 'white' area further west):

> It's a lovely mix ... relatively relaxed people with different backgrounds. There are many with an education ... who in a way are wealthy. And most are Nordic ... And then there are many actors, artists and creatives ... It's the golden mean. (Karen)

She emphasizes that she seldom goes to Grünerløkka, preferring instead to visit 'the area that I'm from ... I do my shopping in the western parts'. She adds that St. Hanshaugen is safe, and a quiet and unpretentious place, adding that 'I really feel at home here'. Karen also points out that it is an attractive area, something the local estate agents confirm. St. Hanshaugen is indeed attractive to people like Karen—young, urban, middle-class and upper-middle-class Norwegian families. As one of the estate agents noted, 'birds of a feather flock together'.

Conclusion

Ceren, living in the ethnic heterogeneous but far from poverty-stricken Linderud, worries about her children's future. She has also had some unpleasant experiences with a neighbour, which challenged her comfort and well-being. Likewise, she does not trust the local environment to improve her children's chances in life. It is far from certain that she would find comfort in an ethnically homogeneous neighbourhood, but others have. Heidi, whom we saw in passing, moved from the mixed inner east, avoiding the likewise mixed outer east in order to settle in a working-class and lower-middle-class suburb. There, life is good and she is certain her children will attend a good school, nothing like the schools that feature regularly in the media coverage of the East End. Karen too, is very much at home among her own kind in St. Hanshaugen. It is significant that she does not know her neighbours that well, but they are like her and they interact without any friction. Similarly, Liv living in Vinderen trusts her neighbours, not because she knows them as individuals, but because they are like her: she identifies with them.

Heidi, Karen, and Liv all trust that their neighbours will not be disruptive and that together they make up a safe environment. However, theirs is not an unconditional trust that implies or requires a certain degree of relational intimacy, such as between a mother and child (Kohn 2008, 2); rather, it is a non-intimate, socio-demographically restricted trust. In suburban and West End neighbourhoods such as Vinderen, parents seem to be certain that their families' social and cultural reproduction (Atkinson 2006) is secure, since they are communities of sameness and of socio-economic and ethnic stability. The point is that among our respondents, it was normal to seek out certain environments—often characterized by ethnic or 'racial' (Hylland Eriksen 2012), and to some degree socio-economic, homogeneity (Andersen 2014). In these spaces, a comfortable and conflict-free life is guaranteed—or such environments may be perceived to afford a sense of local cohesion (Uzzell et al. 2002, 42). Such everyday tactics run counter to the ideal of a general urban social sustainability. This ideal implies first that the city's neighbourhoods, schools, and public spaces are diverse melting pots, and, second, that Oslo is a just, conflict-free zone. The legacy of residential segregation, as well as the actions of contemporary actors such as the media and property developers, likewise counteracts the creation of an integrated city. It should also be stressed that these processes and tactics undermine the ideals of urban cultural and social diversity and inclusion so frequently highlighted as an asset in strategies for creating creative cities or attracting the creative class (Florida 2005). Oslo's sustainability strategy is indeed part of its ambition to be a competitive city in the Florida sense (Municipality of Oslo 2014, 14–15).

When looking at both the actions and ideals of our respondents, they nominally adhere to the national ethos of an egalitarian society and agree with the policy ideal of a more inclusive city. Few of these adults, however, seem to develop strong, close ties with people categorized as 'others'. Many trust their neighbours, but amongst East Enders, distrust is no less omnipresent. This is especially true of neighbourhoods in flux, where the demographics are continually changing. The decision to move in, leave, or stay is heavily influenced by the nature, stability, or changes to the demographic composition of a neighbourhood. This again is linked to perceptions of whether it will be possible to generate sought-after social capital, securing social reproduction and *local* social cohesion. The relationship between social and cultural composition, locally based social capital and cohesion, and social and physical mobility may develop into self-reinforcing circles, which in Oslo may be generalized as the West End neighbourhoods and their residents being stable or getting 'better', and the East End neighbourhoods and their residents being stable or getting 'worse'. In other words, whereas the West Enders we met were comfortable and stable in their neighbourhoods, the East Enders' environments can be said to be uncomfortable or risky, and even for those who enjoyed living there, their well-being was conditional: things might change, and they would then have to move.

In conclusion, at the individual level, a comfortable life and a conflict-free city seem to be contingent on a social and preferably spatial distance to those who are seen as too different. Not unlike Austin, Texas (after the city's transformation according to its 1928 master plan), the historic 'East–West split' (Long 2014, 11) evident in Oslo will in all likelihood continue, probably exaggeratedly so in some cases. The media has a significant role in magnifying or weakening the discourses regarding specific areas of the city. This is evident in the case of the eastern outskirts, but also with respect to high-status areas. The latter, by *not* being problematized, is naturally fine (Andersen 2014, 147–150).

Oslo's historical legacy, the strategies of its property developers, its image in the media, and its citizens' values and actions all seem to run counter to an ideal of inclusion and the probability of creating what we have termed city-wide trust or accumulating bridging capital. In other words, if social inclusion or integration is a crucial condition, inequalities are unlikely to be reduced. Consequently, whereas Long (2014, 20) indicates that Austin can realize its vision of becoming a socially just city, a socially sustainable Oslo seems to be a mere utopia.

Notes

1 In 2015, about 650,000 individuals lived within the city's limits. In Oslo, socio-spatial boundaries are often drawn with reference to (perceived) cultural and phenotypical differences (Andersen 2014; Eriksen 2012). Moreover, different 'groups' are more or less explicitly ranked in what we with Bleich (2009) call a ethno-racial hierarchy.
2 Official city statistics have a category of 'people with a different national background than Norwegian … This group consists of immigrants and Norwegian-born individuals with immigrant parents, and they are called the immigrant population' (Municipality of Oslo 2015). Statistics Norway speaks of the same group as individuals 'with an immigrant background' (Andreassen et al. 2013). The term 'non-Western' refers to people who have parents from, or who themselves have emigrated from, a country that is not classified as 'Western'; even though the term is no longer used by Statistics Norway, it is still widely used in public discourse.
3 The full understanding of what social sustainability (ideally) should imply, according to Basu (2013, 48), is 'an inclusive and conflict-free city; a physically and economically accessible city; and a culturally and politically engaged city, with equitable access to public services and institutional support'. This is largely consistent with the Norwegian policy ideal discussed in the following section.
4 All translations from the Norwegian are the authors' own.
5 A White Paper is the government's case presented to the Storting (the Norwegian Parliament) on various matters that it wishes the Storting to consider. Reports to the Storting are used when the Government wishes to raise a matter in the Storting without a draft resolution.
6 One reason why the level of income does not necessarily match house prices may be because St. Hanshaugen is popular among students (who often rent).

References

Andersen, B. (2014) 'Westbound and eastbound. Managing sameness and the making of separations in Oslo' (Ph.D. diss., Department of Social Anthropology, Oslo: University of Oslo).
Andreassen, K. Kvarv, M. T. Dzamarija & T. I. Slaastad (2013) 'Stort mangfold i lille Norge', *Samfunnsspeilet*, 5/2013, 11–19.
Atkinson, R. (2006) 'Padding the bunker: Strategies of middle-class disaffiliation and colonisation in the city', *Urban Studies*, 43/4, 819–832, doi: 10.1080/00420980600597806.

Basu, R. (2013) 'In search of nimmathi for social sustainability? Imagining, building, and negotiating spaces of peace in Toronto's diverse neighbourhoods', *Canadian Journal of Urban Research* 22/1, 44–66.

Bleich, E. (2009) 'Where do Muslims stand on ethno-racial hierarchies in Britain and France? Evidence from public opinion surveys, 1988–2008', *Patterns of Prejudice*, 43/3–4, 379–400.

Blom, S. (2012) 'Innvandrernes bostedspreferanser—årsak til innvandrertett bosetting?' (Rapporter 2014/38, Oslo: Statistisk Sentralbyrå, SSB).

Council of Europe (2014a) 'Intercultural Cities Charts', Council of Europe, <http://www.culturalpolicies.net/web/intercultural-cities-charts.php>, accessed 27 March 2015.

—— (2014b) *Intercultural cities index: A methodological overview* (Strasbourg: Council of Europe).

Eurocities (2010a) 'Eurocities integrating cities charter', Eurocities <http://www.integratingcities.eu/integrating-cities/integrating_cities_charter>, accessed 27 March 2015.

Eurocities (2010b) 'EUROCITIES Charter on Integrating Cities', Eurocities, <http://nws.eurocities.eu/MediaShell/media/CharterforWebFINAL.pdf>, accessed 27 March 2015.

Florida, R. (2005) *Cities and the creative class* (New York: Routledge).

Hansen, T. & A. Sæterdal (1970) *Ammerud* (Oslo: Pax).

Hylland Eriksen, T. (2012) 'Xenophobic exclusion and the new right in Norway', *Journal of Community & Applied Social Psychology* 22/3, 206–09.

Kjeldstadli, K. (1990) *Den delte byen: fra 1900 til 1948*, iv (Oslo: Cappelen).

—— & Jan Eivind Myhre (1995) *Oslo—spenningenes by: Oslohistorie* (Oslo: Pax).

Kohn, M. (2008) *Trust: Self-interest and the common good* (Oxford: OUP).

Ley, D. (2012) 'Social mixing and the historical geography of gentrification', in G. Bridge, T. Butler and L. Lees (eds.) *Mixed communities: Gentrification by stealth?* (Bristol: Policy Press).

Long, J. (2014) 'Constructing the narrative of the sustainability fix: Sustainability, social justice and representation in Austin, TX', *Urban Studies*, online publication ahead of print.

Meld.St. 6 (2012–2013) *En helhetlig integreringspolitikk: Mangfold og fellesskap* (Barne-, likestillings- og inkluderingsdepartementet; Oslo: Regjeringen).

Moen, B. (2009) 'Tilhørighetens balanse: Norsk-pakistanske kvinners hverdagsliv i transnasjonale familier' (NOVA Rapport; Oslo: NOVA).

Municipality of Oslo (2011) *Oslotrender 2011: Vedlegg til høringsutkasrt til planstrategi og planprogram for Kommuneplan 2013* (Byrådsavdeling for finans og næring; Oslo: Municipality of Oslo).

Municipality of Oslo (2014) 'Smart, trygg, grønn. Kommuneplan for Oslo: Oslo mot 2030', Municipality of Oslo <http://www.kommuneplan.oslo.kommune.no/getfile.php/Kommuneplan%20for%20Oslo%20%28KPO%29/Internett%20%28KPO%29/Dokumenter/Vedlegg%201-H%C3%B8ringsutkast-Kommuneplan%202030-web.pdf>, accessed 13 April 2015.

Municipality of Oslo (2015) 'Befolkningens landbakgrunn', Municipality of Oslo <https://www.oslo.kommune.no/politikk-og-administrasjon/statistikk/befolkning/landbakgrunn/>, accessed 13 April 2015.

Myhre, J. E. (1990) *Hovedstaden Christiania: fra 1814 til 1900*, iii (Oslo: Cappelen).

Norwegian Ministry of Local Government and Modernisation (2012) 'Governance for sustainable development and social inclusion—the case of the Grorud Valley Programme' <http://www.nordregio.se/Global/Events/Events%202014/TIPSE/Presentations%2025%20Nov/Grorud%20Valley%20Programme_Nordregio_Marianne%20Gjørv_final_241114.pdf>, accessed 28 May 2015.

NOU (Norges offentlig utredning) [Norwegian Official Report] (2011:14) *Bedre integrering: Mål, strategier, tiltak* [Improved integration: Goals, strategies, measures] (Oslo: Barne-, likestillings- og inkluderingsdepartementet).

Putnam, R. D. (2007) 'E pluribus unum: Diversity and community in the twenty-first century: The 2006 Johan Skytte Prize Lecture', *Scandinavian Political Studies*, 30/2, 137–74.

Savage, M., G. Bagnall & B. Longhurst (2005) *Globalization and belonging* (London: SAGE).

Stortingsmelding (2012) Meld.St. 6, 2012–2013, *En helhetlig integreringspolitikk* [A comprehensive integration policy] (Oslo: Barne-, likestillings- og inkluderingsdepartementet, 26 October).

Tretter, E. M. (2013) 'Contesting sustainability: "SMART Growth" and the redevelopment of Austin's eastside', *International Journal of Urban & Regional Research*, 37/1, 297–310.

Uzzell, D., E. Pol & D. Badenas (2002) 'Place identification, social cohesion, and environmental sustainability', *Environment & Behavior*, 34/1, 26–53.

Wacquant, L. (1996) 'Red belt, black belt: Racial division, class inequality and the state in the French urban periphery and the American ghetto', in E. Mingione, *Urban poverty and the underclass* (Oxford: Blackwell).

Wessel, T. (2013) 'Hvilken betydning har nabolaget for barns utvikling og livssjanser?', in *Oppvekstrapporten 2013* (Oslo: Barne- ungdoms- og familiedirektoratet).

CHAPTER 6

'Ghettoization' and 'parallel societies' in Denmark
Public rhetoric and lived lives

Tina Gudrun Jensen

The development of multi-ethnic neighbourhoods due to the dual processes of immigration and diversification in Denmark since the 1980s has raised extensive public debate. The debate focuses directly on 'ghettoization' and 'parallel lives' in the sense of 'bad integration', for example unemployment, crime, segregation, and social isolation. The context for this debate is a widespread perception of immigration and cultural diversity as a threat to social cohesion, and of immigrants' cultures as a problem for social integration. Central to the last Danish government's strategy to combat ghettoization and parallel lives was the attempt to vary the composition of residents according to social status and ethnicity.

The endeavour to ensure diversity in residential areas must navigate the general challenge of managing diversity through urban planning (Germain 2002; Sandercock 1998). The heterogeneity of contemporary cities may be envisioned in various ways, such as assimilation, integration, separatism, and mixity (Grillo 2005); urban diversity often tends to be seen as a problem—which is reflected in discussions about multiculturalism (Sniderman & Hagendoorn 2007)—but also as a condition for co-existence (Back 1996; Hewitt 1986). These considerations raise some questions relevant to the Danish case. What are the ideas behind the planning of cultural diversity envisioned in the strategies against ghettoization and parallel lives, particularly in residential areas? Indeed, what are the visions of cultural diversity, interethnic relations and co-existence?

And what is the relationship between the rhetoric of public debate and the reality on the ground?

Given that identities and places are constructed in the interplay of internal and external discourses and experiences (Jenkins 1996; Mazanti 2002), the purpose of this essay is to explore the relationship between the public debate on integration, ghettoization, and parallel lives on the one hand, and the personal stories of people living in multi-ethnic residential areas on the other. Such a perspective assumes that integration and ghettoization are empirical terms rather than analytical terms, and that different actors use them in various ways (Fog Olwig & Pærregaard 2007). The essay focuses on the way cultural diversity, integration, and co-existence are formulated in the Danish public debate and lived lives, and whether it does indeed have an effect on people living in an area that may potentially be defined as a ghetto. It transpires that the case study used here questions the existence of parallel lives by focusing on the relationships between residents who are so often referred to as ethnic majority and minority citizens. The essay thus explores the identities and relationships at stake in Denmark's multi-ethnic neighbourhoods, and how these identities interact in the context of ghettoization, integration, and cultural diversity, by examining the public debate about integration and ghettoization and then looking at the detail of lived lives in a multi-ethnic neighbourhood.

The case study comprises fieldwork in 2010 and 2011 in Green Park in Copenhagen, a residential area of social housing that for many years has been characterized as a multi-ethnic neighbourhood consisting of equal numbers of ethnic minorities and ethnic Danes (Jensen 2015). The research methods included participant observation, qualitative interviews, and focus-group interviews with residents of diverse ages, genders, ethnicities, and socio-economic status, with all data duly anonymized.

Immigration, cultural diversity, and integration

Immigrants constitute 11 per cent of the Danish population, with major groups from countries such as Turkey, Germany, Iraq, Poland, Lebanon, Bosnia-Herzegovina, and Africa, and in particular Somalia,

Pakistan, former Yugoslavia, and Norway. Of the immigrants and their descendants, 58 per cent come from non-Western countries (Danmarks Statistik 2014).

Immigration and social integration are highly politicized issues in Denmark. Danes position themselves among those Europeans who are most sceptical of immigration (Goul Andersen 2002). The challenge it poses seems primarily to be that immigrants represent cultural diversity. It is not uncommon to hear the existence of cultural diversity negated, with references to Denmark as an old and culturally homogeneous nation-state. Heterogeneity, as represented by immigrants, is thus often seen as a threat to the country's social cohesion and welfare. Consequently, 'integration' is a political project aimed at absorbing immigrants into majority society and its norms (Fog Olwig & Pærregaard 2007).

The rhetoric of 'right' and 'wrong' culture and values has dominated the integration question. The same voices like to hint that immigrants' culture is an obstacle to their integration into Danish society, while emphasizing Danish values as rightly predominant and necessary for social cohesion. The debate represents both a politicization of culture, whereby culture is represented as a politically necessary functional homogeneity, and a culturalization of politics, by which political values are legitimized as culture (Mouritsen 2006, 73). The integration debate thus revolves around the question of immigrants' cultural capacity to harmonize their values with Danish values. The concept of integration is generally used in the sense of assimilation as 'cultural sameness', as a process whereby one becomes part of society. The Danish integration debate reflects the ways that civil culture there and in other Scandinavian countries is characterized by the notion of equality in the sense of 'imagined sameness' (Gullestad 2002, 83), and indicates people's unease in the face of difference.

The paradox is that Denmark's official integration policy also emphasizes the necessity of 'making room' and being 'open to other cultures'. All told, discourses on integration mirror a fundamental tension between formal openness and strong demands for assimilation—between multiculturalism as an ideal and assimilation as a necessity (Jensen 2010). The next sections illustrate how urban planning for pluralism mirrors the tension between cultural diversity and assimilation.

Strategies against ghettoization

Immigrants and their descendants have primarily settled in the urbanized parts of Denmark. About 60 per cent of immigrants, primarily non-Western, live in social housing in estates (Skifter Andersen 2006). This council housing was constructed back in the 1960s as part of the welfare dream of providing what at the time were considered 'luxurious' homes, with hot water and showers, for ordinary Danes. However, as residents got better jobs and higher incomes they moved out of the estates, and since 1984 have been replaced by a growing number of immigrant residents. Today, some 22 per cent of Denmark's immigrants live in multi-ethnic residential areas of social housing, 40 per cent of whose population is made up of different immigrant groups (ibid.).

In the mid-1990s, the government's Urban Commission was set up to lead a concerted effort to counteract the development in what is generally termed 'vulnerable' neighbourhoods (Christensen et al. 2010), characterized by residents who are unemployed, mentally ill, drug addicts, criminals, ethnic minorities, etc. From the outset, urban renewal strategies focused on putting a stop to 'negative resident development' by attracting more resource-strong residents to these neighbourhoods. Although social housing is multi-ethnic and therefore cannot be defined as 'ghettos' (Skifter Andersen 2006), the key term used for describing the challenges in the housing estates is 'ghettoization', comprising the problems of segregation, social housing, and social isolation (Pløger 2004). In 2004, the government launched its first strategy against ghettoization directed at vulnerable residential areas (Regeringen 2004). The government singled out eight potential areas of ghettoization in Denmark, characterized by a concentration of ethnic minorities and adult residents living on transfer payments (ibid. 4). During the 2000s, the then government intensified its focus on ghettoization and 'bad integration'—lack of education, unemployment, criminality, segregation, parallel lives, and radicalization—hand in hand with increasing references to Danish values and norms in the debate problematizing immigrants' culture as an obstacle to integration. In 2010, the government launched a 'ghetto plan' (*ghettoplan*), and published its second strategy against ghettoization, where even the title talked of a 'showdown' (Regeringen 2010). Defining ghettos as 'parallel societies' in residential areas with a high concentration of immigrants, where 'Danish values are not rooted', the aim of this strategy was to make these areas become 'a more integrated part of Danish society' (ibid. 5).

The Danish media describe this 2010 strategy as consolidating the government's debate by focusing on everyday values. Whereas the 2004 strategy was vague about the term 'ghetto', the 2010 strategy tightened up the use of the term 'ghetto': where previously 8 'potential ghetto areas' were singled out (Regeringen 2004, 4), the 2010 strategy stated that 'we have today 29 residential areas that face such great challenges that they warrant the term ghettos' (Regeringen 2010, 5). The second strategy also differed from the first by openly mentioning in its discussion of residential areas the issues of parallel societies, integration, and Danish norms and values.

The 2010 strategy to combat ghettoization concentrated on achieving a 'balanced composition of residents' (Regeringen 2010, 14) by their 'dispersal' from vulnerable residential areas. This was to be achieved by a variety of measures, including assigning flats to 'resource-weak' people in less vulnerable areas, for example those run by housing associations, and making it easier for 'resource-strong' people to move into council estates.

These endeavours raise the question of how cultural diversity, interethnic relations, and co-existence were envisioned in the strategies against ghettoization and parallel societies. In focusing on ghettos as parallel societies devoid of Danish values, the government's strategy refers to 'distortion' and 'balance' in residential areas, emphasizing that the balance in residential areas must not tip over to norms and behaviour that are non-Danish:

> The composition of residents in the ghettos is very distorted in comparison to the rest of society. Today, more than six out of ten residents in the 29 ghettos are immigrants or their descendants from non-Western countries. This is not acceptable. No area should have

a preponderance of immigrants and descendants from non-Western countries. And it should be the norm to speak Danish. ... The government will not accept that there are areas where the norm is to be supported from the public purse. (Regeringen 2010, 15)

The strategy thus expects Danish norms to rule in residential areas, implying essentialized and polarized notions of culture and integration that presuppose that people do not have contact with Danish society and thus live 'parallel lives'. The notion also holds integration to be assimilation into majority culture and society, neglecting the ethnic minority networks and institutions that could contribute to this integration, along with any thought of integration as a reciprocal process that affects both ethnic minorities and majorities.

The attempt to ensure diversity in residential areas comes under the broader heading of managing diversity as a challenge facing metropolitan centres (Germain 2002; Sandercock 1998). Different local and national authorities can have different positions on diversity, of course, and in Denmark, urban planning is divided between the government and the municipalities. The management of diversity in residential areas in Denmark reflects the disjuncture concerning integration and diversity, particularly at the state and municipal levels. While the government had its strategies against ghettoization, the municipality of Copenhagen in a variety of ways seemed to distance itself from the government and its vision of integration. Copenhagen's own integration policy generally saw the capital as a site for fruitful coexistence and interaction between citizens from different ethnic backgrounds—one that allowed for diversity (Københavns Kommune 2006). It emphasized 'inclusion' and 'citizenship', and defined integration as 'a dynamic and reciprocal process, where citizens with different backgrounds meet and create future communities' (Københavns Kommune 2010, 12). This integration policy particularly focused on Copenhagen as 'an intercultural city', a site of diversity, interethnic relations, and mixity (ibid.).

In contrast to the capital's own integration policy, the government's strategy against ghettoization and a parallel society makes no mention of diversity or interethnic relations. Where Copenhagen envisioned cultural diversity in terms of mixity, the government stressed separatism. This discrepancy in the management of diversity mirrors an essential ambiguity in Danish integration policy that stems from the fundamental questions of the nature of integration and how to handle cultural diversity, and the tension between the diversity represented by immigrants and the equality (for which read 'sameness' and 'assimilation') represented by the general notions of integration (Jensen 2010).

Focusing on the relationship between abstract debate and lived lives, I will now explore the ways ghettoization, integration, cultural diversity, and interethnic relations are envisioned and practised, using the example of a residential district that is characterized by a high degree of ethnic diversity. The existence of 'parallel lives' is called into question by focusing on the relationships between residents in ethnic minority or majority positions.

Green Park

Green Park is a residential area on the outskirts of Copenhagen. When it was built in 1966, it was one of the new, modern residential areas just like so many other social housing projects at that time. Green Park's approximately thousand residents are made up of an almost equal balance of ethnic Danes and ethnic minorities primarily with non-Western backgrounds, who are mixed in Green Park's blocks of flats. About 40 per cent of residents are on low incomes, and about 23 per cent are unemployed.

Green Park is not technically defined as a vulnerable area or a ghetto, but has attracted some attention as an area at risk of negative development, be it vandalism, crime, or ghettoization, and consequently it has been an official 'social project' since 2004. The present council master plan has picked out several social problems in Green Park: a lack of dialogue between different ethnic groups and between vulnerable and strong residents, vandalism, and the neighbourhood's generally bad image. Compared to other multi-ethnic council estates, Green Park is a conspicuously 'white' area. There are no signs that ethnic minorities live there. For instance, there are no satellite dishes. In 2008, the board of Green Park's Livewell housing association and its residents voted to ban all satellite dishes. The ethnic minority residents were angered by the ban, which they felt was discriminatory, being intended to disconnect them from their countries of origin. The board itself had various explanations for the ban, but many others tended to agree that the underlying reason was to remove the indications of an ethnic minority presence that would associate Green Park with other 'ghettos', and as such the ban was part of the general attempt to make areas like Green Park attractive for 'resourceful' ethnic Danes. Similarly, the use of foreign languages in Green Park was a provocation for the board, who liked to say 'In Livewell, we speak Danish', yet at the same time they went out of their way to show multicultural respect. They were careful to serve halal meat and non-alcoholic drinks at the estate's activities such as summer parties and holiday celebrations, and were keen to learn about the ethnic minorities' cultural and religious traditions: in 2010, for example, they asked Muslim residents to hold a public celebration of Eid ul-Fitr to mark the end of Ramadan. The board thus demonstrated a reserve on the question of cultural diversity that was matched with an openness, an ambiguity between wanting to recognize cultural differences and refusing to do so. In that sense, Green Park reflects the general tensions between assimilation and diversity in the integration debate, and, more specifically, the discrepancies in how diversity is managed.

Narratives about Green Park

> We have a bit of everything. We have the drug addicts and we have the alcoholics. And then we have the ethnics. (Martin, Green Park resident)

The residents' sense of Green Park was formed by internal experiences and external attitudes (Mazanti 2002) to it as a multi-ethnic residential area. When the study's respondents talked about it and its residents, they told stories about vandalism, crime, assault, drinking, and noise, but also about community spirit and good relations. They characterized their fellow residents as 'drunkards', 'drug addicts', 'the mentally ill' or 'the crazy ones', 'the resourceless and resourceful', 'the foreigners', 'the troublemakers', and 'the elders', although the most basic distinction was between 'Danes' (*danskere*) and 'foreigners' (*udlændinge*), mirroring a general distinction in Danish society.

The respondents had many different stories about Green Park. Their main narrative was about then and now: how it used to be and how it is today. They said there used to be more children and more social cohesion, including between different ethnic groups. They spoke of the great numbers of immigrants, refugees, and vulnerable people who arrived in the 1990s, increasing the distance between people, particularly between ethnic Danes and ethnic minorities.

They were also conscious that the media might have an influence on their own and other residents' sense of developments in Green Park. They reflected upon the relationship between the broader public debate and local people's attitudes, noticing that as people became more outspoken on immigration and integration, the residents of Green Park became more anxious. The neighbourhood had seen a great deal of vandalism and crime in the 1990s, which, being associated with immigrant youth, added to the air of ghettoization.

There was an awareness that the term 'ghetto' might possibly apply to Green Park, and respondents spontaneously reflected on whether it was indeed a 'ghetto' or not. Although they started from very different positions on the issue, they all ended up accusing 'the foreigners' for making Green Park a bad place, a ghetto, thus reflecting the wider moral panic about ghettoization. For ethnic Danish residents, the key issue was the number of 'foreigners' living there. They had their own guesses as to the numbers of other residents and their backgrounds, and their own horror stories about being outnumbered by residents from ethnic minorities; indeed, they closely mirrored the government's concern about 'distortion' and 'balance' in ghettoized residential areas, and the fear that it might tip in the ethnic minorities' favour and make them more visible.

With their preoccupation with the area's social composition—primarily 'resourceful' contra 'resourceless' people—the presence of ethnic minority residents, and ghettoization, and their vigilance about the ethnic minority numbers, the respondents' discourses and representations of Green Park broadly reproduce Denmark's public discourse about vulnerable residential areas and ghettoization. Theirs was a rather simplistic, monolithic image of ethnic minorities versus ethnic majorities. However, as will be seen, the reality of Green Park was far more complex than that; the residents' sense of their community was only *partly* shaped by the public debate in the media.

Identities and relationships in Green Park

When speaking about 'the foreigners' in Green Park, respondents from the Danish majority often reproduced the dominant stereotypes of immigrants as 'problems': 'unintegrated', violent, repressive (particularly towards women), unemployed, and with 'different mentalities'. They often singled out Muslims as markers of radical difference and dis-integration (Silverstein 2005).

Respondents who were in a minority were in turn very aware of their categorization by others, and opposed it vigorously. When speaking about themselves and their lives, they would emphasize that they were not 'a problem'. Some argued that they were being excluded from Danish society. Many had lived there most of their lives, and yet the difficulties of being recognized as a Dane rather than a foreigner were central to their life experiences. In our first encounters, they would tell me about the number of years they had lived in Denmark and in Green Park, emphasizing that they spoke Danish and had Danish citizenship. They spoke of themselves as Danish, far removed from the outsiders' definitions of them as 'foreigners'. They spoke of their ethnic Danish neighbours having requested that they assimilate, thereby associating them with the dominant discourse on integration as being assimilation into Danish culture and society. They also said their ethnic Danish neighbours were reserved and anti-social, indicating that they had no interest in them. They also touched on the issue of whether ethnic Danish residents were 'racist' or not. Their narratives thus also reflected the major public debate over Danish attitudes to foreigners; for example, the question of whether Denmark has gone from being an 'ethnically tolerant' country to being a 'racist' one (Hervik 2004; Nielsen 2004).

However, respondents were also very aware of their own stereotypes and prejudices against one another, and the ways they were informed by the media and the public debate on immigrants and their integration into Danish society. Lykke, a 39-year-old woman who had lived in Green Park her entire life, was one who showed some awareness of the ways that immigrants were defined as problems:

> I think it's a pity … because it's as if you lump them all together. When somebody's a different colour, or a different hair colour, well then they're all likely to be burglars or drug dealers, or 'everybody is sure to do that', or 'it's all those Turks' … But it isn't. I really think it's a pity for the ones who behave properly and who may be feeling that others are pointing fingers at them every day. I think it's a pity. I think it's hard. (Lykke, Green Park resident)

Similarly, ethnic minority respondents spoke of the necessity of rising above their own stereotypes of ethnic Danes. For instance, Thanaa, a 45-year-old woman who had immigrated from Lebanon when she was in her twenties and had lived in Green Park for the last 15 years, said that 'Every Dane, every person, has an opinion. You can't talk about "all Danes". Some Danes think this way. Others think other ways.'

Thus respondents often went against culturally essentialist representations of 'Danes' and 'foreigners' to acknowledge the complexity of others' identities and the multifarious ways of being 'Danes', 'immigrants', 'Muslims', and so on. Majority Danes could show empathy for what their ethnic minority neighbours went through, an insight that also led them to express ambivalent positions on ethnic minorities and integration, because it caused them to wonder about major issues in the Danish public debate on immigration and integration—for example, the number of immigrants or the Mohammed cartoons controversy. Their ambiguity thus stemmed from their simultaneous internal and external insights. For some, this even led to the realization that ethnic minorities were generally discriminated against. All told, respondents were capable of expressing a culturally complex understanding that often challenged the rigid categories used in the integration question and the relationships between 'us' and 'them'.

Green Park's residents generally seemed to agree that 'Danes and foreigners don't really have any neighbourhood relations'. Respondents said they did not know one another well, lacked contact, and did not feel that others were 'open'. Yet while this discourse of the non-existence of interethnic relations echoed the public discourse of separatism and parallel lives, the lack of contact seemed to be more general among Green Park residents, as they tended to refer to the limits of neighbouring as an occasioned activity, implying a distant relationship with their neighbours (Laurier et al. 2002). Then there was the discrepancy between what the residents said and what they did in terms of interethnic relations. Whereas respondents tended to formulate interethnic relations as non-existent, in practice the conditions of sharing a residential district as neighbours necessitated several forms of relation-making. The main forms of interaction—as in other residential areas—were contact situations (occasional meetings in or around the blocks of flats), which nevertheless made a difference by giving people who at the outset were strangers a relationship of a kind (Hansen et al. 2010). The commonest forms of neighbourhood relations were defined by shared experiences with the neighbours, and derived from living in that particular neighbourhood.

Positions on integration and cultural diversity

As part of the study, I asked people in Green Park about the public debate on integration and cultural diversity. The respondents had many different positions on the government's integration policies. All of them shared or rejected the dominant discourses on integration in a variety of ways. Generally, they shared a rather abstract notion of integration in the broadest sense as 'conforming to Danish norms and rules', which mirrored the standard definition of integration in the public debate. Some used a very rigid rhetoric, referring to integration as assimilation into Danish culture, and were clearly against the existence of cultural differences; yet there was a disparity between this and the way they talked about the cultural differences of their ethnic minority neighbours.

Indeed, there were very interesting answers to the question of cultural diversity in Green Park. Above all, respondents talked about diversity in terms of language, food, smells, alcohol, noise, furnishings, and gender roles. 'Cultural differences' in the neighbourhood were something they had all had to relate to; however, while certain subjects and episodes were potentially contentious, they rarely led to real confrontations. Furthermore, residents sometimes showed multicultural respect towards others: majority residents would cook halal food for communal activities and knew to take off their shoes before entering their neighbours' homes; minority residents were conscious of Danish habits, with some Muslim residents choosing to drink beer with their Danish neighbours, perceiving the drinking of alcohol as a condition for interaction.

When I asked if it was possible to live together in Green Park in spite of their cultural differences, the ethnic majority residents generally answered that they did not find cultural diversity in Green Park problematic 'as long as people behave themselves', often adding something to the effect that it was possible to 'follow the rules in Denmark without having to abandon one's own culture'. Some were emphatic that culture was something private that should be muted in public, but others did not feel strongly about this private–public distinction. Either way, respondents did not engage in the public debate about 'right' or 'wrong' culture, or culture as an 'obstacle' to integration: the general attitude was that cultural diversity in Green Park was a fact. Most of the time, people did not really notice, think, or care about diversity, and remained pragmatically neutral on the issue. Their perceptions were characterized by 'commonplace diversity' (Wessendorf 2013), as something they experienced as a normal part of life.

Yvonne, a 50-year-old woman, said that the question of ethnic identity or diversity was basically subordinate to the question of living, and living together, in Green Park:

> I think it's totally unimportant what my neighbour's nationality is, but I also assume that ... well, we have our lives here ... Well, we're perfectly able to be friends even though we don't have the same nationality and language and political convictions and religion and sexuality and so on. In fact, I couldn't care less about that. But what we do have in common is that we live here, and that we want to have a nice place to live. It's our home, this place. (Yvonne, Green Park resident)

Her main priority was Green Park as a residential area, where people could get on with living their daily lives, and not bothering so much about the rest. Her attitude toward issues such as cultural diversity seemed to depend on how neighbourhood relations were practised, based on the shared experience of living in that particular neighbourhood, and the general moderation of private, personal neighbourhood relations. The residents' indifference to cultural diversity went hand in hand with the general forms of community that arise from sharing a place. These were consociate relations, based on what people had in common, regardless of their differences—in this instance, by sharing a residential area (Amit 2002; Germain 2002).

Generally, the residents did not make much of an issue out of relations between ethnic majorities and minorities in Green Park. Some felt that it should not be an issue, either. These were the residents—mainly from the ethnic majorities—who were weary of the public debates about integration and ghettoization. People like 50-year-old Jens, who both lived and worked in Green Park, and said, 'Don't focus on [integration], and it will happen automatically. It's our focusing on it that creates insecurity.'

Conclusion

This essay has explored the relationship between Denmark's public debate on integration, ghettoization, and parallel lives and the personal stories of people living in a mixed residential area, focusing on discourses and practices of integration, cultural diversity, and interethnic co-existence. In public debate, 'ghettoization' and 'parallel lives' have become epitomes of bad integration—an essentialist and polarized understanding of culture and ethnic relations coined in terms of 'parallel lives' and 'social isolation.'

At the same time, the various local and governmental visions of integration and urban planning bear witness to the tensions between cultural diversity and assimilation. The different positions on the existence of cultural diversity reflect urban planning's challenges in managing cultural diversity: management practices are either tuned to 'universalism' or 'cultural differences' (Germain 2002) or to separatism and mixity (Grillo 2005). The multi-ethnic residential area of Green Park in many ways reflects these tensions, as well as the general integration rhetoric, as people are torn between wanting to recognize cultural differences and not wanting to. The public discourse of integration and ghettoization was reflected in the residents' general awareness of the possible external categorization of Green Park as a 'ghetto' and in their definition of immigrant neighbours as 'problems'. At the same time, they were aware of the negative influence of public debate on immigration and integration, and thus of the prejudices and stereotypes they and others used about people who were, first and foremost, their neighbours. This was prompted by their personal understanding, acquired in their everyday interactions with their ethnic minority neighbours.

The residents of Green Park did not have much to say about integration per se. They recognized the public discourse on integration and cultural diversity, and were even influenced by it, but were as likely to oppose it. Some saw the public focus on integration as undermining interethnic relations in Green Park. While they reproduced the public notion of integration as coming to an accommodation with Danish norms and rules and the rigid rhetoric of assimilation into Danish culture, they also related to 'cultural differences' as not really being a problem—they opposed the public debate about immigrant culture as wrong and running counter to their integration into Danish society. However, they also voiced cultural complexity based on the multiple influences and cultural interplay between different groups and meaning systems (Hannerz 1992).

All told, culturally complex Green Park presents a very different picture of a multi-ethnic neighbourhood than the impression of essentialist cultures and polarization given by the governmental debate on ghettoization and parallel lives. The two images represent different visions of urban cultural diversity, emphasizing separatism and mixity respectively. Their communication of interethnic relations and co-existence was thus in stark contrast to the debates about 'ghettoization' and 'parallel lives'.

References

Amit, V. (2002) 'An anthropology without community?', in V. Amit & N. Rappaport, *The trouble with community. Anthropological reflections on movement, identity and collectivity* (London: Pluto Press).
Back, L. (1996) *New ethnicities and urban culture* (London: UCL Press).
Christensen, G., M. Falk Mikkelsen, K. Buchholt Pedersen, A. Amilon (2010) *Boligsociale indsatser og huslejestøtte. Kortlægning og programvaluering af landsbyggefondens 2006–10-pulje* (Copenhagen: SFI, the Danish National Centre for Social Research).
Danmarks Statistik (2014) *Indvandrere i Danmark 2013* (Copenhagen: Københavns Statistik).
Fog Olwig, K. & K. Pærregaard (2007) *Integration: Antropologiske proceser* (Copenhagen: Museum Tusculanum).
Germain, A. (2002) 'The sustainability of multicultural cities: A neighbourhood affair?', *Belgeo* 4, 377–86.
Goul Andersen, J. (2002) 'Danskernes holdninger til indvandrere. En oversight', *Amid Working Paper Series*, 12 (2002).
Grillo, R. (2005) 'Backlash against diversity? Identity and cultural politics in European cities', *Working Paper 14* (Oxford: Centre on Migration, Policy and Society/COMPAS).
Gullestad, M. (2002) *Det norske sett med nye øyne* (Oslo: Universitetsforlaget).
Hannerz, U. (1992) *Cultural complexity* (New York: Columbia University Press).
Hansen, K. E., A. Heron Hansen, H. Kalkan & W. Rasmussen (2010) *Om at bo sammen i et multietnisk boligområde* (Hørsholm: Statens Byggeforskningsinstitut).
Hervik, P. (2004) 'The Danish cultural world of unbridgeable differences', *Ethnos* 69/2, 247–67.
Hewitt, R. (1986) *White talk, black talk* (Cambridge: CUP).
Jenkins, R. (1996) *Social identity* (London: Routledge).
Jensen, T. G. (2010) '"Making room": Encompassing diversity in Denmark', in A. Silj (ed.) *European multiculturalism revisited* (London: Zed Books).
Jensen, T. G. (2015) 'The complexity of neighbourhood relations in a multi-ethnic social housing project in Copenhagen', *Identities: Global studies in culture and power*, online publication ahead of print.
Københavns Kommune (2006) *Københavns Kommunes integrationspolitik* (Copenhagen: Københavns Kommune).
Københavns Kommune (2010) *Bland dig i byen. Medborgerskab og inclusion: Integrationspolitikken 2011–14* (Copenhagen: Københavns Kommune).
Laurier, E., A. Whyte & K. Buckner (2002) 'Neighbouring as an occasioned activity: Finding a lost cat', *Space & Culture* 5/4, 346–67.
Mazanti, B. (2002) *Fortællinger fra et sted* (Hørsholm: Statens Byggeforsknings Institut).
Mouritsen, P. (2006) 'The particular universalism of a Nordic civic nation: Common values, state religion, and islam in Danish political culture', in T. Modood,

R. Zapate-Barrero & A. Triandafyllidou (eds.) *Multiculturalism, muslims, and citizenship* (London: Routledge).

Nielsen, H. J. (2004) *Er danskerne fremmedfjendske? Udlandets syn på debatten om indvandrere 2000–2002* (Aarhus: Rockwool Fondens Forskningsenhed, Aarhus Universitetsforlag).

Pløger, J. (2004) 'Planlægning i en kompleks of plural verden—og for den meningsfulde by', in H. Skifter Andersen & H. T. Andersen (eds.) *Den mangfoldige by* (Hørsholm: Statens Byggeforskningsinstitut).

Regeringen (2004) *Regeringens strategi mod ghettoisering* (Copenhagen: Ministry of Economic and Business Affairs).

Regeringen (2010) *Ghettoen tilbage til samfundet: Et opgør med parallelsamfund i Danmark* [The ghetto back to society: A showdown with parallel societies in Denmark] (Copenhagen: Regeringen).

Sandercock, L. (1998) *Towards cosmopolis: Planning for multicultural cities* (Chichester: J. Wiley & Sons).

Silverstein, P. A. (2005) 'Immigrant racialization and the new savage slot: Race, migration and the new Europe', *Annual Review of Anthropology*, 34, 363–84.

Skifter Andersen, H. (2006) *Etniske minoriteters boligvalg* (Hørsholm: Statens Byggeforsknings Institut).

Sniderman, P. M. & A. Hagendoorn (2007) *When ways of life collide: Multiculturalism and its discontents in the Netherlands* (Princeton: PUP).

Wessendorf, S. (2013) 'Commonplace diversity and the ethos of mixing: Perceptions of difference in a London neighbourhood', *Identities: Global studies in culture and power*, 20/4, 407–22.

CHAPTER 7

Invading our homelands
New beggars on the streets of Oslo

Ada I. Engebrigtsen

Nowhere, says Zygmunt Bauman (2000), is the dream of home as a secure place, protected from the unexpected and unsafe encounters in the streets, so prominent as among modern city-dwellers.

In this essay I will discuss the arrival of new types of migrants in Norway: 'tourist' beggars who challenge social, intellectual, and emotional boundaries by breaching unspoken rules of conduct and practice. These new migrants are particularly disturbing because they make visible the permeability of national borders in an EU system that Norway is reluctantly part of, and the inherently fragile achievement of human society (Appadurai 1996). I will argue that breaches of tacit spatial agreements between city-dwellers and the new migrants challenge the production of locality and neighbourhood, and thus the processes of 'selfing and othering' (Baumann & Gingrich 2004), or how Norwegian city-dwellers perceive themselves and 'others'.

The essay draws on a recent pilot study of Romanian streetworkers; beggars, peddlers, and gatherers—in Oslo in Norway (Engebrigtsen 2012). Speaking Romanian and some Romanes, my approach has been a combination of observing beggar practices and discussing begging and the situation of streetworkers in Oslo with as many streetworkers as I could find, but necessarily in a rather unsystematic way. (I use the term beggars and streetworkers interchangeably, but it is important to note that most 'beggars' occupy several niches besides begging). I also refer to my Ph.D. fieldwork among Roma and villagers in a Romanian village in 1996/97 (Engebrigtsen 2007), as this segment of the Romanian Roma population is very similar to the Roma who are begging in the streets of Oslo today.

Interviewing streetworkers is not an easy business. Their marginal position, combined with the paternalistic position of the researcher, bending down to street level, is not a recipe for close communication about personal matters. Their position as beggars does necessitate talking about personal matters, but in a rather depersonalized way. The same stories of hungry and freezing children, sick wives and husbands, flooded houses and leaking roofs are told repeatedly. They may be true or false; the point is that they reproduce beggar stories that are very difficult to circumvent in order to talk about their social organization in Norway, freedom of travel in Europe, relations with the authorities, and other issues of interest to the researcher. A general mistrust of authority, journalists, and other representatives of the majority also makes interviews a meagre source of knowledge. Accordingly, the data produced by this unsystematic fieldwork are anchored in my long-standing work with different Roma populations, combined with my many discussions with Norwegian friends and acquaintances about how they feel and think about these new beggars. The animated media debates, including my own participation in a number of them, and several reportages on the conditions of migrating 'beggars' also form part of my empirical data for this essay.

The essay opens with a discussion of public space in Bauman's sense, and how this insight can provide some understanding of the exchange between citizens and foreign beggars in urban space. I will then present aspects of the migrating beggars' backgrounds and their situation in Oslo. I discuss the contestation of locality in Oslo in terms of Appadurai's analysis of the production of locality (1996), and Bauman's notion of 'strangers *ante portas*' (1995). Power ratios between citizens and strangers are uneven, and with the sociologist Certeau (1984) I analyse this relationship in terms of two modalities of action: those of the powerless and those in power. The essay closes with a discussion of whether these new encounters in public space have influenced the processes of 'selfing and othering' of Norwegians city-dwellers and thereby the collective Norwegian self-image.

The ambiguous stranger and the production of locality

Bauman's point of departure for his discussions of postmodern urban life (1995, 2000) is that the city is not possible without strangers, and, more precisely, urban life is where strangers meet and stay strangers to one another. This renders the urban milieu an uncontrollable and unpredictable place; the unknown, the stranger, and the villain may pop up anywhere, which makes necessary strategies to meet, ward off, or avoid danger. Yet strangers also constitute the charm of urban life; they represent the pleasures of risk and the opportunity for new interesting experiences, and even new friends and lovers. Thus, strangers are Janus-faced–dangerous and attractive. The idea of home as the most secure place transforms those living outside, on the fringes, into potential enemies. Nevertheless, as city life means living with strangers, we manage our lives by turning some of them into our friends and by disregarding the others. Some strangers, however, can neither become friends, nor can they be disregarded. They are the strangers who make themselves visible by forcing themselves into our field of vision by overstepping the boundaries that 'keep the civilized from the barbaric' (Bauman 1995, 143).

In Bauman's terms, privatizing public space is about controlling the borders between barbarity and civility: it is an ordering and civilizing process, which aims at protecting certain city-dwellers from the unpredictability of disorder; it is about turning space into place—a territorialization or invasion of unmarked space (Certeau 1984). Appadurai (1996) discusses these processes in terms of 'the production of locality', which in his perspective is a structure of feelings; it is about producing reliable social subjects and neighbourhoods within which subjects can be recognized and organized. This is a fundamental property of social life, and boundary maintenance is one of its techniques (ibid. 181). In the encounter between begging migrants, the nation-state, and the Norwegian public, competing productions of locality and neighbourhoods materialize. Several border-crossing and border-controlling processes are going on simultaneously, all aimed at colonizing and localizing public space.

Romanian migration to western Europe

Begging was banned in Norway in 1907, a ban that was only lifted in 2006 by a liberal government. Begging has been an aspect of urban life in spite of the ban, of course, but beggars were predominantly alcoholics or drug addicts and almost all men. Since about 2007, however, the urban scene has changed dramatically. When Romania joined the EU in 2007, emigration from Romania steadily increased. Romanians migrate as academics, as skilled or experienced workers, and as tourists (according to the migration regime) but for economic reasons. This last category is largely made up of Roma and other Gypsy populations as well as some ethnic Romanians (according to their own denominations or ethnonyms). Here called streetworkers, most of them earn a living as street musicians, beggars, peddlers, and gatherers. They enter Norway as EU citizens, and have rights and obligations under the European Economic Area (EEA) regulations that apply to Norway as a member state. They may stay in the country for three months without applying for work permits or work; after 6 months without a contract they must leave. As there is no registration when they enter the country, they may in practice stay for an unlimited period as long as they can support themselves. They do not receive welfare support, but do have access to emergency healthcare. They are to be found all over Norway, from the 'deep south' to the far north, but tend to concentrate in the major cities. The capital, Oslo, has about one million inhabitants, and in spring, summer, and autumn there are somewhere between 300 and 1,000 beggars working on the streets, with fewer in winter.

As Roma and other minority populations from Romania, they are economically marginal and must always be on the alert for new opportunities, because every resource is meagre or inaccessible (Engebrigtsen 2007). They are not necessarily from the poorest segments of the Romanian population: they are not homeless, they are generally settled, and they are frequently part of large family networks with some who stay in Romania and others who migrate. Neither is migration an entirely new livelihood for these minorities. Many travelled the Romanian countryside up to the 1950s, when a ban on 'vagrancy' was issued by the Ceauşescu regime, while work migration to Turkey and other neighbouring countries has been quite common. Yet the majority of Romanians have been isolated in Romania for decades due to internal and external political circumstances. When the doors finally opened with EU membership in 2007, a Romanian celebrating in the streets exclaimed to the author, 'This is a great moment of freedom for us', and in so doing he also expressed the feelings of many Roma. Finally, they could legally travel out of the country.

Gender relations

A conventional and generalizing idea about minority women is that they are victims of double discrimination, as women and as minorities. According to this model, one might expect those who become migrant streetworkers to carry a third burden, as migrants. Yet this discourse of victimization is being challenged by new insights into the life of migrant women that reveal resourcefulness and agency (Krummel 2012; Pantea 2012; Tesar 2011; Vlase 2013). Ionela Vlase has studied return migration among Romanian migrants to Italy. She found that for women, migration meant the opportunity to send remittances and gain some level of economic independence, especially from parents-in-law. She also found that although local gender regimes did not change substantially after their return: 'Contrary to all appearances, women who return do not passively submit to men's authority. Even if the possibility of women's agency remains slim, as women become dependent on their husbands upon return, they try, nevertheless, to counter the asymmetrical balance of power' (Vlase 2013, 755). Maria-Carmen Pantea has interviewed Roma women from Transylvania who migrated to western Europe, and finds that Roma women experience empowerment by migration, but that it comes at a social cost. To gain respect as migrants, women have to balance the respect they can gain by supporting their families as breadwinners with the challenges of adhering to local expectancies of gendered morality at home. She concludes that women's migration, and their empowerment by migration, is dependent on the gender regimes in their home communities (Pantea 2012).

My own experience working with Roma in Transylvania and Norway leaves me wary of generalizing about their gender relations

(2007). Roma communities vary according to the national and cultural context they have adapted to, their socio-economic position, and their basic occupations. The Roma and other minorities who beg in Oslo are from a socio-economic level where women are breadwinners alongside the men. Women supply the household with daily food, begging and bartering in the villages and often working as farm hands, weeding and harvesting for Romanian peasants, in exchange for food, while men often take on the more long-term economic projects such as waged work and business projects (Engebrigtsen 2007). All the Roma communities I have known could be characterized as patriarchal and male-centred, but it is married couples, the heads of extended families, who are the backbone of Roma community. As girls and young wives, women come under the authority of their husbands and in-laws, but as breadwinners, cooks, and principal child carers, and with age, women gain power and become rulers with their husbands. Migrating Roma keep to the same structure, albeit men's and women's roles are more similar, and if the men are not musicians or do not have paid work, they beg like their wives and daughters. In some senses, sleeping rough is harder for women because of menstruation, pregnancy, and their relative physical weakness; however, women are not shamed by begging, where that may be the case for men. In Romania, begging is generally carried out by women going from door to door, and falls somewhere in between begging and barter. Begging in the streets is illegal and mostly left to the disabled or the very elderly.

The women's position and the fact that they generally travel with male relatives to protect them from abuse from other men and the police protects them to a certain extent, but it does not protect them from abuse from their own family. This, however, is the plight of all women, and there is no evidence that Roma women (Romni) are more vulnerable to abuse than women in general. The fact that some women even travel alone or with their children across Europe to beg or work in Norway is of course a sign of desperation, but also of agency and independence. I asked the women how they experienced being women living on the streets in such a precarious situation. They seemed surprised by the question, and told me they were fine except for the health problems many suffer from, and the pain of being separated from their children. None of the stories they told gave any indication of exploitation or abuse, except for some incidents involving abusive by-passers. This is not evidence that there is no exploitation, of course; it only illustrates that exploitation is difficult to identify in conversations and interviews. In Norway, the majority of women begging are in their late thirties and forties, which means that many still have young children and others have grandchildren. The difficulty of leaving their children with their in-laws or even with neighbours, while they are away begging in countries that forbid children on the streets, is probably one of the heaviest burdens on these women. However, the usual impression gained by the public that the women are victims and less threatening than the men means that they can expect to get more from begging than the men do.

Begging in Oslo

Most streetworkers travel all over Europe looking for opportunities to make money. They generally travel in family groups and send their earnings back to Romania. There are different kinds of streetworkers in Norway as elsewhere: the street musicians, who are expected to earn good money and generally rent mattresses in overcrowded flats often owned by immigrants; some families travel by van, where up to ten people sleep, eat, and live; and the poorest sleep outside, under bridges, motorway junctions, in parks, and in the woods surrounding the cities often in makeshift shelters and tents. Some even stay through the winter when temperatures are far below freezing. Most families travel voluntarily and leave their young children at home with grandparents. Some say they are in a kind of bondage, having borrowed money with interest that must be paid back, and some say they are in Norway to find work. Shoplifting, according to police reports, is widespread among some groups. The majority, however, seem to rely on a combination of begging, busking, collecting empty bottles for recycling and other valuables from dustbins and containers, by selling party stashes to young people at night, or by selling a street newspaper produced specially for them—all of it what I term streetwork—and by taking illegal daywork.

It is important for a beggar to find and keep a 'good spot', and the unwritten rule is that the first person to occupy a place has the right to it. There are rumours among the beggars about people, not beggars themselves, who chase away the 'rightful' occupant of a good begging spot in order to install 'his or her beggar' there. This may indicate that some beggars have protectors, possibly exploiters, but little is known about actual power relations on the streets.

Outside a metro station in central Oslo, Mr Romescu has been sitting begging for the last 5 years. He is Romanian and not a Gypsy, he tells me. In his 1950s, he first came here with his wife and two grown children, but for the last two years he has been here alone. He goes home to Romania for Christmas, Easter, and sometimes during summer, but the rest of the year he spends sitting on the street from 8 in the morning to 4 in the afternoon. This is how he supports his family in Romania. He and his wife and children earned enough by begging in the first years to buy a house for the family; now he is collecting money to buy new teeth. He rents a mattress in a flat that he shares with many others, and he sleeps in the parks in summer. This spot in the centre is this man's 'rightful place', and when he visits Romania he agrees with someone he knows to hold his place for him. When he gets back, the substitute leaves for somewhere else. Having his own place seems to be a good strategy: when he arrives back from his visits home, passers-by greet him and seem happy to see him. His cup is always full of coins and notes.

Mariana lives with her husband, sister, and brother in-law in a van that they drive to a different car park every night, in order not to be fined by the police or the traffic wardens. She is in her late thirties and has four grown children and a number of grandchildren to support in Romania. When we talked one January afternoon she told me that the money she and her family had managed to collect during their 3-month stay before Christmas had all been spent on firewood and food. At least they had had pork for Christmas.

Some Romanian beggars arrive in cars that they hired in Bulgaria, but it is difficult to find places to park. When they do, they generally congregate and set up a 'gypsy camp', preparing food on an open fire, washing clothes, and generally having to live family life in full view in a public space.

In 1997 a Norwegian organization, the Kirkens Bymisjon (Church City Mission), conducted a striking if limited study in which a journalist interviewed a Romanian woman begging in the streets of Oslo several times over the course of one year, and visited her in her home village when she returned home. Her appearance had changed from the generally impoverished look of a beggar in Oslo to a traditionally dressed Romni in her home town. She told the journalist that she had bought two cows for the money she collected in Norway, and she could now sell milk to her fellow villagers.

'Why don't they work?'

The public debate about Romanian streetworkers in Norway is heated. There is despair and contempt expressed from some quarters; others support the beggars and point to their vulnerable position and their problems in Romania; while others doubt that they really are poor, but are certain they must be swindlers and criminals. A majority of politicians and the public seem to think it reasonable to ban begging and send the beggars home, or to restrict begging to certain areas and in certain ways. Most people say that they find it humiliating to pass beggars in the streets, not knowing how to relate to them: should one give money and risk being conned, or should one neglect them altogether? Should one be humane and give, or will it encourage laziness instead of diligence? Both solutions to this challenge stem from the Norwegian welfare ethos, according to which waged labour is the only really morally sound activity for adults, and begging risks jeopardizing this work ethic. In addition, begging is an explicit expression of poverty and should not exist in a modern welfare society. Destitution is an unthinkable condition in a rich country like Norway, and meeting the poor in the streets comes as a shock—an accusation that many cannot handle. In a welfare society, the state is meant to deal with poverty, so that citizens are protected from coming face to face with the ambivalence associated with destitution. Norwegian society is habitually described as extremely private and home-centred, but at the same time there are permeable boundaries between private life and public control. Family life, for example, is more heavily monitored in Norway than in most countries (Gullestad 2006). And very little that is private is expressed in public spaces. The streets and urban space in general are kept neutral, disciplined, and formal—at least by day.

Embattled processes of locality production

Public streets are the workplaces of streetworkers where they often must compete with one another and with Norwegian beggars for the best spots and simultaneously avoid crossing paths with the various guardians of public order—in Appadurai's terms, the defenders of locality.

Mr Romescu, who has had the spot outside a central metro station for the last five years, occupies what has become 'his place' and has 'his own clients'. He is allowed to sit there, but if he tries to move to a dry spot under the half-roof by the entrance to the station, he is chased back out as soon as the security guards appear. Back into the rain or snow. Then there is the young man who often sits outside an exclusive hotel in the city centre, not leaning against the wall of the building, but against the lamppost opposite the entrance. He says that the hotel staff allow him to sit there at night, but not in daylight hours.

The city shopping centres are generally off-limits to the foreign streetworkers, as are restaurants, coffee shops, and bars. In some supermarkets, staff stop them from using the reverse vending machines to recycle the bottles they have gathered. The people who sleep under the city's bridges and motorway junctions on mattresses and newspapers are chased away, sometimes by the police, sometimes by 'cleaning the city' brigades. Their property—mattresses, bedding, clothes, food—is confiscated and burned. Recent research (Nasjonal institusjon for menneskerettigheter, 2015) finds that homeless Roma and Africans in Oslo are more often expelled from their sleeping places and by rougher methods than Norwegians are.

These are public strategies whereby public space, often unmarked by any specific social activity, is colonized by the state or by state-supported bodies and incorporated into the urban locality. From being space that is open to all, but still unmarked, this territorialization or colonization turns public space into private property, creating boundaries that streetworkers who are not citizens may not cross. This is not only the privatization of public space; it is the nationalization of public space, defining boundaries of citizenship and the nation as a locality (Brubaker, 1996; Løfgren, 1999).

For their part, the streetworkers are engaged in ongoing processes, not producing localities as such, but what we may term dwelling places (Urry 2000). They are squatters. Squatting on existing localities, and thereby challenging both local boundaries and the norms that guide reliable citizens in these localities. In a town outside Oslo, I visited a family living under a motorway junction. They have lived there off and on for the last four years, between 10 and 20 people, all from the same family. When I arrived, they were serving dinner: grilled steak and potatoes. I was invited, in the usual Rom way, to sit down (on a stone) and share their meal. Behind the 'table' a low concrete platform ran along the whole of the back of the 'house'. The front was open to the street. On this platform, mattresses and bedding were laid out and clothes piled up. They were living their private family life in full public view.

Outside Oslo's Natural History Museum, the Romanian streetworkers who have cars often meet and eat together before driving off to find somewhere to park up for the night. Passers-by are pulled into their dinner preparations, washing up, or family squabbles: the fence surrounding the museum is often decorated with drying laundry. Rubbish and excrement often litter the surroundings.

Are these 'dwelling processes' (Urry 2000) challenging the production of locality by trespassing on the boundaries of existing neighbourhoods and social subjects? By acting out their private family lives in full public view, they at least destroy what Bauman has described as the courtesy of public or city life. The courtesy of city life implies the creation of a space where people can be together without interfering in one another's lives and, crucially, without being bothered by other people's problems or trivialities. Bauman writes that civil courtesy implies wearing a public mask in order to protect ourselves from one another (Bauman 2000, 114). In that way, the streets and public spaces can be kept neutral and civilized, free of private emotions and other expressions of 'the wild'.

Respectable beggars, unreliable beggars

While the streets are public places to most citizens, to some they are also neighbourhoods. The Norwegian non-migrant beggars and peddlers, most of them drug addicts, have for many years produced central parts of Oslo as their locality. They have more or less sewn up the distribution of good begging spots, where to sell their street newspaper, and where to sleep. The negotiation of accepted begging strategies and proper conduct on the streets are all part of the business of securing their locality and producing reliable social subjects within their field: regular passers-by who recognize them as reliable drug-addicts and 'colleagues' who behave in acceptable ways. These beggars do not sleep in doorways or under bridges, and do not bother their clients by shoving their products or their demands into their faces, and they do not exhibit wounds or handicaps. They have become part of the cityscape: welfare recipients, deviant, but predictable.

The migrant streetworkers intrude on these beggar neighbourhoods, not only by colonizing their market, but also by colonizing their streets. 'Look at them, they're everywhere, we're being pushed out of our own city.' One such beggar complained that if he could not make enough money selling his magazine, he would have to go back to breaking and entering. The migrants not only take over some of the most profitable spots, they also overstep the mark of proper beggar conduct by displaying wounds, peddling, begging, and by talking different languages.

Strangers ante portas

Among my Norwegian friends and colleagues, the usual response when confronted by foreign beggars is to feel a mixture of shame and contempt. Shame because of the intolerable economic and social differences between them and the beggars, and their own reluctance to be involved; contempt because the beggars passively display their poverty instead of 'doing something about it'. Some acquaintances have told me that they avoid passing beggars in the street out of sheer embarrassment, some feel angry and invaded, and others surrender and give money. The Norwegian beggars are accepted by politicians, the media, and I would argue by most people—as drug addicts, they are seen as being in some way the 'deserving poor'. The Romanian beggars, on the other hand, seem to undermine people's sense of 'urban freedom'. They are 'strangers *ante portas*' (Bauman 2000).

There are two lines to the public debate. The most visible and authoritative one refers to the beggars as different, dangerous, unsanitary (they are unhygienic and leave their rubbish everywhere), and a menace to public order (they are thieves and frauds): in short, they eat rats and defecate in the parks. The other line sees beggars in terms of poverty, powerlessness, and compassion: they too are human, and must be helped to get off the streets and into welfare society. How can we understand the strong reactions evoked by the beggars? What makes generally sensible and empathic persons quite literally go out of their way to avoid meeting beggars in the streets?

As Bauman (2000) and others have pointed out, strangers are what makes life in the city 'free', in the sense of a certain freedom from the mutual obligations of small-town and rural life. Yet in order to live with strangers they must be 'pacified'. The unpredictability and threat posed by strangers must be arranged as 'background' in order for the city to appear as a 'defensible space', a relatively safe place. As a backdrop, strangers may engage in that special mode of city courtesy, where strangers are able to mix without revealing their true selves. This disinterested courtesy enables us to sit squeezed in next to total strangers on the underground—only because we are in the same place at the same time—without feeling shame. I would quote Bauman—'This courtesy helps strangers to mix separated from relations of power, feelings of dislike or private emotions'—and Bauman quotes Sennet—'The purpose of courtesy is to protect other people from being burdened with yourself' (2000, 95). Courtesy in the urban milieu is about creating space where people can be together without being involved, without being personal, without being forced against one's will to show one's emotions, thoughts, weaknesses, or worries. To make this possible, Bauman claims, everyone involved must be so materially and culturally equal that they do not challenge one another's desires or tear off the mask of convenience. Such cleansed public spaces, where no surprise can dislodge the rigid mask of polite disinterest that is the accepted mode of exchange, are ideal for consumption because they encourage shopping, not social interaction. Indeed, the *raison d'être* of modern urban space is shopping, and strangers are essentially disturbing elements in the individual act that is retail therapy. In the temple of Mammon the pilgrims must not be disturbed: properly guarded, it is an island of order, free from beggars, vagabonds, persecutors,—or at least, free from people expected to be like that, according to Bauman.

The Romanian beggars are the very embodiment of strangers *ante portas*. They are the not yet pacified strangers. By throwing themselves on our mercy they tear away the mask of relative equality and make us witnesses to the bare destitution under our noses. To pass a beggar with your shopping bags full of food and not to give anything? That demands steely resolve or a legitimate reason. As Daniel Miller (2001) emphasizes, shopping is not void of moral dilemmas and considerations, and in the presence of impoverished beggars, our purchases suddenly demand moral legitimacy. Originally, the spots 'dwelt in' by foreign streetworkers were non-places; it is by dwelling in them that the beggars make them visible parts of the neighbourhood. That said, it is not primarily the physical aspects of a locality that are thus threatened; it is the social aspects. As Appadurai explains,

> The capability of neighbourhoods to produce contexts (within which their very localizing activities acquire meaning and historical potential) and to produce local subjects is profoundly affected by the locality-producing capabilities of large-scale social formations (nation-states, kingdoms, missionary empires, and trading cartels) to determine the general shape of all neighbourhoods within the reach of their power. (1996, 187)

Thus the beggars' locality-producing efforts are entirely restricted by, or at least at the mercy of, those being produced by the nation-state and their legitimate contexts. It is not by producing locality in a spatial sense, but by producing foreign, unreliable, and immoral social subjects that the 'beggar localities' threaten Norwegian citizens' neighbourhoods.

The production of locality is at once a social, a material, and an emotional process, designed to secure one's life in uncertain and threatening environments (Appadurai 1996). The nation-state secures its external boundaries against 'unwanted invaders', and tries to control its internal boundaries by protecting the rules of 'proper citizenship' and by patrolling public space; however, both these locality-producing strategies are hampered by the laws, regulations, and norms that are the outcomes of other locality-producing processes. Norway's partnership with the EU through the EEA agreement is a way of widening the Norwegian state as a locality, reaching out to other localities for the economic and social benefit of wider social networks. The beggar-migrants are unwanted subjects of this enlarged locality, and cannot be avoided without breaking the agreements on how EU citizens should behave. Monitoring internal boundaries is also complicated. Any ban on begging will hit the 'legitimate' Norwegian beggars and the large number of NGOs that in effect beg in the streets as well. Any attempt to clean up the places that beggars frequent, confiscating their belongings and forbidding them to sleep rough, would challenge the Norwegians' self-image as 'do-gooders' (Tvedt 2007) and question the authorities' commitment to the fight against poverty 'at home and abroad'.

Tactics of movement and strategies of force

The power ratios of citizens to migrant streetbeggars are not equal. The place-making efforts of hotel staff, shop-owners, civil servants, the police, and other public bodies all represent legitimate ordering at the instigation of political and economic forces, and while their place-making strategies are not sanctioned by the authorities, they are still accepted and even approved. They are the strategies of the powerful, acting on the strength of a legitimate and well-produced place: the nation-state. Certeau discusses two modalities of action that are both temporal and spatial: strategies and tactics. It is open to social formations such as nation-states to employ planned actions—strategies—in the places or territories they hold or create as their own, and they can govern those places by affixing a common past and future to them and monitoring their boundaries, thus controlling them temporally and spatially. Tactics, unlike strategy, are calculated actions or a manipulation of power relations in the absence of a proper locus (one's own place), for the space of tactics, says Certeau, is the space of the other (1984, 37). Thus tactics must follow the lie of the land (for which read rules and conditions) as ordained by the law of the 'other'. Tactics are thus manoeuvrings within the enemy's field of vision and within enemy territory.

The streetworkers' very public 'home-making' represents the tactics of the powerless. They are not a unified subject and have no place they can call their own. They take advantage of opportunities and exploit the cracks in the system; they are continuously on the move, playing hide and seek with power, sliding in and out of dwelling places according to the movements of their persecutors. This relationship between 'state power and nomadism' (Deleuze & Guattari 1986) takes the form of wordless negotiations, where endurance and creativity may be the best weapons, and where the traditional power-holders may well lose their grip.

This slipperiness is noticeable in the politicians' reluctance to take action. Every action may evoke a counteraction that is not easy to control, or it may spur a situation that is worse than the current one. To ban begging would mean using scarce police resources (at least from the institutions' point of view) to control relatively innocent crime at the cost of losing their grip on serious criminal offences. It would also mean embarking on criminal proceedings against perpetrators and eventually prison sentences for those found guilty—a lengthy and costly process that would far outweigh any inconvenience the beggars cause at present. Set up cheap housing or latrines and they would attract more beggars and require staff to keep them in order. Such are the discussions.

Selfing and othering

We have seen how the question of place and how to behave in public spaces is contested between citizens and begging strangers in Oslo. In spite of the uneven power ratio between them, the foreign beggars touch a raw nerve in the modern Norwegian self-understanding. Using Bauman's perspective on 'the stranger' as a threat in urban life, I would argue that the Romanian beggars in Oslo threaten the production of neighbourhoods, and with it the production of reliable social subjects that is crucial if citizens are to feel secure and at home. By turning public space into 'mobile homes', constantly changing dwelling place, and playing hide and seek with the authorities, beggars also confront state power, but in a 'slippery way', playing on the population's ambivalence.

When the first tourist beggars appeared in Norway after the ban on begging was lifted in 2006, one right-wing politician argued for a new prohibition in order to protect the 'innocence' of the Norwegian public. He argued that were Norwegians to become used to seeing the poor begging in the streets, they would become blind to poverty and harden their hearts against it: they would lose their 'innocence'. This idea of innocence is related to the notion of Norwegians as 'do-gooders' and the Norwegian welfare state as 'a do-gooder regime' (Tvedt 2007). The ongoing public debate is split between those who want to help the beggars live dignified lives in Norway by offering them work and accommodation, and those who want to reinstate the ban on begging. The government is treading a fine line. It wants to maintain its image as a humanitarian state, while simultaneously controlling and limiting the opportunities to beg in the streets. The result, of course, is contempt from all quarters. The hidden and open debates (whether on television or in the press, Facebook, Twitter, and so on) about the begging problem have, in my view, opened Norwegians' eyes to the full implications of EEA integration and the global situation. Sending money and aid to poor people on the other side of the world has strengthened the humanitarian self-image of most Norwegians, while encounters with poor, unwanted beggars within Norway's own borders may have put an end to their 'innocence' as humanitarians. So have these encounters changed Norway's national self-image and impressions of 'the other'? I do not think so. But I do believe the unwanted enlargement of what is generally conceived of as Norway's neighbourhood, the EU, by 'uncivilized others', has brought to the fore the moral issues of poverty and inequality that most of the world's citizens, without a welfare state to their name, have to face in their daily lives.

References

Appadurai, A. (1996) *Modernity at large: Cultural dimensions of globalization* (Minneapolis: University of Minnesota Press).
Bauman, Z. (1995) *Life in fragments: Essays in postmodern morality* (Oxford: Blackwell).
—— (2000) *Liquid modernity* (Cambridge: Polity).
Baumann, G. & A. Gingrich (2004) (eds.) *Grammars of identity and alterity: A structural approach* (New York: Berghahn).
Brubaker, R. (1996) *Nationalism reframed: Nationhood and the national question in the New Europe.* Cambridge: CUP).
de Certeau, M. (1984) *The practice of everyday life* (Berkeley & Los Angeles: University of California Press).
Deleuze, G. & F. Guattari (1986) *Nomadology: The war machine* (New York: University of Minnesota Press).
Engebrigtsen, Ada I. (2007) *Exploring gypsiness: Power, exchange and interdependence in a Transylvanian village* (New York: Berghahn).
—— (2012) *Tiggerbander og kriminelle bakmenn eller fattige EU-borgere?* (Norsk institutt for forskning om oppvekst, velferd og aldring (NOVA), Notat, 2; Oslo: NOVA).
Gullestad, M. (2006) *Plausible prejudice* (Oslo: Universitetsforlaget).
Krummel, S. (2012). 'Migrant women: Stories of empowerment, transformation, exploitation and resistance', *Journal of Ethnic and Migration Studies*, 38(7), 1175–1184.
Löfgren, O. (1999) 'Feeling at home: The politics and practices of national belonging', *Anthropological Journal of European Cultures*, 8/1, 79–97.
Miller, D. (2001) *The dialectics of shopping* (Chicago: University of Chicago Press).
Nasjonal institusjon for menneskerettigheter (2015) *Kriminalisering av hjemløse i Oslo* (Norsk senter for menneskerettigheter: Juridisk fakultet; Oslo: University of Oslo).
Pantea, M. C. (2012). From 'making a living' to 'getting ahead': Roma women's experiences of migration, *Journal of Ethnic and Migration Studies*, 38/8, 1251–68.
Tesăr, C. (2011) 'Tigan bun traditional in Romania, cersetor de-etnicizat in strainatate. Politici ale re-prezentarii publice si etica muncii la romii Cortorari', in T. Stefania & L. Fosztó (eds.) *Spectrum: Cercetari sociale despre romi* (Cluj Napoca: ISPMN-Kriterion).
Tvedt, T. (2007) 'International development aid and its impact on a donor country: A case study of Norway', *European Journal of Development Research*, 19/4, 614–35.
Urry, J. (2000) *Sociology beyond societies: Mobilities for the twenty-first century* (London: Routledge).
Vlase, I. (2013) '"My husband is a partiot!": Gender and romanian family return migration from Italy', *Journal of Ethnic and Migration Studies*, 39:5, 741–758.

CHAPTER 8

The production of deportability

Klara Öberg

This essay examines deportability and legal status as factors that shape social relations and transactions with employers and brokers in the informal employment market in the Swedish city of Gothenburg. It argues for the importance of a local perspective on the meanings of legal status, especially as these meanings might be localized within general processes of the state such as neo-liberal developments or increasing privatization, the informalization of work, atypical labour contracts, and so on. The essay considers deportability as a crucial factor in the organization of a labour market that is increasingly coloured by precariousness, insecurity, and unstable relations between employer and employee. The focus here is on men who live with the risk of being deported—asylum seekers and irregular migrants who work in the informal economy.

The locus of the study, Gothenburg on the Swedish west coast, is a post-industrial city with a population of 500,000 and a growing service market. A city that just like other cities is more attractive for those looking for jobs than the countryside. Furthermore, an urban context that provides greater anonymity and possibilities to expand one's social networks and essential contacts to find work and accommodation. In Gothenburg, as elsewhere, neoliberal economic processes have led to privatization and segmentation of the labour market. At the same time, the measures designed to tackle the economic crisis in 1991 live on, including the stimulation of increased self-employment, particularly of unemployed immigrants (Slavnic 2004; Schierup & Ålund 2011:50). These changes have driven the emergence of a sector within the informal economy of those who cannot support themselves as self-employed without the use of cheap unregulated labour.

The essay builds on ethnographic data from fieldwork in 2010–

2012 among asylum-seeking and irregular migrant men who work in the informal labour market in Gothenburg. The informants came from Iraq, Iran, Afghanistan, Syria, Eritrea, and Somalia. They were unmarried and aged between 20 and 56, and the majority did not have family or friends or any other prior contacts living in Gothenburg. None of the asylum seekers lived in accommodation provided by the Swedish Migration Board, having moved to Gothenburg to look for work and possibilities in general—and to escape the official accommodation they had been allocated, which was far out in the countryside in cramped apartments, with little chance of finding work. The uncertainty of what the future might hold, and especially whether their asylum applications would be approved, was an important part of the reason to look for work, both as a strategy to manage the future as well as their everyday lives.

I would argue for the importance of a local perspective when it comes to understanding the men's legal status. The example of these particular asylum seekers and irregular migrants, all of whom work in the informal labour market, points up the importance of *deportability* as the key factor in a specific organization and stratification. Here, for example, legal status and deportability represent economic values in terms of salaries, possibilities to negotiate, and working conditions. The essay thus illustrates an example of social disintegration in an urban context.

Categories of asylum seekers and irregular migrants

> What politics does to life—and lives—is not just a question of discourses and technologies, of strategies and tactics. It is also a question of the concrete way in which individuals and groups are treated, under which principles and in the name of which morals, implying which inequalities and misrecognitions. In other words, to prolong the Wittgensteinian reference, it is indeed a question of form but it is also a question of life. (Fassin 2009, 57)

Although immigration law separates out the categories of asylum seekers and irregular migrants, I would argue that there are valid reasons to include both categories in this example. One is that in the Swedish context, irregular migrants are very strongly linked to the asylum system—a majority of irregular migrants in Sweden are former asylum seekers whose applications were rejected. Migration to Sweden and other Nordic countries is primarily achieved through the asylum system, in contrast to migration to the south of Europe. Thus irregular migration to Sweden can arguably be thought of as a product of the asylum system. Of course, the categories used by the asylum system are arguably what Wimmer and Glick Schiller (2002) refer to as national methodological tools. To understand the role of the nation-state in relation to migration, it is important to understand the asylum system precisely as a tool that lives in symbiosis with larger economic and social processes and transformations.

Asylum seekers may have the formal right to work in Sweden. In reality, only about 50 per cent of male asylum seekers aged between 20 and 64 obtain this right (Öberg 2015). To obtain the formal right to work, one of the conditions is to be able to prove your identity. The national background of the asylum seeker is thus an important factor, since Sweden does not accept the majority of identity cards from some countries, such as Afghanistan.

The formal right to work does not automatically lead to work in the formal economy; however, it might be an asset when finding work in the informal economy, as it minimizes the legal consequences that an employer faces if raided, as the employer can always argue that the person is applying for a job or an internship.

The labour market and its social structures are shared by asylum seekers and irregular migrants. Finding work may be more acute for irregular migrants, but asylum seekers too can hardly survive on the monthly allowance of about EUR 200, a sum that is not enough to cover rent in the city, and of course it is in the city that the majority of jobs are to be found. Asylum seekers, just like irregular migrants, often face the reality of having to pay off loans taken to fund their migration. Also, being an asylum seeker includes not knowing whether your application will be approved or not. Thus work is a crucial strategy if asylum is not granted as there is a potential risk of deportation. For irregular migrants the risk and threat of deportation is even more acute in everyday life.

Deportability

Nicholas De Genova is without doubt the researcher who has done most to chart the meanings of the term deportability and bring it into contemporary academic usage. Writing mainly from an American perspective, his texts are dominated by examples of Mexican irregular migrants in the US. I interpret De Genova's (2002, 2013) use of the term deportability as flexible and contextual, and as permeating the everyday lives of those who are rejected. The acts of deportation and border control are described by De Genova (2013) as the spectacle of deportation, and it is the spectacle that keeps the imagination, the fear of being deported, vivid—not forgetting that many people actually *are* deported, so that the fear of deportation is not a phobic fantasy but a real potential outcome. Many more persons are not deported, however, and are left to subsist in the grip of fear of being deported.

It is the local state of deportability and its effects that I seek to describe. In the present example, I consider deportability to apply to asylum seekers as well as irregular migrants. Asylum seekers have access to emergency health and dental care,[1] a monthly sum of money (albeit low), the chance to live in accommodation arranged by the Swedish Migration Board, and the right to work legally if their identity can be established. And asylum seekers are afforded greater protection than the irregular migrants, who have a very limited set of rights—emergency healthcare,[2] protection by the police, and the possibility of demanding fair salaries from employers.

All these rights, though officially proclaimed, tell little of their accessibility. Hence the asylum seekers who have work permits but do not stand a fair chance of finding a legal job given the competition, or those who are denied work permits altogether. Hence the irregular migrants who do not dare seek medical attention for fear of the consequences, or do not have realistic access to help in order to claim a fair salary in return for work done.

Asylum seekers have a temporary legal status, which means they could potentially be deported or become irregular migrants. Irregular migrants face even more uncertain outcomes. That uncertainty is itself a factor that affects people's choices and drives them to accept unreasonably low wages—you only know what you have, not what will come. The uncertainty that comes with these two different legal statuses is thus an important factor in deportability.

When examining the informal labour market and the relations between employers and employees, deportability is the stick with which employers can beat a cheap, docile, and flexible labour force into submission. It becomes a value in itself in the informal economy, resulting in lower salaries, poor working conditions, and general uncertainty. In that sense deportability is an institutionalized concept that verges on being commoditized: its meanings and values are evident to employers, landlords, middlemen, and irregular migrants.

The spectrum of possible manifestations of deportability is at its most visible in actual deportation, but otherwise comes in all shades and opacities. The production of deportability vis-à-vis asylum seekers and irregular migrants creates hierarchies, which bring with them very concrete facts such as lower wages, longer hours, poor working conditions, and above all the risk of dismissal, labour being so readily available.

Social segregation and self-employment

By understanding the processes that David Harvey (2008) describes as accumulation by dispossession, together with increasing precariousness (Standing 2011) in relation to a chain of important interlinked nodes—an expanding service market, the increased use of subcontractors, informal and formal forms of labour, forms of citizenship (Isin 2009), migration law, forms of capital ownership—the structures of social and economic organization become clearer. And I would argue that it is an organization which is highly fragmented.

Naturally, these processes affect society in general, but in the example of asylum seekers, irregular migrants, and their employers in the informal economy their action becomes particularly clear. Rather than discussing asylum seekers' and irregular migrants' work in the informal sector as belonging to an underground 'ethnic economy', I focus on how legal status and deportability in the informal employment sector dictate interethnic relations and working conditions for those who find themselves at the very bottom of the economic system. This raises serious questions about the chances of creating sustainability when so many live under such conditions.

In times of labour segmentation and increased competition, it is challenging to find a permanent job, and the number of self-employed has dramatically increased, as has the number of small and medium-sized businesses. Many of the newly self-employed are immigrants who have had little or no choice but to become self-employed (Slavnic 2004; Khosravi 1995, 1999). Ironically, they are frequently cited as evidence of a truly successful integration model (Abbasian 2000; Slavnic 2004). Being self-employed, they are no longer counted among the numbers of unemployed nor are they eligible for benefits. They are thus ideal citizens from the state's perspective. However, they are working harder for less money and less security than if they had been in regular employment.

The state's enthusiasm for self-employment dates from a specific economic crisis in Swedish history. In the 1990s Sweden nearly went bankrupt. The private property market collapsed and interest rates on bank loans and mortgages soared. Those who were sitting on substantial capital or owned their property outright were relatively unaffected; the rest—those who could not afford to pay their mortgages—were forced to sell cheaply to those who still could afford to buy. With an economy that was highly dependent on a few large industrial companies to buoy it up, Sweden was hard hit. The government promoted the idea that Sweden's route out of the crisis would be a large number of small entrepreneurs, who would also ensure it would not be as fragile in future. And migrants were targeted as potential entrepreneurs since their presence on the official job market was below average. There were other processes at work too, which, taken with the economic crisis when Sweden teetered on the brink of bankruptcy, drove up the number of self-employed people dramatically.

It was especially in relation to the 1990s' crisis that the government specifically targeted small businesses and the need for increased flexibility in the workforce. Confronted with an untenable situation—a strong public sector and a few large companies, albeit major brands such as Volvo, Saab, and SKF—the chosen solution was articulated as a need to steer away from economic meltdown, a course that was reliant on the strength of the emergent small businesses (Slavnic 2004). This was introduced as a transformation of the Swedish economy and labour market, a concept which, while it focused on unemployed immigrants, was also about adaptation to global markets, with atypical labour contracts and a growing temporary manpower services sector. This is not something limited to Sweden, of course.

The resultant transformation of the state has seen a restructuring of the economy, but also new forms of risk-taking, with demands for what Slavnic (2004) terms the 'elasticity' of the self-employed and small businesses. At the same time as the self-employed and small businesses are stretched to cut costs, they are compelled to behave as taxpayers, playing by the same rules as the larger concerns higher up in the hierarchy of production. While competition and the growth of subcontracting push prices down, which benefits large corporations and a public sector (the elite) that has partly been or is being privatized, small businesses are expected to produce more cheaply. Thus in the hierarchy of subcontracting, the relevance of producing social and labour segmentation, of segregation, is vital.

Until the early 1990s, the decommodification of labour was something that had been upheld by an active labour market (Schierup & Ålund 2011). But to understand these changes we must first go back to the reforms of 1976, which paved the way for an inclusive citizenship that proclaimed equality, anti-racism and, implicitly, multiculturalism. Migrants were to be politically acknowledged as a cultural resource and an asset to multicultural Sweden. Obviously, there were several problematic issues with this model, including cultural essentialism and the risk of exclusion, as Schierup and Ålund (2011, 49–50) point out in their investigation of how the Swedish welfare model was changed and how these processes affected large sections of the migrant population in Sweden.

One problem was that the political agenda, for all its multicultural values and equality, drifted increasingly apart from certain political actions that little by little diminished the state's responsibility towards its citizens. The state was bent on liberalizing the nature of its relations and, as elsewhere, multiculturalism was the buzzword. Yet the multiculturalist political ideology tended to create differences and enclaves (Carlbom 2003) rather than equal rights based on multicultural values: as an ideology, it stemmed from the notion that people were essentially different (SOU 2006:79) instead of creating a just society, regardless of citizens' cultural backgrounds. This was nothing new, of course. Think only of the classic example of Furnivall's work (1948) on how the colonial administration created a plural society and at the same time differences, both social and economic.

The Swedish welfare state has changed in more ways than one since the economic crisis of the 1990s. Primarily, the burden of risk has been shifted from the state to the individual citizen—a process bound up with the decommodification of values (Slavnic 2004). Where the welfare state once served to protect citizens and market values in relation to labour, services, goods, and so on, it is now the citizens themselves who have to adjust to the recommodification of labour, fluctuating markets, and competition in price-sensitive goods and services, while the service and construction sectors have been deregulated. The employment situation has changed too, and again it falls to the individual's lot to be the risk-taker, as the new forms of employment include short-term and even zero-hour contracts, profit-based salaries, and employment agencies specialized in professions such as teaching, healthcare, and administration.

Immigrant populations were hit hard by unemployment, especially during the crisis in the 1990s. Unemployment insurance is such that those who have not entered the labour market are excluded, the logic being that one has to have paid national insurance from a regular job for a given period in order to have access to unemployment benefits. The result is that large sections of the immigrant population are either trapped in casual work or the informal labour market (Schierup & Ålund 2011, 50).

While many of the self-employed persons and small businesses that I came across during my fieldwork are busy 'saving' themselves from unemployment and struggling to become middle class, there is a reaccumulation of capital whereby the state saves money and the new classes are left almost déclassé—a new economic and social order where the demand for cheap consumer goods and services has increased. The example of Sweden's self-employed and small businesses can be said to be part of what David Harvey terms accumulation by dispossession (Harvey 2008), and how capital is dispossessed by the elite (who are those with power and capital aplenty). Unregulated labour in the informal economy generates little profit, since it is only when it transfers into the formal economy that the real market value enters the scene. That is, when the contractors who are further up the hierarchies—property developers, investors—translate value from the informal economy into formal salaries, values, collateral, and financial return.

This is not a uniquely Swedish situation. It is seen elsewhere in the EU, as are cosmopolitan elite politics under the banner of 'free movement' (see Schierup 2010). The ideological basis is the European legislation on the free movement of labour and services within the EU; the liberalizing regulations apply to labour-related, third-state, circular migration to the member countries of the EU. It is an example of the results of Castell's morphologic network society (2000); however, my informants have not experienced the spaces of free flow that Castell envisages as part of a network society, but instead are governed and controlled so they remain on the margins and at the bottom of the production chain.

Numerous studies show that large corporations and companies at the top end, rather than producing themselves, use specialist subcontractors and specifically immigrant-owned small businesses, leaving them to shoulder the risks and responsibilities of production. Additionally, they are tacitly expected to do the work at a competitive price by breaking health and safety regulations and using informal labour or sweatshops (see Fakiolas 2000; Slavnic 2004; Schierup et al. 2006). Again it is all about avoiding risk and keeping down production prices—and the accumulated capital rises to the top, and not only becomes profit, but profit in the *formal* market. This is a transnational phenomenon, and applies as much to large corporations that use smaller companies as subcontractors, as to the private service sector that now operates what used to be the classic state apparatus—education, healthcare, day care, care for the elderly, and so on—or the example of small businesses that drive the informal market where my informants work.

This particular example of the informal economy can also be

understood as a result of dispossession by accumulation. Competition and subcontracting push prices down, benefitting large corporations and a partly privatized public sector. The small businesses, of which many are subcontractors, are expected to produce more for a lower price, and it is among these businesses that a majority of my informants find work. This is a space where the non-rights and vulnerabilities of irregular migrants and asylum seekers become very visible. It is equally a space where the structures, transactions, and social relations expressed in everyday acts can produce and reproduce an extreme social and labour segmentation. Precariousness (Standing 2011) is what faces people who have been pushed out of safe jobs into unstable, short-term employment, while benefits and rights are increasingly associated with regular, long-term employment alone. My informants are at the absolute bottom of the precariat (Standing 2011), which nonetheless can be argued to be constructed as a hierarchy, depending on what rights are open to the individual. My informants' employers also belong to a self-employed precariat that is partly in the informal economy, since they too are afforded so little protection, their few rights being solely connected to current or past regular employment.

Working in the informal labour market

It is not easy for asylum seekers or irregular migrants to find work; just as difficult as finding work in general in fact, for it too demands social contacts, networks, and a solid source of information, good references, and so on. Their situation is even more precarious, however, because of the vulnerabilities that go with migration, starting with the lack of local knowledge, social contacts, accredited references, experience, and, crucially, language.

The first period searching for work, when reliable, multiple social resources are fewest, is commonly described as exhausting, and often follows immediately on arrival in the city. Sometimes the newcomer's first contacts in the city are made through other asylum seekers, whom my informants had met early upon arriving in Sweden. In some examples these early contacts are invaluable, but in other cases they do not lead to reliable work or accommodation, which was the situation facing Atif in the first months after his arrival in Gothenburg.

> I asked for work and I needed work ... I had no money. It [the city] was expensive. I thought that I could, you know, ask [his employer] for more money. But I tell you, I did not even know the salary. It was one day you work and then the boss gives me money ... sometimes longer days and sometimes shorter ... one day 70 kronor and another day 100 kronor. In this place you do not ask the boss why ... then I think ... that there is no more work. (Atif)

Work in the informal labour market is beset by multiple risks. Wages are not paid as agreed; work is unregulated, with irregular breaks and no limits on the number of hours worked per day or week; health and safety is ignored and the working environment is insecure, nor is the worker provided with the necessary footwear, clothing, masks, helmets, etc. And, ultimately, all working conditions are governed by the worker's deportability, as the following example shows. At the time of our interview, Mansoor from Iran had lived as an irregular migrant for a year. He told me about one of his jobs in a restaurant:

> I went to the restaurant in the morning and we did, you know, preparations for lunch. Before we opened, everyone, the boss too, sat down to eat for maybe twenty minutes. Then it was lunch and then washing dishes. And then more preparation. And I reckoned it's time to knock off. I was very tired. It's hard, working in a restaurant. And the boss said to me, 'Mansoor, today you must stay late.' I stayed the whole evening. I stayed until the restaurant closed and we had finished washing dishes and cleaning. ... After work it was late and I had to walk from [a place in Hisingen] to get to [the tram station], very cold and dark. And it was Saturday night. Lots of young people going to the city to parties and, you know, being very drunk, not nice drunk. I was scared, I was thinking that perhaps the police would come because people were screaming and throwing beer bottles. And they talked to me and I did not know what to say. ... And then the next day the boss asked again and the next ... I was thinking many things: perhaps I will have no more

work. Also the boss told me he could help me find a place, a flat ... Perhaps if he gets angry he will call the police, I don't know ... Then one day I go to work, we prepare lunch, and then the boss says that he has no more work for me. He gives me my money and I leave. (Mansoor)

Such working conditions and interactions build upon social relations negotiated from a position of deportability, not legal contracts. If all the criteria are met with proof of identity and the like (not always possible for migrants who have no papers at all), asylum seekers are able to obtain work permits. As an irregular migrant in need of work, one has to fall back on non-regulated labour in the informal economy, which is also the reality for many asylum seekers, work permit or not.

Wage brackets and working conditions differ depending on the employer and the type of work, but also the worker's legal status, individual social contacts, and so on. Many employers claim that, out of solidarity, they prefer hiring an irregular migrant over all other hopefuls. As one employer said,

> I do not hire Swedish people and not asylum seekers, they can survive anyway ... But those who have no work permits, they have nothing! All human beings have a right to eat ... To eat you must work. (Mustapha)

Social relations between employer and employee

The social relations between employers and employees seemed paradoxical in many ways, with informants referring to their employer or would-be employer as a brother, father, or friend, while it was obvious that their relations were not equal. Informants might work endless hours and only be paid for a fraction of them, insisting that the extra hours were only to 'help out' by carrying boxes, delivering goods, or something else that was simply hard to describe but that fell into the category of actions that would normally be the informant's private business. Work was not only disguised as voluntary help, for at times it clearly tipped over into the employer's private sphere, as when an informant cooked for an employer's elderly father or cleaned his home.

There were actions of nominal reciprocity between employer and employee. It could take various forms, but commonly the employer offered access to a certain amount of waged work, advice, money, goods, food, or contacts, which amounted to the value of social relations. Thus labour, time, support, friendship, and so on are forms of capital that can be used by the asylum seeker or irregular migrant to manage everyday life.

It was evident that status as an asylum seeker itself brought a particular capital and place in the hierarchy, as asylum seekers are less of a risk to employers since their physical presence is not illegal. Thus legal status is worth something on the informal labour market. Not only are asylum seekers 'safer' for employers to hire, being potentially legal employees and with the legal right to be within Swedish borders: the legal status of asylum seekers, even if it minimizes access to protection by the state, highlights the fact that, irregular migrants, even more than asylum seekers, cannot afford to say no to poor working conditions, low or unpaid wages, and other abusive behaviour on the part of employers. Thus the legal status articulated by the state is in surprisingly close symbiosis with the informal labour market.

Strictly speaking, irregular migrants and asylum seekers are legal categories, with associated sets of legal rights. Whereas the mere physical presence of irregular migrants on Swedish soil is illegal, they have the formal right to seek the protection of the police from abusive employers who refuse to pay wages. Yet even though it is a formal right, it is profoundly unrealistic to expect an irregular migrant to report a crime to the police, when he or she will risk being deported as a result.

Asylum seekers have rights, such as the right to emergency health or dental care, and if eligible they may seek formal employment, but in reality their chances are slim. The daily allowance for an unmarried asylum seeker who does not live in accommodation provided by the Swedish Migration Board is 71 SEK a day, or about SEK 2,130 (EUR 200) a month, a sum that has to cover everything: food, rent, health and dental care, clothing. The average cost of private accommodation, even in a shared room, is greater than that figure. Without private savings or loans from friends or family it is impossible to survive without earning money on the informal labour market. What realistic chance does an asylum seeker have other than to look for work in the informal market?

The regulations concerning asylum seekers and irregular migrants frame everyday life for these non-citizens, who actually live as citizens, performing citizen actions (Holgersson 2011) in the city. This framework limits non-citizens, preventing them from working legally, signing contracts, and the like, but is also connected to the market value put on the asylum seeker or irregular migrant, partly by affecting rents and wages on the informal market, but also in terms of physical danger and threats. The regulations and the status of the migrant in the recipient country—whether an asylum seeker (regularized migrant) or an irregular migrant—foster competition between asylum seekers and irregular migrants, and do much to determine salaries and possible risks, where the irregular migrants receive the lowest wages and take the greatest risks (Khosravi 2010).

Employers in the informal economy

A majority of the employers among my informants were immigrants themselves, or children of immigrants. Among the employers I met there were people from a variety of professional backgrounds: the majority of self-employed men who ran businesses where my informants worked had came to Sweden as adults, and as first-generation immigrants had an advanced educational background having trained as teachers, scientists, engineers, etc. There were also men who prior to migrating had had a long-term profession—farmers, teachers, engineers, mechanics, estate agents—that they had not been able to pursue in Sweden. It was typical of the majority of their businesses that they were small and, due to the harsh economic realities of life, had to be flexible in terms of occupation, number of staff, hours worked, and so on.

The businesses fall into two groups. The first is the type of business that sells or produces and then sells directly to customers or distributors. Common businesses here are restaurants, coffee shops, hairdressers, grocery stores, corner shops, delis, car washes, and garages. To expand their opportunities to make a profit, business owners were always on the lookout for sidelines: restaurants and coffee shops offered catering or organized events; grocers became importers and distributors, and periodically needed to take on more staff to unpack, repack, and deliver goods.

The second type of business is the company that works as a subcontractor, often for other subcontractors. Here we find building firms, electricians, painters, plumbers, tiling companies, cleaning companies, and so on. These companies vary considerably in size. Some subcontractors work alone with a flexible staff of workers, a yard as a base, and a mobile phone; others have a more established profile, and a small but regular and formally employed workforce with extra hands hired informally if needed. It is especially the tasks that are time-consuming and only demand unskilled labour that are more commonly performed by irregular migrants, who also are the ones who experience high rates of unreliability—their wages for a certain job of work can be disproportionally small when roughly calculated in advance. Not only is this a common experience for workers at the bottom of the chain, but subcontractors are also exposed to similar economic pressures from the companies that hired them.

Certain kinds of work are felt by informants to be particularly stressful and risky. One example is cleaning, where the unregulated workers who do the work also represent the company when cleaning for clients. This may require communicating with other staff and answering questions. One informant—an irregular migrant who worked for a cleaning company—spoke of dreaming up different answers to potential questions when he was at work in a shopping centre. What he feared most was being asked about his legal status, and what he should answer that would give a credible impression. In his mind there was a great risk that someone would 'see that he had no permit' and that he did not know how to answer questions about where he came from, why he did not speak better Swedish, and so on.

Although it is not possible to draw an absolute distinction between these different types of businesses, I would argue that the social relations between employer and employee, transactions, trust, reliability in terms of unpaid or low wages, health risks, and the like in the working environment are patterned according to the company structure. In the case of subcontractors, they are forced to be flexible towards their contractors and to hold their costs down, which can create unreliable situations for workers, who have little or no chance to resist. These businesses are part of the informal economy because of their use of unregulated labour, undeclared income, and their violation of labour rights such as a safe working environment or reasonable wages. Their business activities, however, are not illegal. My informants' employers argued that their businesses could not survive if they hired staff formally, because it is not profitable enough.

The question is then why employers choose to become self-employed, since they invest an enormous number of hours in projects that only can be realized if they break the law. The answer is that they have not been able to enter the formal labour market. Neither the men who had an educational and professional background in their country of origin, nor the young men who often had not completed their education in Sweden and had no professional experience, subsisting on work experience placements that could potentially be transformed into full jobs, but never were.

The local production of deportability

Deportability is a consequence of legal status—that is, legal status either because of irregularities or because of the risk of not being granted asylum. In what way, then, can deportability be argued to be the product of local structures? And in what way are legal status and deportability the key factors in social relations and transactions?

Deportability is perhaps best described as the risk of being deported, but it is only when we understand deportability in context that we see its full meaning. The example of the informal labour market and its social networks is useful in this, because it reveals that not only is deportability a potential risk, but also how it is a value.

The value of deportability is to the employer, in the shape of lower wages, poor working conditions, and general insecurity. My informants have employed different strategies in order to create stronger bonds with their employers, thus seeking to ensure some measure of security. In some cases informants have tried to hide their deportability from their employers, something that might be risky if a situation arises that calls for proof of identity.

In relation to legal status and deportability, the different realities that asylum seekers and irregular migrants face when working leave the irregular migrants at the bottom of the hierarchy, being the most docile and exploitable labour force. We might as well turn the situation on its head. Being the most docile and exploitable labour force can actually be an absurd advantage when looking for work. It all comes down to competitive edge.

Deportability as a value and a stratifying denominator can be said to be produced through legal status, in conjuncture with the specific organization of the informal economy. That organization is part of a national structure and active policies that have created a segment of the population who have no rights to social security because they are self-employed, no paid holidays, no sick pay, no parental leave—none of the benefits that go with a real salary, taxed at source, and governed by a long-term contract or similar.

Concluding remarks

This essay sheds light on the ways in which the excluded can be understood as part of a structure. Even the outcast plays an important role for the tools of social control. People who are deportable, either because of their temporary legal status as asylum seekers or because they are irregular migrants with no legal right to be in the country, are controlled by their exclusion from formal rights. Meanwhile, in the present case, their employers have the formal right to work, but have not succeeded in entering the formal labour market.

To me it seems that the processes that have stimulated the structures of inequality seen here are the result of active political choices in response to intensified global neoliberalism and integrated economic markets and their impact on value, production, capital, and profit. In Sweden, privatization and neoliberal redistributions such as tax credits for domestic services are only a few examples that have stimulated a service market for a growing body of consumers keen to maximize the value of their property. The current state of subcontracting and its place in the informal economy is reflected in the fact that contractors have seen a chance to cut costs and thus increase profits by using the labour of cheap subcontractors, which makes them competitive on the formal market. This leads subcontractors to specialize in different sectors and tasks—something that is evident in my material, where self-employed subcontractors in the construction business are often called in to do the jobs that are dirty, dangerous, and time-consuming.

Formal ownership and capital go together. It is plain that the work my informants do generates neither substantive capital nor formal ownership for their employers, which is still the main way to accumulate capital. The self-employed in the informal economy do not have a fully declared income and have a hard time getting the business to make a profit. It is in relation to the questions of who makes the profit and who has the formal ownership of the business, capital, and any property that we must understand phenomena such as the informal economy and its stratification.

Central to the issues this essay addresses is the question of access to rights. Either access is formally barred, as in the example of irregular migrants, or, as in the example of asylum seekers, they have the right to a work permit, but only if all the requirements are met in the shape of valid proof of identity—an inherent problem for the majority of migrants worldwide. In the case of the self-employed, they have the formal right to work, but self-employment has persisted as the only real option, a choice made of necessity although egged on by the state.

Legal status, blocking people from accessing rights by a variety of formal and informal means, is what gives deportability its value in this local example of an informal economy. Equally, it is what shapes the informal economy's social relations and transactions. In the light of this, I would argue for the importance of abandoning national tools and methodologies as given denominators when understanding how a nation-state handles migration. Rather than looking at structures and phenomena using the standard perspectives—ethnicity, say, or the legal categories of asylum seekers and irregular migrants—I would suggest that in transcending those categories, other structures become visible. Anthropology in its more ethnographic moments is a valuable tool in understanding the meanings of social networks, as it reveals not only what capital might be and how it is produced and transacted, but also the fuller meaning of structural inequalities and how they are produced in specific, if complex, parallel processes and practices. It thus makes it possible to understand deportability as a local phenomena, and not as something external to the nation.

Deportability appears as one factor that socially and economically stratifies the informal economy where irregular migrants become the most docile workers. Beyond this we might additionally understand the position of my informants' employers, who have become self-employed due to unemployment, as part of a production of social disintegration on a national scale.

Notes

1 This was, however, not the case when the data was collected for this study. It was only recently, in 2013, that irregular migrants were given the right to subsidized healthcare.

References

Abbasian, S. (2000) *Bosättningsmönster, eget företagande och integration* (Kulturgeografiska institutionen, Handelshögskolan, 124; Gothenburg: University of Gothenburg).
Björklund-Larsen, L. (2010) *Illegal, yet licit: Justifying informal purchases of work in contemporary Sweden* (Studies in Social Anthropology, NS 2; Stockholm: Stockholm University).
Boissevain, J. (1966) 'Patronage in Sicily', *Man*, 1/1, 18–33.
Boverket (2008) *Asylsökandes eget boende* (Karlskrona: Boverket).
Carlbom, A. (2003) *The imagined versus the real other* (Lund: Lunds universitet).
Castells, M. (2000) *The information age: Economy, society and culture. Vol. 1, The rise of the network society* (Oxford: Blackwell).
De Genova, N. (2002) 'Migrant "illegality" and deportability in everyday life', *Annual Review of Anthropology*, 31, 419–47.
—— (2013) 'Spectacles of migrant illegality, the scene of exclusion, the obscene of inclusion, *Ethnic and Racial Studies*, 36/1, 1180–98.
Fakiolas, R. (2000). 'Migration and unregistered labour in the Greek economy'. *Eldorado or fortress*, 57–78.
Fassin, D. (2009) 'Another politics of life is possible', *Theory, Culture & Society*, 26/5, 44–60.

Furnivall, J.S. (1948) *Colonial practice and policy: A comparative study of Burma and Netherlands India*. (Cambridge: Cambridge University Press).
Fassin, D. (2009) 'Another politics of life is possible', *Theory, Culture & Society*, 26/5, 44–60.
Granovetter, M. (1978) 'Threshold models of collective behavior', *American Journal of Sociology*, 83/6, 1420–43.
—— (1983) 'The strength of weak ties: A network theory revisited', *Sociological Theory*, 1, 201–33.
—— (1985) 'Economic action and social structure: The problem of embeddedness', *American Journal of Sociology*, 91/3, 481–510.
Harvey, D. (2008) 'The right to the city', *New Left Review*, 53.
Holgersson, H. (2011) *Icke-medborgarskapets urbana geografi* (Gothenburg: Glänta).
Isin, E. (2009) 'Citizenship in flux: The figure of the activist citizen', *Subjectivity*, 29, 367–88.
Khosravi, S. (1999) 'Displacement and entrepreneurship: Iranian small businesses in Stockholm', *Journal of Ethnic & Migration Studies*, 25/3, 493–508.
—— (2010) 'An ethnography of migrant "illegality" in Sweden: Included yet excepted?' *Journal of International Political Theory*, 6/1, 95–116.
Öberg, K. (2015) *Meanings of social networks and the local production of deportability: The example of asylum seekers and irregular migrants in the informal labor market in Gothenburg, Sweden.* (Paris: École des hautes etudes en sciences sociales).
Sassen, S. (1992) 'The informal economy', in J. H. Mollenkopf & M. Castells (eds.) *Dual city: Restructuring of New York* (New York: Russell Sage Foundation).
Schierup, C.-U., P. Hansen & S. Castles (2006). *Migration, citizenship, and the European welfare state: A European dilemma* (Oxford: OUP).
Schierup, C.-U. (2010) 'Diversity' and social exclusion in third way Sweden: The 'Swedish model' in transition, 1975–2005 (The MES working paper 35; Linköping: Linköping University).
Schierup, C.-U. & A. Ålund (2011) The end of Swedish exceptionalism? Citizenship, neoliberalism and the politics of exclusion. *Race & Class*, 53/1, 45–64.
Slavnic, Z. (2004) *Immigrant and small business research in Sweden: An overview* (Linköping: Linköping University Electronic Press).
Standing, G. (2011) *Prekariatet* (Gothenburg: Daidalos).
Wimmer, A. & N. Glick Schiller (2002) 'Methodological nationalism and the study of migration', *European Journal of Sociology*, 43/02, 217–40.

CHAPTER 9

Inclusion and exclusion in a residential narrative of 'us' and 'them'

Anne Harju

This essay examines the tensions between citizens in a narrative of 'Swedes' and 'immigrants'. The point of departure is fieldwork in Landskrona, a post-industrial city in southern Sweden with a population of 40,000. In recent decades, the city has undergone radical economic and social changes. Until the mid-1970s, it had several large-scale industries, including a huge shipyard; since then, Landskrona has steadily declined in economic importance, leading to high unemployment and considerable population losses (Johansson 2011; Salonen 2011; Scarpa 2011). Other cities in the region, such as Malmö, have gone through the same transformation, but Landskrona has not benefited from its location to the same extent. In fact, it has higher unemployment and greater numbers on benefits than elsewhere in the region (Scarpa 2011). The decline in the economy and the population losses have left flats vacant in the city. By way of a solution, the city council agreed to house refugees, who had their living expenses covered by the state and therefore would not, in the short term, be a burden on the local economy. Since the 1980s, Landskrona has thus experienced new population gains by taking in refugees (Johansson 2011; Salonen 2011; Scarpa 2011). People of foreign background now account for approximately 30 per cent of the city's population (Statistics Sweden 2013).

The essay is based on empirical material from extensive ethnographic fieldwork to explore residents' experiences of everyday life in Landskrona, the positive and negative aspects of life in the city, and relationships between residents. The fieldwork was divided into two phases. In the first phase, residents' experiences were investigated as open-mindedly as possible: observing what happened, listening to what was said, and asking questions in informal conversations and interviews. The documentation consisted of field notes of observations and conversations. Right from the beginning of this first phase, it was clear that the demographic changes had created a heterogeneous and complex social situation, and a dominant narrative of the category 'immigrants' was one outcome. The second phase of the fieldwork was to strategically collect data relating to this narrative by concentrating on the relationship between people in three major categories, who were identified as central actors in the narrative: people who had moved to the city in the 1980s or later as refugees, and subsequent arrivals as part of family reunification (newcomers); people from other countries who moved to the city in the 1950s, 1960s, and 1970s to work (labour migrants); and people of Swedish origin.

A sense of fear and feelings of insecurity were a recurrent theme in relation to the narrative of 'immigrants', who were blamed for causing all the problems. Perceived behavioural factors such as involvement in violence, criminality, and gangs were often cited when the category was described, as was bad behaviour such as rowdiness and loudness (Wiklund 2005; Burcar & Wästerfors 2007; Harju 2011, 2013; Lundberg 2011; Viscovi 2011). As other studies have shown, blaming 'immigrants' for being the cause of feelings of insecurity and insecurity is a common national and global narrative (for example, Abrahamsson in this volume; May 2004; Lappalainen 2005; Kamali 2006; Finney & Simpson 2009; Back et al. 2012). This essay goes beyond this common assumption to explore it from another angle, for here it is argued the narrative has to do with residents' power relations—that is, that residents create and maintain power positions by means of the narrative. Control of the narrative is central to the establishment and maintenance of these positions, and the aim of the essay is to explore the circumstances that have to be fulfilled in order to have a chance of controlling the narrative.

Conceptual framework

Norbert Elias's figuration of the established and outsiders is used here to explore the circumstances in which narrative can be controlled. Based on a study of a suburban area of an English industrial town pseudonymously called Winston Parva (Elias & Scotson 1965), Elias (1994) claims that communities consist of networks of mutually dependent groups bound by changing and asymmetrical power balances. At its most basic, the model is that groups of people become dependent on one another because of external circumstances such as an inflow of new residents. This dependence inevitably leads to an internal ranking, in which certain groups stigmatize and exclude others. Elias (1994) calls this a figuration of the established and outsiders, proceeding from the existence of a power imbalance, which means that the established are able to set the norm and dominate the outsiders by treating them collectively as inferiors. In this way they make a distinction between themselves and 'the others'. The process is made possible by strong group cohesion driven by social 'oldness', social control, and key positions in institutions. Time also plays a key role here, because a common past provides a stock of common memories and attachments. To help them, the dominant group has a number of stigmatization techniques, of which two are crucial: group charisma, which is ascribed to one's own group on the basis of its nomic part, that is, its 'best' members; and group disgrace, which is ascribed to 'the others' on the basis of their anomic part, that is their 'worst' members. This is what Elias (1994) calls moral differentiation. His model focuses on the way that those with power, the established, stigmatize and exclude those with less power, the outsiders, while their actions have their origin in the sense of threat to their internal cohesion (established norms, values, and way of life) and position of power.

Elias (1994) suggests that it is the sociodynamics of inter-group relationships that are central not only to the figurations of the established and outsiders, but also their power differences. He argues this from his findings in Winston Parva, where the figuration included residents with similar backgrounds: Elias's stance is that the sociodynamics of groups bonded to one another are determined by the manner of their bonding, not by group characteristics. It could thus be argued that it is the sociodynamics of inter-group relationships that are central to power positions in a residential figuration, and not group characteristics such as class, ethnicity, or cultural background. This means that differences in physical appearance or socio-economic position are subordinate to sociodynamics. A focus on such characteristics is peripheral, according to Elias, and diverts attention from what is central—differences in power balances and the exclusion of groups inferior in power (Dunning 2004). However, in the light of the findings from the city of Landskrona discussed here, this assumption is open to question.

The established in Landskrona

During the fieldwork it was possible to discern a figuration of the established and outsiders, in which people of Swedish background and people who arrived in the 1950s, 1960s, and 1970s can be defined as being established, and people who had arrived since the 1980s are outsiders. In this figuration, just as in Elias and Scotson's study (1965/1994), a distinction was made based on time. In relation to this, people whose families had been in the city for generations and those who moved there to work starting in the 1950s, when the city was prospering, talked about themselves as 'us'. The distinction was performed in almost all interviews with residents in these two categories. It was especially apparent in the interviews with labour immigrants, including Darko, who emigrated from former Yugoslavia in the 1960s and worked in the local shipbuilding industry until he retired:

> There are some Swedes who've sort of learned things about immigrants. A bit of background and things like that, and they make an exception especially for us old immigrants. ... I've heard a lot of them saying, 'No, you old ones are no problem. You've worked your arses off.' (Darko)

This echoes the general statements about labour immigrants—they are now categorized as respectable. Just as for Darko, their having come to Sweden in the 1960s to work, and thus having 'done their bit', legitimated their inclusion and confirmed their favourable position.

The cohesion between the two categories was based on the existence of a narrative about a harmonious past in which residents got along, in contrast to the present, when insecurity and change had become the focal issues. In other words, the narrative was strongly connected to memories of the so-called 'good old days'. Dragan described how the city used to be in the following way:

> I thought it was a really great town. It was a small town, but with a lot of industry. There was no work crisis, there was no unemployment, there were no, you know, troublesome lads and people. There were no burglaries, no muggings or things like that. It was a really, really nice quiet town. (Dragan)

Generally speaking, Landskrona in the 'good old days' was said to have been a safe, friendly, and quiet place. Other studies confirm the existence of this collective memory of the city (Johansson 2011; Viscovi 2011). At the same time, this does mean that previous antagonisms had to be denied. Thus Johansson (2011) shows in his historical study of Landskrona that when it was prosperous and recruiting labour, above all from Europe, there was an obvious sense of 'us' and 'them' between the labour immigrants and those who had lived there longer. The labour immigrants were seen as 'ill-suited' to life there and culturally different, and represented the category of 'them'. These antagonisms were denied, both by individuals of long-standing Swedish background and by the older labour migrants who had been newcomers at the time. Indeed, people in both categories even talked about their past social relations as having always been harmonious. As Klara, a woman of Swedish background, who was a schoolgirl at that time, said, 'I don't remember when I went to school there being antagonism between Swedes and foreigners'. In other words, there was an absence of any past of 'us' and 'them' in today's collective memory.

The cohesion between 'Swedes' and labour immigrants was thus based on a belief in the good old days and a harmonious past, and on denied antagonisms. The existence of the category of 'almost Swedes' also helped to maintain the sense of cohesion between the two categories. One man of Swedish background illustrates the common perception of labour immigrants as 'almost Swedes':

> Anders: I don't actually think about that because I see them almost as Swedes. Their parents came here in the seventies. We actually have some among the adult group in the club who are immigrants, or their parents are immigrants at least.
> Interviewer: But they don't count, do they?
> Anders: But they have become a part of society. They are in principle Swedes. OK, they might have a surname like Whatsovich but—

This was a recurrent theme in the interviews: labour immigrants and their children were counted as being 'almost Swedes'. It was a measure of the degree of their establishment. Being 'Swedish' was synonymous with being a part of society. The category of 'Swedes' was viewed as the norm, a yardstick of establishment, from which comparisons with other categories proceeded. There thus existed a hierarchy in which people who define themselves and others as Swedish are ranked highest, followed by labour immigrants, and then those who came later.

The shared memories and existence of the category of 'almost Swede' provided a common reference point and helped to create and maintain strong internal cohesion, which according to Elias (1994) is one requirement if a group is to successfully maintain a power balance in a figuration. In his and Scotson's study of Winston Parva, the solidarity of the established was based on the fact that they lived in clearly separated and demarcated neighbourhoods, in which they could stick together by using social rewards and control. In Landskrona, the difference was not noticeably maintained by strong social cohesion in a specific residential area, nor did it seem to be dependent on everyday face-to-face interaction; instead, it was maintained by perceptions of similarity and memories of a harmonious past. Talja Blokland (2001) argues that processes of collective remembering serve to reconstruct place and its identity; even without knowing one another, shared memories of changed places create a collective memory. This not only gives those sharing the memories a sense of community, it also makes a difference to the newcomers, who are strangers to local history. In Landskrona, the cohesion between 'Swedes' and labour immigrants favoured their chances to define and differentiate the 'others', and thereby maintain their power positions in the residential figuration.

The construction of difference

During the fieldwork, it became clear that the dominant narrative of the immigrant category did not include everyone who came from an immigrant background, but only those who had recently arrived, who were defined on the basis of what Elias (1994) called moral differentiation—'we' were considered to behave more correctly than 'they' did. The way this was done was that the newcomers were viewed on the basis of the anomic members of the category. One example of the use of the anomic members in order to condemn the whole group, according to Elias (1994), is to perceive outsiders as unruly, breaking the law and ignoring norms. Such perceptions were apparent during the fieldwork: for example, people often equated immigrants with criminals, as in an interview with a couple and their daughter living in an affluent, white ('Swedish') neighbourhood. The mother explained the reasons behind much of the residents' sense of insecurity:

> Monika: Because I think that the problem, the fact that many people feel insecure, has to do with immigrants.
> Interviewer: Is there a connection?
> Monika: Yes, I think so, and the statistics show that a lot of the crimes committed are connected to the fact that there are far more immigrants here perhaps in [the city] than there have been, than what you find in other cities of the same size.

What she is referring to is the narrative, repeated over and over again, which says that insecurity has increased because there is more crime, and that increase is linked to immigrants, by which is meant people who have moved to the city since the 1980s: they were the ones, especially the young men, who were thought responsible for the gangs, muggings, and burglaries and all the associated insecurity. Perceived behavioural factors such as involvement in violence, criminality, and gangs were often cited when they were described (see Wiklund 2005; Burcar & Wästerfors 2007; Viscovi 2011). Some years ago, there was a group of adolescents who mugged people in the city. By the time of the fieldwork this had all but ceased (Citizens survey 2010), yet, according to Elias (1994), in making distinctions it is not important that the events referred to are real, invented, or no longer relevant—the point is that events in the constructed ideas are affirmed, while non-confirmed events are ignored. Thus during the fieldwork, residents constantly returned to that group of young muggers, using them as a model for the whole category, and the narrative was kept alive with the aid of rumours that confirmed it. One woman with a Swedish background offers a typical example of this kind of talk:

> And you hear things. For a while it was fairly common that people were mugged and knocked down. I've heard of people who've gone out, both midweek and at weekends, and they were assaulted beaten and robbed. (Susanna)

Although she does not openly lay the blame at the immigrants' door, they are the ones she means. In almost all interviews, feelings of insecurity and fear were related to this one category, as was others' bad behaviour such as rowdiness and loudness. As one woman of Swedish background put it:

> There are times I'm in a shop and they're so noisy and they don't behave the way we do, and then I think maybe it's easy to get the impression, 'Well of course, it's an immigrant again'. For we have slightly different temperaments and different views of what is proper behaviour. (Karin)

Karin explicitly refers to differences in temperament and perceptions of correct behaviour, which can be directly related to endlessly repeated distinction between 'rough' and 'respectable' seen in other studies (Elias & Scotson 1965; Skeggs 1997; Blokland 2003; Watt 2006; May 2008; Cheshire et al. 2010). One source of information in the present study was the local newspaper. In a study of the same paper, Dino Viscovi (2011) found a discourse in the letters to the editor (where 'immigrants' were nearly non-existent) focused largely on the behavioural deficiencies of 'immigrants', who were described as problem-makers, criminals, and drug addicts. Many of the references were to one specific neighbourhood, which was singled out as the source of most of the crime. Located in the city centre, the neighbourhood had high rates of unemployment and benefit takers and a high proportion of newcomers. In the dominant narrative, it was described as dilapidated and dangerous—in a recent local survey by the police (Polisen 2010), for example, it was described as being the least safe place, due to the fear of being attacked or robbed. The following exchange with one couple highlights this particular line of reasoning:

> Saara: We lived there for 36 years, and we would still be living there.
> Markku: If those darkies hadn't come. The whole neighbourhood was ruined, and the house, well, you couldn't live in it any longer.
> Saara: You couldn't live there.
> Interviewer: What happened?
> Saara: They have a completely different way of life. The laundry room: they went there any time of day. They didn't go when it was their own time. And they wrecked the garden.

The couple, who had moved to work in the city in the 1960s, had lived in the neighbourhood until a few years ago. They echo the general talk of the area as 'ruined', including putting the blame on the people who had moved in most recently, who are said to be incapable of taking care of the place, and thus are not behaving correctly.

While one requirement if you are to keep your grip on the power to differentiate and define, and thus your power position in a residential figuration, is to have a strong internal cohesion (Elias 1994), another is for 'others' to have none. In Elias and Scotson's study in Winston Parwa (1965), they found that the residents who were defined as outsiders had little cohesion, and were therefore unable to close ranks and fight back. On the contrary, aware of their status, they tried to avoid being 'polluted' by it by distancing themselves from the category. This resonates with Loïc Wacquant's thoughts on stigma management in stigmatized neighbourhoods (1996), for he argues that territorial stigmatization stimulates behavioural patterns, which lead to increased social differentiation and distancing within the neighbourhoods that are stigmatized, as residents try to manage the stigma by mutual avoidance, micro-hierarchies, and scapegoating. By emphasizing their own high moral value while devaluing others, they try to regain their dignity and ensure their own status in the eyes of society. An interesting aspect of Saara and Markku's remarks is that they stigmatize a neighbourhood and a category that they themselves could be associated with. This form of stigmatization, according to Elias (1994), especially affects groups who aspire to become established, and not being identified with the 'others' is an important step in the right direction. The couple's horror at the state of the neighbourhood and subsequent move can therefore be interpreted as a strategy to avoid identification. The same kind of avoidance was apparent in the interviews with newcomers, who distanced themselves from other newcomers. This was evident in an interview with a mother and her 17-year-old daughter. The mother explained why she preferred her daughter to socialize with 'Swedes':

> Liri: But boyfriends. I've said it many times, go out with Swedes.
> Ana: I'm allowed to go out with Swedes, but not Albanians, and what's wrong with Arabs?
> Liri: I don't think Arabs are good. I'm a Muslim, but it's not the same thing as them. Arabs are totally different.

The family, who were originally from Kosovo, came to live in Sweden, and Landskrona, in the early 1990s. The mother is in effect telling her daughter that having Swedish boyfriends will be better for her, and in explaining why she prefers 'Swedes', she implies that there is a sliding scale where Swedes are good and Arabs and Albanians, who are the newcomers, are bad. The mother was thus voicing prevalent negative beliefs about the category that she herself was defined as belonging to. In doing so she effectively accepted the status and the characteristics attributed to the category she belongs to, while at the same time trying to distance her family from it.

This kind of distancing is also found in an interview with a couple from Afghanistan who had lived in the city for five years. The husband wanted to move out of the neighbourhood. One reason was that the residents with a Swedish background were moving out, leaving only immigrants behind. From his perspective, the new immigrants did not know how to behave—young people were making trouble, parents did not care about their children, and the streets were filthy. Another reason was that he wanted his own children to socialize with 'Swedish' children, and he explained why:

> My daughter wants to be a writer, but society has deceived her. Society has deceived her by claiming she has chances she doesn't have, because of bad schooling, bad people. The problem is there are too many immigrants. There should be a mixture, fifty-fifty. Swedes are good: they tell children what is right and what is wrong. Immigrants don't do that. (Namir)

Namir's explanation echoes the general view of 'immigrants' as troublesome. For him, the society of 'Swedes' would determine his children's opportunities: from his point of view, to be identified as 'immigrants' would be a disadvantage for them. Both Liri's and Namir's explanations smack of the attempt to avoid being polluted and of stigma management (see Elias 1994; Wacquant 1996), but also, as we will see, of the effort by immigrants themselves to attain a stronger position in the new hierarchy of belonging by differentiating themselves from other immigrants (see Back et al. 2012).

Discussion

In focussing on Landskrona, a city in southern Sweden, where the narrative of 'immigrants' as the cause of the city's woes has had a direct impact on residential relations, the purpose of this essay is to explore the narrative in relation to the establishment and maintenance of residential power relations. Elias's figuration (1994) of the established and outsiders has proved a useful analytical tool: it focuses on the basic mechanisms by which those who have power can stigmatize and exclude others. In this sense, our attention is limited to what the established do, away from 'the others', who are often left with the blame for the problems associated with the relationship. When the narrative in Landskrona is analysed more closely using Elias's model (1994), it is possible to see that the more established residents had the power to strengthen their position in the residential figuration by using their control of the narrative. The results show that strong cohesion among the established and weak cohesion between newcomers, combined with distancing processes, are central for the one group's ability to define who members of the other group are.

However, as much as the results indicate the potential of Elias's model (1994) in charting power relations and their effects, there is at least one aspect of it that remains to be addressed. The model is generally taken to mean that 'real' or 'material' differences between groups are irrelevant to the creation of established and outsider figurations. According to Elias (1994), factors such as socio-economic status, race, or ethnicity are not central to such figurations, whereas the sociodynamics of inter-group relationships are. This means that differences in physical appearance or socio-economic position are subordinate to the sociodynamics. Elias (1994) bases his argument on findings from Winston Parwa, where residents were very similar in ethnicity, nationality, and class, but still differentiated in their internal social ranking. One example from Landskrona is the changed position of labour immigrants. They may have largely the same ethnic characteristics as the newcomers, but today have a relatively strong position in the residential figuration; however, the findings here indicate that an internal social ranking that spans different categories of residents is closely interrelated with ethnicity and socio-economic position. When residents refer to the problematic image of 'immigrants', physical appearance and cultural differences are mentioned, as are the most recent immigrants living in socio-economically vulnerable neighbourhoods. It could therefore be argued that inter-group relationships in Landskrona are not only a matter of sociodynamics, which are based on the manner in which groups bond, but also of assumptions about ethnicity and socio-economic position. Suppositions about residents based on these factors thus matter for residential power positions and the inclusion or exclusion of residential groups.

These findings are in line with Back et al. (2012), who argue that minority communities are positioned differently in (new) hierarchies of belonging, for they are ordered by race and established through the ranking of immigration status. This leaves some immigrants invisible and others marked out for distinction and differentiation, thus conferring the status of 'insiders' on some and 'outsiders' on others. The judgements about who belongs or could be included are made routinely in everyday life: according to Back et al. (2012), such judgements pack the micro-spaces of social life, with all the resultant shame, displacement, and status anxiety. This in turn encourages existing immigrants to rank recent immigrants beneath themselves in the hierarchy of belonging, despite their striking similarities—the upshot of the distancing processes discussed in this essay. The enemy becomes the 'new immigrant' rather than the powerful groups who benefit from local injustice and global inequality (Back et al. 2012). Here again, Elias's figuration (1994) of the established and outsiders can help us to lift our gaze from the 'immigrant' to what the established have to gain.

Evidently, by controlling the narrative, the more established residents—the city's 'Swedes' and long-standing labour immigrants—can strengthen their position in a residential figuration by blaming newcomers for any and all problems. Those defined as newcomers were morally judged and differentiated by residents in the two other categories, and this was only possible because of the strong cohesion among the more established and the weak cohesion among the newcomers. Crucial to the maintenance of such power positions was the distancing process engendered between newcomers: newcomers were aware of their status, and, by distancing themselves from other newcomers, tried to avoid being 'polluted' (Harju 2011, 2013). Elias's model of the established and outsiders has been useful in understanding residential power relations in the city, and suggests that it could be valuable as an analytic tool when looking at the heterogeneous cities of today, where uneven power relations and space have become an increasing point of tension (Hanley et al. 2008).

References

Back, L., S. Sinha & C. Bryan (2012) 'New hierarchies of belonging', *European Journal of Cultural Studies*, 15, 139–54.

Blokland, T. (2001) 'Bricks, mortar, memories: Neighbourhood and network in collective acts of remembering', *International Journal of Urban and Regional Research*, 25/2, 268–83.

—— (2003) 'Ethnic complexity: Routes to discriminatory repertoires in an inner-city neighbourhood', *Ethnic & Racial Studies*, 26/1, 1–24.
Burcar, V. & D. Wästerfors (2007) *Lugnt på stan? En studie av trygghetsarbetet i Landskrona centrum* [Quiet in town? A study of work for security in the centre of Landskrona] (Sociologiska institutionen, Lund: Lund University).
Cheshire, L., P. Walters & T. Rosenblatt (2010) 'The politics of housing consumption: Renters as flawed consumers on a master planned estate', *Urban Studies*, 47/12): 2597–614.
Dunning, E. (2004) 'Aspects of the figurational dynamics of racial stratification: A conceptual discussion and developmental analysis of black–white relations in the United States', in S. Loyal & S. Quilley (eds.), *The sociology of Norbert Elias* (Cambridge: CUP).
Elias, N. (1994) 'Introduction: A theoretical essay on established and outsider relations', in N. Elias & J. L. Scotson *The established and the outsiders* (London: SAGE).
—— & J. L. Scotson (1965/1994) *The established and the outsiders* (London: SAGE).
Finney, N. & L. Simpson (2009), *'Sleepwalking to segregation'? Challenging myths about race and migration* (Bristol: Polity).
Hanley, L. M., Blair A. Ruble & A. M. Garland (2008) *Immigration and integration in urban communities: Renegotiating the city* (Washington, DC: Woodrow Wilson Center Press).
Harju, A. (2011) '"Vi" och "Dom": Kollektiva föreställningar i staden' ['Us' and 'Them': Collective Images in the City], in T. Salonen (ed.) *Hela staden: Social hållbarhet och deintegration?* (Umeå: Borea).
—— (2013) 'Children's Use of Knowledge of Place in Understanding Social relations', *Children & Society*, 27/2, 150–60.
Johansson, J. (2011) '"Det var bättre förr": Samhällsförändring och nostalgi' [It was better in the past: Societal change and nostalgia], in T. Salonen (ed.) *Hela staden: Social hållbarhet och deintegration?* (Umeå: Borea).
Kamali, M. (2006) 'Den segregerande integrationen' [Integration that segregates], in M. Kamali (ed.), *Den segregerande integrationen: Om social sammanhållning och dess hinder* [Integration that segregates: On social cohesion and obstacles to it] (SOU 2006:73; Stockholm: Fritzes).
Lappalainen, P. (2005) *Det blågula glashuset: Strukturell diskriminering i Sverige* [The blue-and-yellow glass house: Structural discrimination in Sweden] (SOU 2005:56; Stockholm: Fritzes).
Lundberg, A. (2011) 'Svensk, invandrare eller katolik?' [Swede, immigrant or catholic?], in T. Salonen (ed.) *Hela staden: Social hållbarhet och deintegration?* (Umeå: Borea).
May, D. M. (2008) 'The interplay of three established-outsider figurations in a deprived inner-city neighbourhood', *Urban Studies*, 41/11, 2159–79.
Polisen (2010) *Polisens medborgarundersökning* [Citizen survey by the Police], <www.landskrona.se/bra>, accessed 18 November 2010.
Salonen, T. (2011) 'En blågul stad? Myter och sanningar om staden' [A blue and

yellow city? Myths and truths about the city], in T. Salonen (ed.) *Hela staden: Social hållbarhet och deintegration?* (Umeå: Borea).
—— (2011b) (ed.), *Hela staden: Social hållbarhet och desintegration?* (Umeå: Borea).
Scarpa, S. (2011) 'Statlig påverkan på den lokala arenan' [State influence on the local arena], in T. Salonen (ed.) *Hela staden: Social hållbarhet och deintegration?* (Umeå: Borea).
Skeggs, B. (1997) *Formations of Class and Gender* (London: SAGE).
Statistics Sweden (2013) <www.scb.se>, accessed 2 June 2013.
Viscovi, D. (2011) 'En vanlig och en ovanlig stad med problem' [An ordinary and unordinary city with problems], in Salonen 2011b.
Wacquant, L. (1996) 'Red belt, black belt: Racial division, class inequality and the state in French urban periphery and the American ghetto' in E. Mingione (ed.) *Urban poverty and the underclass* (Oxford: Blackwell).
Watt, P. (2006) 'Respectability, roughness and "race": Neighbourhood place images and the making of working-class social distinctions in London', *International Journal of Urban & Regional Research*, 30/4, 776–97.
Wiklund, S. (2005) *Främlingsfientlighet! En studie om majoritetskulturens uttryck och värderingar om mångkulturella Landskrona* [Xenophobia! A study of the majority culture's expressions and evaluations concerning multicultural Landskrona] (Sociologiska institutionen, Örebro: Örebro University).

III

INEQUALITY MANAGEMENT
IN SCANDINAVIAN CITIES

CHAPTER 10

The whole city or the city as a whole?
Questioning the conceptual assumptions of social sustainability in urban governance

Randi Gressgård

The visionary goal of many urban planners is to develop an attractive and sustainable city, socially, economically, and ecologically. This essay discusses the conceptual assumptions of social sustainability in Swedish urban governance, and the urban strategy of the city of Malmö in particular.[1] Social sustainability programmes in Malmö take as their starting point 'the whole city' when identifying structural mechanisms of marginalization and spatial segregation, as opposed to circumscribing the problems to so-called problem areas and marginalized groups. However, when the social sustainability agenda is incorporated into the visionary urban strategy, 'the whole city' translates into 'the city as a whole', which invokes a unifying notion of *one* future for the city as a single entity. The overall goal of a social sustainability agenda, in the frame of urban strategy, is to progressively transform immigrant-dense 'problem areas' of the city into 'innovation areas', according to given criteria of success. I shall argue that unless the social sustainability agenda discards the spatiotemporal coordinates of visionary urban strategy, it risks reproducing the status quo and contributing to further marginalization of targeted populations.

The analysis is based on a study of urban policy in the two-year period between the pre-launching of Malmö's comprehensive strategy plan in 2011—when it was circulated for public comment—and its official approval by the Malmö City Executive Board in 2013. The massive consultation programme included stakeholder meetings, public debates, film screenings, exhibitions, briefings, blogging, online consultation portals, and media debates. In addition, I draw on the local media reports, policy documents, and research publications on the social sustainability agenda in Malmö between 2011 and 2015.

The framing of sustainability in urban policy

Sustainability has emerged as *the* key word in urban and social policy in the past decade: a catch-all term around which policy is formulated (Davidson 2010a, 390–91). Timothy Beatley (2012, 121–2) remarks that sustainability is permeating and penetrating the cultural consciousness in a way that earlier visions did not, creating 'a space in which different stakeholders in the planning process are able to come together and develop a practical future vision (different to the status quo)'. According to Tony Manzi et al. (2010, 2), urban strategists have started talking about sustainable development in terms of the (many) overlaps in the interactions between economic, social, and environmental issues, and the need to consider long-term change. This policy integration is sometimes illustrated using the overlapping circles of a Venn diagram. Sustainable development is said to be about balancing the three dimensions and achieving some kind of trade-off between them in the prioritization process (Manzi et al. 2010, 2–3). The back blurb of *The Social Sustainability of Cities* (Polèse & Stren 2000) announces that 'policies conductive to social sustainability should, among other things, seek to promote fiscal equalization, to weave communities within the metropolis into a cohesive whole'. This holistic ambition (Lithman 2010) is characteristic of social sustainability literature. It is also reflected in the national Swedish initiative, the Delegation for Sustainable Cities (Delegationen för hållbara städer), which was appointed by the Swedish government in the autumn of 2008, and finalized its work in December 2012. Its mission statement emphasized the interconnection between ecological, social, and economic sustainability:

> The mission of sustainability embraces three mutually dependent dimensions: ecological sustainability for a good environment and limited climate impact; social sustainability, which relates to empowerment, welfare, safety and security, and ... economic sustainability, which presupposes a well-functioning and creative business sector, trade and service. (ISSUU 2010, 7)

In her analysis of municipal planning in divided cities in Sweden, Dalia Mukhtar-Landgren (2008, 150) draws attention to how local authorities have endeavoured to make disparate transformations into a 'whole' by imagining a desirable future in terms of visions. She refers, for instance, to *Vision Malmö 2015*, which served as the policy programme for the city's previous development strategy (from 2000). Reflecting on the process leading up to this vision, Mats Olsson and Göran Rosberg (2007, 30) from the Malmö City Planning Office comment that 'considerable focus has been directed on the construction of a strategic infrastructure base, which is also a precondition for economic growth'. What remains, however, is to convert cultural diversity from a 'problem' to a 'resource' by way of integration: 'To further develop Malmö as an attractive knowledge city, some major steps towards a more multicultural and integrated Malmö have to be taken' (Olsson & Rosberg 2007, 28).

In line with what Thorkild Ærø and Gertrud Jørgensen (2005, 127) identify as trends in Nordic urban policy, the planning officers emphasize the strengths and potential of the city rather than its weaknesses, 'with an implicit expectation that "the strengths will ameliorate the weaknesses"'. Although poverty and social problems dominate areas with a large number of immigrants and ethnic minorities—and the socio-economic gaps continue to grow—the main focus is on potential rather than problems (Dethorey 2013, 313). It is assumed that cultural diversity represents a competitive advantage for the city (as a whole). Characteristically, Malmö's most recent urban strategy document, *Overview Plan for Malmö 2012* (Malmö City Planning Office 2011a), depicts cultural diversity as ambivalently disturbing, a potential source of conflict, a threat to cohesion and safe living, and a potential asset and future resource. Ethnic minorities are by and large presented as some kind of reserve workforce with untapped potential. This corresponds to an urban cosmopolitanism that celebrates cultural difference as long as it is associated with prosperity, progress, and development (Gressgård 2015a; see also Baeten 2012, 37). For the purposes of our argument, it is important to note that in Malmö's long-term urban strategy, cultural diversity is connected to prosperity through the vocabulary of social sustainability. This approach to cultural diversity sits well with governmental ambitions to convert problems associated with immigrant populations (for example, segregation) into resources for urban development, while at the same time transforming the city into a 'whole' (see, for example, Clavier & Kauppinen 2013; Mukhtar-Landgren 2012; Nylund 2014).

In recent years, cultural development has been framed as part of the broader sustainability agenda that includes social, economic, and environmental development. This trend is epitomized by the Swedish Hållbar stad website (Sustainable City 2012), hosted by the Swedish Centre for Architecture and Design and funded by the Delegation for Sustainable Cities (ISSUU). The underlying assumption seems to be that a growing economy will result in a culturally attractive, socially inclusive, and environmentally friendly city (Kornberger & Clegg 2011, 143, 146). For instance, the information folder that promotes Malmö's new development plan, eloquently entitled 'Malmö—Time to take the next step!' (*Malmö—dags för nästa kliv!*), proclaims that the city will be the right place to be for an innovative and creative business life by the year 2032, and its streets and squares will not only be vibrant but also considerably cleaner and quieter (Malmö City Planning Office 2011b).

From planning to strategy

To understand the shape of the discourse of sustainability, it is worth considering the shift from 'planning' to 'strategy' that has taken place in Western urban governance in recent decades. Alongside the shift from industrial society to flexible regimes of production, there has been a general shift in the understanding of governance and planning. Old models of (distant) planning are seen as less useful, whereas strategy as an ongoing process is regarded as more suitable for changing business environments in a flexible economy (Thrift 1999, 46, 47). The Nordic City Network—a knowledge platform where representatives from member cities meet several times a year to discuss relevant themes—may serve to illustrate this general tendency in a Nordic context. The network emphasizes that the transition from industrial to knowledge cities requires a change in the way cities are governed: 'Separating functions and sectorizing responsibilities and administrations is outdated—we now need to set out minds and efforts to structure, shape, organize and govern our cities as knowledge cities' (Nordic City Network 2015).

According to Mark Purcell (2003, 100), the reconfiguration of governmental rationality is characterized by three major transformations: governance is rescaled such that institutions on sub- and supranational scales are taking on greater powers; policy is reoriented away from redistribution towards competition, leading local governance institutions to place increasing emphasis on maintaining their region's or cities' economic competitiveness; and many state functions are transferred to non-state and quasi-state governmental bodies (often depicted as a shift from state-based government to neoliberal governance). In considering this shift from sectorized and controlled planning to contextual, boundary-crossing and self-organizing strategy in urban governance, Martin Kornberger and Stewart Clegg (2011, 139) take strategy to mean a discursive practice that constitutes reality, defines what is meaningful, and legitimates actions and decisions. The first task of strategizing, they argue, is to render the city visible and provide a representation as the necessary frame in which interventions can be discussed and legitimized (Kornberger & Clegg 2011, 144). According to Kornberger (2012), strategy is a space in which epistemology coincides with politics—a regime that connects facts and values. Urban strategy thus stages public events to make people respond to visionary questions (that they might not themselves otherwise pose), such as 'How do you want the city to look in 20 years' time?'(Kornberger 2012, 98), or—in the case of Malmö—'Which future Malmö would you like to see?' ('Vilket framtida Malmö vill du se?') (Malmö City Planning Office 2011a).

'Vision images' are efficient tools for strategists when presenting (commissioned) research reports, polls etc. to mobilize people and enrol them in their agenda (Kornberger & Clegg 2011, 147–8, 150, 155; see also Kornberger 2012, 93). Over the past few decades, urban planners have increasingly made use of persuasive tropes to communicate stories about the future (Throgmorton 2003, 127). Olsson and Rosberg (2007, 30) associate the use of vision images with democratic transparency and a culture of growth:

> An important feature of our communication strategy was the 'vision images', i.e. we invested in exciting images which could communicate our ideas for the future in a simple way ... a democratic development process has to be fuelled by information, and it is the city which has to initiate a transparent communication process. A culture of growth arises from open discussions. (Olsson & Rosberg 2007, 30)

I shall comment on the issue of democratic transparency in due course. Meanwhile, it is important to note that the proposition of developing a sustainable city involves a view that takes social and ecological development to be in the interests of the economy, at least in the long run (Bröckling 2011, 249, 252). For the urban strategists in Malmö, the salient question is 'What makes Malmö the engine of the region?' This was the title of one of three thematic meetings that were organized in connection with the pre-launch of the new urban strategy in September 2011 (Thematic Meetings 2011; see also Gressgård 2015b). Like numerous other city administrations, Malmö City conceives of economic development as a two-pronged strategy that raises revenue for the city, while also improving the quality of life of its residents (Kornberger & Clegg 2011).

Quality of life and sustainability

Nicola Dempsey et al. (2011, 291) point out that Western urban policy hinges on interrelated concepts such as social sustainability, quality of life, social cohesion, liveability, and well-being. In Sweden, this chain-linking of policy terms and fields is evident in urban governance, including the Delegation for Sustainable Cities mission statement referred to above, which states that they 'will work together with other key actors to help create a well-functioning and attractive urban environment, in which high quality of life goes hand in hand with improved environment, economic growth, social cohesion and minimum climate impact' (ISSUU 2010, 6–7).

The emphasis on quality of life, liveability, and well-being is emblematic of urban strategies that take competitiveness to be the benchmark of success. This is the view advocated so notably by Richard Florida (2002), whose book *The Rise of the Creative Class* depicts culture as a driving force of the city economy, in so far as it produces a creative and attractive urban environment. In the preface to the revised edition of 2012, Florida strategically couples the city's creative economy with a newfound interest in sustainability. The respect for liveability and sustainability, he argues, is powered by the same ethos that drives the creative economy, for 'The creative ethos demands that we cultivate and utilize all of our natural and human resources' (Florida 2012, x). He maintains that our fledgling creative economy needs to give way to a fully creative society—a society that is more just, more equitable, more sustainable and more prosperous—because our economic future depends on it (ibid. xiv).

Although this is merely the bare bones of the argument, it still indicates that the vocabulary of sustainability allows wide-ranging, holistic ambitions for a prosperous city which strategically gloss over the possibility that social equity, eco-friendliness, and economic prosperity might be antagonistic goals. Under the heading 'high expectations', Magnus Boström (2012, 7) notes that the win-win framing inherent in the concept of sustainable development—the positive integration of the various pillars on which development rests—'may conceal the fact that clashes or trade-offs between environmental and social goals are sometimes (or even often) unavoidable'. Not only can goals vary according to the pillar, there might also be inconsistent goals within each sustainability agenda (Boström 2012, 8; see also Littig & Grießler 2005, 67). Nevertheless, in the language of sustainability in urban strategy, the city figures as a whole, coupled with ideas of prosperous futurity (see, for example, Massey 2005). It can be argued that sustainability is constituted as a unifying planning idea that serves an important legitimating function in urban governance (Gressgård 2015b; Nylund 2014).

Social sustainability initiatives in Malmö

A Directive passed by Malmö City Executive Board (2010) states that environmental, economic, and social sustainability need to be integrated to mutually strengthen one another, and to this end, it is necessary to focus more on social sustainability. On the basis of this instruction, the local council established the Commission for a Socially Sustainable Malmö, also known as the Malmö Commission, with a view to establishing a knowledge platform for future policies aimed at improving living conditions for the most vulnerable and disadvantaged groups. The Malmö Commission had fourteen members whose areas of expertise were within the social sciences, the health economy, and urban studies, in addition to representatives from the city administration. Over the course of two years, between 2010 and 2012, it produced some 30 research reports with policy recommendations on living conditions for children and young people; residential environment and urban planning; education; income and work; health and healthcare; and changing conditions for sustainable development. It also organized a number of seminars and conferences related to the topics of the reports.

In March 2014, Malmö City Executive Board adopted the Commission's extensive final report, *Malmö's Path towards a Socially Sustainable Future*, which had been submitted one year earlier (CSSM 2013a). The report shows the influence of the World Health Organization (WHO) Commission's report, *Closing the Gap in a Generation* of 2008, led by the British researcher Michael Marmot. Based on the assumption that health inequity is indicative of social inequality, the report sets out to identify social factors that lie outside the field of healthcare and welfare—so-called social determinants (education, profession, income, geographical area, country of origin, and so on)—with the ambition of putting all such socially inequitable conditions on the political agenda. As Per-Olof Östergren (2014, 516) (who was a member of the Commission) points out, the aim was to politicize the consequences of social inequality. Accordingly, the report calls for a shift in focus from a one-sided concern with economic growth to a perspective that problematizes health inequity from a structural point of view. And like the other reports produced by the Commission, the final report includes a series of concrete policy recommendations—74 action points—which provide the detail of two overarching recommendations: that to establish a social investment policy can reduce differences in living conditions; and, in order to achieve this, knowledge alliances must be created between researchers and stakeholders (from the public sector, the voluntary sector, and the business community, for example). The latter recommendation also involves a democratization of management (CSSM 2013a).

To follow up on these policy recommendations, Malmö City Office issued a summary of ongoing and forthcoming processes of social sustainability as decided by Malmö City Executive Board. In the foreword to this document, entitled *Continuing Work for a Socially Sustainable Malmö*, the Chief Executive Officer draws the connection between social sustainability and business development, envisioning new kinds of collaboration in the future, in accordance with the overall urban strategy:

> The work that is to be undertaken requires stakeholder involvement and the development of new collaborative initiatives, in line with the Commission's recommendations. It is also my hope that the short version can be used as a starting point for dialogue, as a support in business development and as a source of inspiration for new endeavours and collaborations in the future. (Malmö City Office 2014, 7)

In addition to the Commission, Malmö City initiated five so-called Area Programmes for Social Sustainability (Områdesprogram för social hållbarhet) that ran for a period of five years between 2010 and 2015. These area-specific programmes engaged local businesses, property owners, Malmö University, community groups, and others in an attempt to improve the general living conditions of local populations. Sabina Dethorey (2013, 313–14), who has been responsible for the Area Programme in the district of Rosengård, remarks that the ambitions are high: the programme does not just concern local development, but also aspires to contribute to the overall development of Malmö—Malmö as a whole. Taken together, the overall goal of the Area Programmes is to transform problem areas of the city into innovation areas, in accordance with the hope of converting problems into resources for the city as a whole (Malmö City 2012). This goal is also emphasized by the Institute for Sustainable City Development (Institutet för hållbar stadsutveckling, ISU), a joint venture between Malmö City and Malmö University, which serves as a forum for researchers and practitioners and promotes a 'holistic' approach to sustainable city development (ISU 2012).

This wide-ranging engagement notwithstanding, when the first interim report on the Area Programmes came up for consideration in 2012, local decision makers raised a number of critical questions in *Sydsvenskan*, the local newspaper, on 13 October 2012: How do the various partners work together? How do the programmes involve local residents? What about businesses? How much do the Area Programmes cost? Have they created any jobs? Given that the reason for the social sustainability programmes' existence is purported to be both renewal and integration, it is somewhat ironic that many elected politicians, including the then-mayor Illmar Reepalu, used the press to characterize the programmes as isolated islands, slightly detached from the municipality's other activities. In contrast to Olsson and Rosberg—the urban strategists who emphasize the democratic element of transparency in strategy and make a connection between open discussion and a culture of growth—the local politicians hint at a democratic deficit inherent in the strategy process. Their criticism, however focused it may be on urban development, indicates that the actual goal of the social sustainability agenda is to mobilize people around a set of predefined ideas, rather than engaging people politically through the established, elected bodies (Kornberger & Clegg 2011).

Many previous efforts to achieve social sustainability in Malmö have not yielded the desired results (Dethorey 2013, 312). The question remains whether the Malmö Commission's call for a democratization of management will effect any substantial change in politics, let alone whether the relationship between growth and welfare will be substantively altered towards a more distributive model that highlights social investment, as suggested by the Commission's final report (see also Stigendal 2014). Katarina Nylund (2014) is not overly optimistic, remarking that while the previous long-term urban strategy plan advocated special initiatives to offer weak groups influence over their own living conditions, citizen participation as a means of engaging underprivileged groups in planning processes is remarkably downplayed in the most recent policy document. She notes that in the current strategy plan, businesses and property owners are included on an equal footing with residents (ibid. 54).

The strategic framing of social sustainability

Social sustainability initiatives in Malmö might have a certain impact on the definition of goals for sustainable development (substantive aspects) as well as the means to achieve these goals (procedural aspects) (see Boström 2012, 6). However, as Åsa Vifell and Renita Thedvall (2012, 57) argue, when the process of defining social sustainability is moved from the political arena into managerial, bureaucratic hands, then power struggles and the political aspects of negotiation are obscured. They maintain that state actors' meta governance practices constitute 'governance through bureaucratization', as a filter of formalization, precision, and visibility determines how the social dimension of sustainable development could be turned into policy (ibid. 51, 56). More than fostering democratic transparency and discussion, therefore, the strategic framing of social sustainability seems to represent what Aletta Norval (1990, 146) describes as a technocraticism, attempting to depoliticize areas of potential conflict by constructing non-antagonistic identities.

In his study of the newly planned district of Hyllie in the south of Malmö, Guy Baeten (2012, 39) underlines that urban development has become a managerial issue: 'The total convergence of social, economic and political concern is ... what has depoliticised development in Hyllie'. As he sees it, the Malmö planning community risks becoming the administrative wing of a profit-seeking development regime, driven by an unbridled belief in economic growth and the possibility of building away unwanted deprivation (ibid. 22–3). He goes on to argue that urban planning has become a matter of strategy, where communication processes aim to create a single discourse (ibid. 38; see also Gressgård 2015b; Nylund 2014). Recalling the strategic framing of social sustainability described above, this suggests that the sort of knowledge alliances advocated by the Malmö Commission risk turning into what Tove Dannestam (2008, 365), drawing on Maarten A. Hajer (1993), describes as discourse coalitions in urban politics. A discourse coalition is, as Hajer (1993, 45) describes it, a group of actors who share a social construct (such as social sustainability).

Take the political process to be the mobilization of bias, as Hajer does in a British context and Dannestam in a Swedish context, and it becomes clear that communication strategies are deliberately used to change people's understanding of the nature of the city into an all-embracing understanding of problems and opportunities (Dannestam 2008, 358, 363; Kornberger 2012; Kornberger & Clegg 2011). We have seen that there is a wish in policy circles to establish a common standard for urban development, based on a vision of a common future, and as João A. Baptista (2014, 359) reminds us, sustainability is a potent discursive tool in this respect, inasmuch as it is anchored in a powerful trope: the future. He emphasizes that the solutions to identified problems gesture towards an idealized common future—a singular representation of the future brought by sustainability (ibid., 364). With a strategic framing, discourses of sustainability serve to legitimize present interventions, which suggests that the future is a discursive representation that ultimately is used to govern in the present (ibid., 362 ff.). Kornberger (2012, 91) asserts that strategy is not about the future, but about a shared belief in the future.

Instead of asserting—as Schlossberg and Zimmerman (2003, 654) do in their discussion of the different elements of sustainability—that the creation of public policy is inherently political, it seems pertinent to ask whether the inherent vagueness and visionary dimension of sustainability contribute to its broad appeal and depoliticized status (Boström 2012, 3, 11; Gressgård 2015b). For instance, in his study of social sustainability policy in Vancouver, Mark Davidson (2010a, 398–403) found that, irrespective of the actual impact the social sustainability agenda had on housing affordability, social welfare, segregation, and so on, many practitioners carried on working towards, fighting for and implementing social sustainability because it offered a common platform—a feeling of a new coherence—for policy agendas across governmental and non-governmental fields. Davidson's study suggests that the depoliticized social sustainability agenda in fact facilitates connections between expert fields, businesses, and governmental bodies, and its protagonists are often present in several of these arenas at once. Along similar, albeit more optimistic, lines, Michael Cuthill (2009, 364) notes that social sustainability provides an umbrella under which different perspectives could be sheltered because it does not carry any political or academic baggage from previous use (see also Gressgård 2015b). Davidson (2010b, 88), in noting his concern that 'Old antagonisms are seemingly obscured and/or removed thanks to sustainability', underscores the strategic, legitimizing function of sustainability. Paraphrasing Kornberger and Clegg (2011, 149), we may infer that the vocabulary of sustainability serves to legitimate the visionary big picture in which the interests of a few collide with the illusions—or fantasies—of the many.

Above all, the strategic framing of social sustainability works to strengthen the imagination of the city as a coherent entity, with some uneven internal development 'to be smoothed out still' (Massey 2005, 158). A case in point is the Malmö Commission's emphasis on 'the whole city' in its approach to marginalization and spatial segregation, which translates into 'the city as a whole' when discussed within the frame of urban strategy. For instance, at the Commission's concluding conference, which took place in September 2013, its chairman spoke of the future city as a whole ('ett framtida *helt* Malmö'), while others, in talking about a shared ambition and future vision of a sustainable society, emphasized the importance of consensus (CSSM 2013b, 7, 37). The holistic ambition is further underscored in the published conference proceedings, whose editors draw a parallel between the integrated system of social, ecological, and economic sustainability on the one hand and the human organ system or organic whole on the other. In particular, they use the organic metaphor to stress the interconnectedness of welfare and economic growth (CSSM 2013b, 8–9). Similarly, in reflecting on the Final report, Per-Olof Östergren (2014, 521ff.) draws a parallel to the human body—to the biological system—when explaining that there is a tipping point in each society's social sustainability.

Beyond that point, he contends, society stops functioning, the social contract can no longer be sustained, and society falls apart.

Concluding remarks

It is beyond the scope of this analysis to problematize the demand for measurable goals (quantification) implied by research aimed at identifying past failures and initiating restorative action for the future. Neither has it been my intention to fill the empty conceptual space of social sustainability in order to overcome its inherent vagueness and make it more useful for researchers and policymakers (see, for example, Boström 2012, 11; Davidson 2009, 610). The point here is that the strategic framing of social sustainability reproduces idealized and idealizing notions of urban society, while directing attention away from diverging representations of the city and conflicting policy goals. Sustainability's unifying vision is matched by a distinct sense of temporality: a one-trajectory development towards an idealized future—*the* future (Baptista 2014; Massey 2005). Accordingly, differences—especially cultural differences associated with ethnic minority populations—are taken to be alternately disturbing (a problem) or desirable (a resource) for the city's overall development, based on predefined criteria of success. I would argue that as long as the overall goal of social sustainability initiatives is to transform immigrant-dense problem city districts into innovation areas, it is likely that the social sustainability agenda will continue the dominant structure, working to marginalize vulnerable populations rather than challenging the status quo.

Notes

[1] This essay presents findings from the research project 'Planning for pluralism in Malmö', supported by a research grant from the Meltzer Fund of the University of Bergen. I wish to thank the other contributors to the present volume and the members of the Social Sustainability and Social Disintegration in Scandinavian Cities (SSSDSC) network and their convenor Erica Righard for their valuable comments on earlier versions of this essay.

References

Ærø, T. & G. Jørgensen (2005) *Implementering av bypolitik i Norden* [Implementation of urban politics in the nordic countries] (Copenhagen: Nordic Council of Ministers).

Baeten, G. (2012) 'Normalising neoliberal planning: The case of Malmö, Sweden', in T. Tasan-Kok & G. Baeten (eds.) *Contradictions in neoliberal planning, cities, policies and politics* (London: Springer).

Baptista, J. A. (2014) 'The ideology of sustainability and the globalization of a future', *Time & Society*, 23/3, 358–79.

Beatley, T. (2012) 'Sustainability in planning: The arc and trajectory of a movement, and new directions for the twenty-first-century city', in B. Sanyal, L. J. Vale & C. D. Rosen (eds.) *Planning ideas that matter: Livability, territoriality, governance, and reflective practice* (Cambridge, MA: MIT).

Boström, M. (2012) 'A missing pillar? Challenges in theorizing and practicing social sustainability: Introduction to the special issue', *Sustainability: Science, Practice, & Policy* 8/1, 3–14.

Bröckling, U. (2011) 'Human economy, human capital: A critique of biopolitical economy', in U. Bröckling, S. Krasmann & T. Lemke (eds.) *Governmentality: Current issues and future challenges* (London: Routledge).

Clavier, B. & A. Kauppinen (2013) 'Art for integration: Political rationalities and technologies of governmentalisation in the city of Malmö', *Identities: Global Studies in Culture and Power* 21/2, 10–25.

CSSM (Commission for a Socially Sustainable Malmö) (2013a) *Malmö's path towards a sustainable future: Health, welfare and justice* (*Malmös väg mot en hållbar framtid*), <http://www.malmo.se/kommission>, accessed 12 February 2014.

CSSM (2013b) *Malmös väg mot en hållbar framtid: Dokumentation från Malmökommissionens konferens på Slagthuset den 10 september 2013* [Malmö's path towards a sustainable future: Report from the Malmö Commission's concluding conference at Slagthuset, 10 September 2013], <http://malmo.se/download/18.29aeafd-91411614c896da0b/1383647131879/Malm%C3%B6kommissionen+10+september+dokumentation.pdf>, accessed 16 March 2015.

Cuthill, M. (2009) 'Strengthening the "social" in sustainable development: developing a conceptual framework for social sustainability in a rapid urban growth region in Australia', *Sustainable Development*, 18/6, 362–73.

Dannestam, T. (2008) 'Rethinking local politics: Towards a cultural political economy of entrepreneurial cities', *Space and Polity*, 12/3, 353–72.

Davidson, M. (2009) 'Social sustainability: A potential for politics?', *Local Environment*, 14/7, 607–619.

—— (2010a) 'Sustainability as ideological praxis: The acting out of planning's master-signifier', *City: Analysis of urban trends, culture, theory, policy, action*, 14/4, 390–405.

—— (2010b) 'Hacking away at sustainability: Science, ideology and cynical blockage', *Human Geography*, 3/2, 83–90.

Dempsey, N., G. Bramley, A. Power & C. Brown (2011) 'The social dimension of social sustainable development: Defining urban social sustainability', *Sustainable Development*, 19/5, 289–300.

Dethorey, S. (2013) 'Malmö: Giving social sustainability substance—the district programme in Rosengård', in M. J. Lundström, C. Fredriksson & J. Witzell (eds.) *Planning and sustainable urban development in Sweden* (Stockholm: Swedish Society for Town & Country Planning).

Florida, R. (2002) *The rise of the creative class, and how it's transforming work, leisure, community, and everyday life* (New York: Basic).

—— (2012) *The Rise of the Creative Class* (10th Anniversary edn., New York: Basic Books).

Gressgård, R. (2015a) 'The instrumentalization of urban sexual diversity in a civilizational frame of tolerance and cosmopolitanism', in N. Dhawan, A. Engel, J. J. Govrin, C. Holzhey & V. Woltersdorff (eds.) *Global justice and desire: Queering economy* (London: Routledge).

—— (2015b) 'The power of (re)attachment in urban strategy: Interrogating the framing of social sustainability in Malmö', *Environment & Planning A*, 47/1, 108–20.

Hajer, M. (1993) 'Discourse coalitions and the institutionalization of practice: The case of acid rain in Great Britain', in F. Fisher & J. Forester (eds.) *The argumentative turn in policy analysis and planning* (Durham: Duke University Press).

ISSUU (Delegation for Sustainable Cities) (2010) 'Sustainable cities: Experiences and conclusion so far' (Stockholm: Delegation for Sustainable Cities) <http://issuu.com/delegationen/docs/sustainable_cities_english/3?e=3988031/3467888>, accessed 5 June 2012.

ISU (Institute for Sustainable City Development) (2012), <http://www.isumalmo.se/isu/>, accessed 5 June 2012.

Kornberger, M. & S. Clegg (2011) 'Strategy as performative practice', *Strategic Organization*, 9/2, 136–62.

—— (2012) 'Governing the city: From planning to urban strategy', *Theory, Culture & Society*, 29/2, 84–106.

Lithman, Y. (2010) 'The holistic ambition: Social cohesion and the culturalization of citizenship', *Ethnicities* 10/4, 488–502.

Littig, B. & E. Grießler (2005) 'Social sustainability: A catchword between political pragmatism and social theory', *International Journal of Sustainable Development*, 8/1–2, 65–79.

Malmö City (2012) *Områdesprogram* [Area programmes], <http://www.malmo.se/Kommun--politik/Sa-arbetar-vi-med../Omradesprogram/Vad-ar-Omradesprogrammen.html>, accessed 5 June 2012.

Malmö City Executive Board (2010) *Directive 2010/11/09 on the Commission for a Socially Sustainable Malmö*, <http://www.malmo.se/download/18.29c3b78a132728ecb52800018806/Direktiv%2BKommissionen%2Bf%C3%B6r%2Bsocialt%2Bh%C3%A5llbart%2BMalm%C3%B6.pdf >, accessed 10 October 2015.

Malmö City Office (2014) *Continuing Work for a Socially Sustainable Malmö: An Approach for the City of Malmö from 2014,* <http://malmo.se/download/18.7de6400c149d2490efb23ad3/1416817001145/Continuing_work_socially_sustainable_Malmo.pdf>, accessed 1 July 2015.

Malmö City Planning Office (2011a) *Översiktsplan för Malmö 2012* [Overview plan for Malmö 2012], Planning Strategy 2012–2032, <http://www.malmo.se/Medborgare/Stadsplanering--trafik/Stadsplanering--visioner/Oversiktsplaner--strategier/Forslag-till-ny-oversiktsplan-OP2012.html>, accessed 1 September 2011.

—— (2011b) *Malmö—dags för nästa kliv!* [Malmö—Time for the next step!], <http://malmo.se/download/18.29c3b78a132728ecb52800013322/%C3%96P2012-broschyr.pdf>, accessed 10 October 2015.

Manzi, T., K. Lucas, T. Lloyd-Jones & J. Allen (2010) *Social sustainability in urban areas: Communities, connectivity and the urban fabric* (Washington, DC: Earthscan).

Massey, D. (2005) *For space* (London: SAGE).

Ministry of Integration (2002) *På rätt väg? Slutrapport från den nationella utvärderingen av storstadssatsningen* [Moving in the right direction? Final report from the national evaluation of the metropolitan policy] (Rapportserie 2002:05; Stockholm: Integrationsverket).

Mukhtar-Landgren, D. (2008) 'Kommunal planering i delade städer: Målkonflikter i urbana visioner och kommunala roller' [Municipal planning in divided cities], in G. Graninger & C. Knuthammar (eds.) *Samhällsbyggande och integration: Frågor om assimilation, mångfald och boende* [Formation of society and integration] (Linköping: Stiftelsen Vadstena Forum för samhällsbyggande).

—— (2012). *Planering för framsteg och gemenskap: Om den kommunala utvecklingsplaneringens idémässiga förutsättningar* [Planning for progress and community: On the underlying conceptual assumptions of municipal development planning] (Ph.D. diss., Lund Political Studies 167; Lund: Lund University).

Nordic City Network (2015) <http://www.nordiccitynetwork.com/>, accessed 1 July 2015.

Norval, A. J. (1990) 'Letter to Ernesto', in E. Laclau (ed.), *New reflections on the revolution of our time* (London: Verso).

Nylund, K. (2014) 'Conceptions of justice in the planning of the new urban landscape: Recent changes in the comprehensive planning discourse in Malmö, Sweden', *Planning Theory & Practice*, 15/1, 41–61.

Olsson, M. & G. Rosberg (2007) 'Malmö: From blue-collar city to knowledge and culture city', *Topos*, 2/2007, 28–33.

Polèse, M. & R. Stren (2000) (eds.) *The social sustainability of cities: Diversity and the management of change* (Toronto: University of Toronto Press).

Purcell, M. (2003) 'Citizenship and the right to the global city: Reimagining the capitalist world order', *International Journal of Urban & Regional Research*, 27(3): 564–90.

Schlossberg, M. & A. Zimmerman (2003) 'Developing statewide indices of environmental, economic, and social sustainability: A look at Oregon and the Oregon Benchmarks', *Local Environment* 8/6, 641–60.

Stigendal, M. (2014) 'Varför ska Malmö finnas?' [Why should Malmö exist?], *Socialmedicinsk tidskrift*, 91/5, 505–12.

Sustainable City (2012) 'Swedish Hållbar stad webpage', <http://hallbarstad.se/om-oss>, accessed 5 June 2012.

Thematic Meetings (2011) 'Thematic meetings homepage', <www.malmo.se/op-temakvallar>, accessed 5 June 2012.

Thrift, N. (1999) 'The Place of Complexity', *Theory, Culture & Society*, 16/3, 31–69.

Throgmorton, J.A. (2003) 'Planning as persuasive storytelling in a global-scale web of relationships', *Planning Theory*, 2/2, 125–51.

Vifell, Å. C. & R. Thedvall (2012) 'Organizing for social sustainability: Governance through bureaucratization in meta-organizations', *Sustainability: Science, Practice, & Policy*, 8/1, 50–8.

CHAPTER 11

Segregation of living conditions in Nørrebro

Iver Hornemann Møller & Jørgen Elm Larsen

Social sustainability and justice in cities are dependent on many things, not least mutual respect and recognition between different groups, majorities, and minorities, and the ability to create decent living conditions and a relatively fair and equal distribution of resources among its inhabitants. With this and the relations between ethnic Danes and immigrants in mind, we look at the city of Copenhagen, and in particular one of its districts, Nørrebro, where one of the highest concentrations of immigrants and their descendants is to be found. We begin with a brief introduction to the national and local integration policies in Copenhagen in recent decades before detailing the discrepancies between the living conditions of the Danes and immigrants and their descendants in Nørrebro, showing that all the groups—Danes and immigrants alike—consider there to be a high degree of respect and mutual recognition in everyday social interactions, and that immigrants (Muslims) experience the local welfare institutions such as schools and hospitals as accommodating their particular needs. Finally, we address the tensions and discrepancies between the national xenophobic policies and Copenhagen's own policies; the tensions between the inhabitants of Nørrebro and the national policies and the media; and what seems to be the growing tension between immigrants' and Danes' mutual recognition on the one hand and the large differences in their living conditions on the other, which in turn could lead to a growing immigrant precariat. In this, we have drawn on a range of material, including policy documents, demographic data, income and living conditions in general, and a survey of and qualitative interviews with Nørrebro's inhabitants (At Home in Europe Project 2011). First, however, we will detail the analytical tools we have used to analyse integration in terms of recognition and redistribution.

Recognition and justice in the city

The data and the overall understanding of segregation and integration have been interpreted using the concepts of redistribution, recognition, and political representations, as formulated by Honneth (1995) and Fraser (1992, 2000, 2008). Honneth speaks of three patterns of inter-subjective recognition: love, rights, and solidarity. The first pattern centres on basic human relationships, for example love and care between a few people who are close. The second pattern is legal: self-respect can only develop fully where the individual is recognized as an autonomous actor, and has the characteristic of universal equal treatment. The third pattern constituting recognition is self-esteem. The individual has self-ascribed fame, prestige, and recognition that ultimately springs from personal qualities and presentations—the individual is recognized as a person who has capabilities valued by the community. Honneth's theory can be seen as a normative frame of reference when analysing different forms of recognition and its opposite, disrespect. However, his theory cannot stand alone. If we are to address different groups of people's demands for recognition in relation to one another's justifications, then we also need a theory of justification. Therefore, we use Fraser's theory as a supplement to Honneth's, for she speaks about justice requiring both equal distribution and recognition.

According to Fraser, the task is to devise a three-dimensional conception of justice that can accommodate both defensible claims for social equality and a recognition of difference. The leitmotif of Fraser's work is to formulate a theory of social justice, which identifies and defends those versions of the cultural politics of difference that can be coherently combined with the social politics of equality and parity in representation. The three dimensions posit very different conceptions of injustice. Redistribution focuses on injustices that it defines as socio-economic, and presumes to be rooted in the economic structures of society, for example, being denied an adequate material standard of living. Recognition targets injustices it understands as cultural, which it sees as rooted in social patterns of interpretation and communication, for example cultural domination and disrespect. Representation serves in part to account for 'ordinary political injustices', which arise internally within bounded political communities, when skewed rules of decision-making compromise the political voice of some who are already counted as members, impairing their ability to participate as peers in social interaction.

While the remedy for social injustice, Fraser maintains, might involve redistributing income, reorganizing the division of labour, or more radically transforming basic economic structures, the remedy for cultural justice, in contrast, is some sort of cultural change. This latter point is at the heart of Mouzelis's concept of polylogic integration. Mouzelis (1995) distinguishes between a range of ideal modes of multiculturalism, of which, inspired by Habermas, he privileges the polylogic integration that respects the autonomy and internal logic of the various cultural identities and traditions, while insisting on building a two-way bridge of communication between them.

In addition, Titmuss's concept of positive selectivism (1974) will be related to Fraser's concept of redistribution. Titmuss argued that welfare universalism could have problems with meeting the particular needs of specific groups, and legal equality does not always mean equality in outcome. He consequently suggested that universalism should in a number of cases be combined with positive selectivism, where extra resources would make the distribution of income more equal. Thompson and Hoggett (1996) have suggested that in addition to positive selectivism, there is a need for a particularism that goes beyond the limitations of selectivism. This implies a universal/egalitarian welfare state with built-in opportunities for varying standards of special treatment for specific individuals and groups, thus supplementing the principle of positive selectivism.

National and local integration policies in Copenhagen

Especially in the last ten years, Denmark's national integration policy and Copenhagen's local integration policy have in many ways moved in opposite directions. The Danish integration policy towards immigrants and refugees can be divided into three phases (Ejrnæs 2014). During the first phase, from the Second World War until the mid-1960s, only a few refugees and immigrants made their way to Denmark. At the peak of the economic boom there was a shortage of labour, and Denmark started to recruit workers, especially from Turkey. They were expected to return to their home countries when they were no longer needed, and therefore there were no nationally, coordinated integration efforts and immigrants were only granted a handful of civil, social, and political rights.

The second phase was the period from the early 1980s to 1999. During the economic crisis and rising unemployment of the late 1970s and 1980s, it became clear that immigrant workers were not returning to their home countries as expected. Due to new laws on family reunion and a steady flow of refugees, the number of immigrants and asylum seekers steadily rose, especially in the late 1990s. Since the early 1990s, immigrants and refugees from non-Western countries have outnumbered those from Western countries. From 1980 to 2014, the total number of immigrants (including refugees who have been granted permanent residence in Denmark) and their descendants grew from approximately 150,000 to 620,000, or 11.1 per cent of the Danish population (Danmarks Statistik 2014).

During the 1980s and 1990s, integration policies mostly focused on integrating immigrants into Danish society by granting them civil, social, and political rights such as access to benefits, healthcare, education, and suffrage. In this period, the emphasis was not on assimilation. Instead, they were expected to participate in different arenas in the Danish society on equal terms with ethnic Danes, while at the same time being able to uphold their own cultural traditions (Mikkelsen 2008).

The ongoing third phase began in 1999, a time which has seen immigration and integration policies become major political issues, and negative attitudes towards immigration and especially immigrants from non-Western countries have been fuelled by the Danish People's Party's harsh rhetoric and growing political influence on immigration and integration. The focus has been on immigrants' relatively low labour market participation, their ghettoization in large housing estates, and their lack of willingness to integrate into

Danish society—indeed, it has been said that they are creating 'parallel societies' (Andersen et al. 2009). The emphasis was now far more on duties than on rights. In 1999, Parliament passed the Integration Act, which stressed refugees' duty to participate in Danish language courses and activation measures, at the same time as their social benefits were substantially reduced (Müller et al. 2015). This course of action was intensified under the Liberal-Conservative government (supported by the Danish People's Party) in 2001–2011. Integration for both men and women was now almost synonymous with integration into the labour market. The period also saw restrictions on immigration, but due to the increase in refugees and the EU rules of free movement between member states, the number of arrivals continued to rise. Although the centre-left government of 2011–2015 abolished the lower grades of benefits, it still largely followed the same type of integration policy that had been set out by earlier Liberal-Conservative governments.

Copenhagen, meanwhile, has in many ways tried to move in a different, if not almost opposite, direction to the national approach to integration. Copenhagen City Council has been more active than most Danish local authorities in framing and pursuing an immigrant integration policy in terms of religious, cultural, and economic recognition. The first major integration programme was implemented in 2007, because the City Council recognized that Copenhagen in recent decades had become a multi-ethnic city, and it had decided that ethnic diversity had 'the potential to improve Copenhagen's status as a large city in a constantly changing, diversified world' (Københavns Kommune 2007–2010).

The second programme (Københavns Kommune 2011–2014) rests on three principles of integration. The first is that diversity is strength—the diversity of Copenhagen's population can be a force for good in, for example, the workplace, and it is a strength to be able to use two languages. The second is that everyone should have the possibility to participate, meaning that all should be treated equally, if not necessarily in the same manner. Titmuss's conception (1974) of positive selectivism is evident in the statement that if someone needs extra help to be able to participate they shall receive it. The third and last is Mouzelis's ideal of polylogic integration (1995), as when the programme states that 'Citizenship concerns everybody. Everybody has a responsibility for inclusion, and if more people are to identify themselves as Copenhageners, there should be established partnerships across the city where everybody contributes and takes responsibility' (Københavns Kommune 2011–2014, 7). The policy has four stated target areas with specified goals: (*i*) all children and young people should have a decent start in life (as will be seen, it is particularly boys from immigrant families who leave the educational system without any vocational or similar training); (*ii*) inclusion in the labour market (since the employment situation for migrants in Copenhagen is much worse than for ethnic Danes, it comes as no surprise that employment is a key point); (*iii*) a helping hand should be given to socially vulnerable people and areas in the city, exemplifying Fraser's principle of redistribution (1992, 2000), with special attention paid to increasing the number of immigrant children who attend daycare and other child and youth facilities; and (*iv*) an open and accommodating metropolis, with fewer people excluded from participating in community life due to poverty, and fewer experiencing discrimination. As will be seen, the experience of discrimination is especially high among immigrants and their descendants.

As a policy programme for integration, the plan can be characterized as ambitious, coherent, and detailed, with action plans and devolution of responsibility to various municipal departments listed for each vision and policy goal. A central principle of the policy is to enhance the participation of all citizens and thereby contribute to increased communication between immigrants and Danes, which again can lead to more recognition and acceptance of one another's norms and values (Mouzelis 1995). It is recognized by the City Council that socio-economic conditions and inequalities are central issues, although as regards to its redistribution policies, the City Council's hands are often tied, especially when it comes to the redistribution of incomes, which is mainly decided at the national level—a failure of structural capability in Sen's understanding (1992).

Nørrebro

Nørrebro is one of the ten districts of Copenhagen, and the one with the highest population density (18,500 per square kilometre). It has its own specific character. Traditionally, it was a working-class area, but regeneration programmes and slum clearances in the 1970s onwards led to changes in the area's demography, driven by the availability of new social housing, which provided opportunities for many young people, students, and migrant families to move into the area. By 2009, 27 per cent of its 78,000 inhabitants were either immigrants or their descendants (Københavns Kommune 2014), while more than half of the immigrants and their descendants come from countries where Muslims are either in the majority or a substantial minority (Schmidt 2012).

Today, Nørrebro's residents are characterized by a segregation based on both class and ethnicity; however, it does *not* constitute a hyper ghetto in Wacquant's sense (2008), if only because it is not sealed off from the rest of the city. Neither has Nørrebro been abandoned in terms of public institutions, sports facilities, and the like. Many of the residents are old-age pensioners or belong to the industrial reserve army of labour (here defined as people of working age who have been unemployed for at least ten months in the last twelve and who live on benefits). Decades of liberalistic incursions into Danish social policy have pushed a considerable number of the latter below the poverty line, particularly long-term recipients of benefits and immigrants (Møller 2011). Yet there is also a group of residents in Nørrebro who belong to the middle class and predominantly support left-wing policies. At the last municipal elections in 2013, the left-wing parties (including the Social Democrats) received 67 per cent of the vote (Københavns Kommune 2013).

Nørrebro has always been a locus for immigration. A hundred years ago, industrialization saw large numbers of agricultural labourers settle in the area; in recent decades, the majority of immigrants have come from countries with a Muslim majority population (Schmidt 2012). The residents of Nørrebro have always been known for showing strong solidarity with the underprivileged segments of society and have demonstrated against racism and right-wing extremism more than anywhere else in Copenhagen. It is a dynamic area that on several occasions, some as far back as the 1980s, has been the scene of violent clashes between the police and local squatters and autonomous groups. In May 1993, following the Danish yes vote on accession to the EU, the Nørrebro district, which had emphatically voted no, was the scene of riots during which the police shot at demonstrators. In the spring of 2008, it witnessed one of the worst riots in Danish history, this time involving young men from predominantly immigrant communities who expressed their frustration with frequent police stop-and-searches and blamed the police for being 'brutal', 'racist', and exercising 'utterly unacceptable intimidation' (*Politiken* 2008). This and other similar occasions of fierce rioting by young immigrants in the streets and squares of Nørrebro are thus far from new phenomena, but have evolved with the makeup of the area. Clearly, the way in which immigrants in Nørrebro use the space in their neighbourhood to do politics is their approach to building on relationships, especially ones with long historical roots (Schmidt 2012).

In recent decades, as Nørrebro changed character from a traditional working-class area to a multi-ethnic and multi-class district, the neighbouring district, Vesterbro, has undergone comprehensive gentrification programmes that transformed it from a typical working-class area into a district with many middle-class and high-income groups (Larsen & Hansen 2012). And while Vesterbro borders Nørrebro to the west, the Frederiksberg area, dominated by the classic urban bourgeoisie, is its neighbour to the north-west. This contributes to the feeling that Nørrebro is something very specific, and has attracted intense and largely negative media scrutiny over many years, the focus being the simmering conflicts and spectacular clashes between the police and immigrants.

Living in Nørrebro

Despite the Copenhagen City Council's policy of redistribution in favour of the least privileged inhabitants, large differences remain in socio-economic living conditions between immigrants and ethnic Danes, while, as we will see in the case of Nørrebro, there is nevertheless a high degree of interaction and recognition between these two groups.

Copenhagen is among the Danish municipalities with the lowest average disposable income—an average of DKK 211,400 a year (AE Rådet 2012). However, the internal differences are significant. There are almost twice as many households in Nørrebro than in Copenhagen as a whole that have an annual income below DKK 100,000, and in Nørrebro only 4.2 per cent of households have an annual income above DKK 700,000, compared with 8.2 per cent of households in Copenhagen. Around half of the immigrants aged between 15 and 24 have no publicly registered income, compared to around 15 per cent of ethnic Danes of the same age (CASA 2013); the data do not reveal whether they are provided for by their families, or whether they rely on the black economy or criminal activity.

In 2009, Copenhagen was the municipality with the highest percentage of poor people (the poverty line being defined as 50 per cent of the median national income): 7.6 per cent, compared to 4.4 per cent for Denmark as a whole, excluding students (AE Rådet 2011a). Poverty in Copenhagen is very unevenly spread across its districts and parishes. Two out of the five parishes with the highest poverty rates are located in Nørrebro, with 10.1 and 9.8 per cent respectively living below the poverty line. In 2005, adding together the poverty percentages for immigrants and their descendants, measured in relation to their proportion of the Copenhagen population, 30 per cent of all immigrants and their decedents were living in poverty, compared with 17 per cent of Danes—although it should be noted that these data are taken from the Copenhagen Survey (Københavns Kommune 2008) and are thus not immediately comparable with the other poverty data, being arrived at by the budget method, with a poverty line greater than 50 per cent of median income. In response, Copenhagen City Council has tried to combat poverty in various ways, for example by taking the initiative in capacity-building support for NGOs and other organizations that provide information and advice to immigrant communities.

Of the ten Copenhagen parishes with the highest concentration of people with poor health, three are located in Nørrebro (AE Rådet 2010). In these three, visits to doctors and the number and cost of prescriptions are on average 2.5 times greater than for the population of Copenhagen as a whole. However, as a part of

Copenhagen City Council's integration policy there is a separate strategy on healthcare for immigrants, and in the interviews about Nørrebro's health service a large majority of immigrants expressed satisfaction with the service, singling out its recognition of different religious customs (At Home in Europe Project 2011). A number of immigrant doctors have recently been employed at the district's central hospital, the general hospital in Nørrebro has established a multi-faith prayer room, and an imam is available to provide support for patients and their families.

There is a so-called 'ghetto list' of public housing areas in Denmark that are characterized by two out of the following three criteria: (*i*) 50 per cent or more of the residents are immigrants or their descendants; (*ii*) more than 40 per cent of residents have no contact with the labour market or education; and (*iii*) a high rate of criminal convictions (Ministry of City, Housing and Rural Districts 2012). The 'ghetto list' was introduced by the former Liberal–Conservative government in 2010. Of the 33 areas listed in 2012, 8 were located in Copenhagen, and 3 of them in Nørrebro. These 'neglected' residential areas are not ethnically homogeneous, but are to a large extent inhabited by Danes. It could be argued that the 'ghetto list' is both a blessing and a curse. One the one hand, these areas attract special political attention and investment in employment, education, housing, and the like—Copenhagen City Council, for example, has established quite a number of community centres, partly financed by the municipality. On the other hand, the 'ghetto list' also tends to stigmatize these areas and their inhabitants.

Both immigrants and Danes report frequent daily and weekly interactions with people from different ethnic and religious backgrounds than their own (At Home in Europe Project 2011). There is also a clear sense of belonging, both in Copenhagen and in Nørrebro, among all groups. Contrary to Wacquant's observations from the hyper ghetto (1996), a majority of both immigrants and Danes say that some or most of the people in the neighbourhood can be trusted and that they enjoy living in the area. There is a view that neighbours get along well and are willing to help one another. Although the overall picture is far from rosy—witness the levels of discrimination and the enduring tendency in national politics and the media to be increasingly negative to migration—the general picture is that Danes living in Nørrebro, where they have frequent daily interactions with individuals from immigrant minorities, are far less biased towards immigrants than are Danes who live in provincial towns and rural areas. Rafiqi and Frølund Thomsen (2014) find something similar, and have emphasized the importance of neighbourhood and workplace interactions for the majority's tolerance vis-à-vis its minority members.

Regarding the education system, Nørrebro is the city district with the most pronounced segregation in its state schools, and in terms of school grades both boys and girls from immigrant families perform less well than Danes. Most strikingly, young men from immigrant families do not go on to or finish vocational training or the like: by the age of 26, 40 per cent of them have not had any such training whatsoever (AE Rådet 2011b). They appear to be severely marginalized; twice as many of them as Danes are unemployed and do not participate in educational activities. One of the severe problems facing those who do participate in youth training programmes is finding a placement for their obligatory work experience. This explains why so many do not finish the training programmes or even start in the first place.

This leads us to what Honneth (1995) calls disrespect or non-recognition, and which in everyday language is often labelled discrimination. This seems particularly prevalent in the education system, where many Danes from Nørrebro have moved their children to private schools in order to avoid the state schools with a high proportion of bilingual pupils. In general, however, the data on discrimination in Nørrebro are rather thin, and when it comes to the labour market, positively opaque. Sample respondents (At Home in Europe Project 2011) who had been rejected for jobs were asked about the reasons why they had been unsuccessful, and around a third of immigrants cited their ethnic or religious background as the most important factor. There is also some evidence of discrimination against immigrants over housing, in particular with respect to the waiting lists of private housing associations. The Integration Barometer (Københavns Kommune 2011), which covers all ten of Copenhagen's districts, shows that immigrants experience discrimination three times more often than Danes, and that among men that figure is even higher.

The specificity of the City Council's policy on immigrants and integration is underlined when it comes to the education system. While national legislation abolished governmental support for mother-tongue tuition for students from outside Europe, Copenhagen decided to continue its principle of positive selectivism (Titmuss 1974), by which the needs of specific groups could be met by the provision of extra resources, in this instance by offering mother-tongue tuition on an almost equal footing for all bilingual students. A range of other measures has also been initiated: support for schools to update their computer-based learning facilities, programmes involving up-skilling more than 1,000 teachers to teach Danish as a second langue, and courses on multilingualism and interculturalism, while, as an example of the City Council's particularism, there is the programme of provision of Danish-language tuition for older immigrant women.

Turning to the labour market in Nørrebro, 80.2 per cent of the Danes in 2011 were in employment, compared to 48.3 per cent of immigrants and 68.9 per cent of their descendants; whereas 16.2 per cent of the Danes were not active in the labour market (having taken early retirement, for example, or being on benefits) compared to 46.7 per cent of immigrants and 26.6 per cent of their descendants. Large differences are also evident when comparing immigrants' unemployment rates with all Copenhagen residents'. Immigrant women in 2011 had an unemployment rate that was more than one-and-a-half times higher than for all women in Copenhagen, while for men it was more than twice as high (Larsen & Møller 2013).

Recognition and integration

The frequent interaction between immigrants and Danes in Nørrebro, the residents' view that they all get along well together, and their sense of belonging and identification with the district, are taken as contributing to the greater mutual recognition (Fraser 1992, 2000) seen there, far greater than the distance between the two groups, and thus promoting and enhancing the principles of polylogic integration (Mouzelis 1995). These observations challenge one of the most popular perceptions in the national and media discourse that some residential areas in Denmark, including Nørrebro, are developing into isolated 'ethnic enclaves', leading to a 'parallel society'—with Muslims implicitly held responsible for their isolation from society at large and their lack of interest in integrating (Andersen et al. 2009).

These tensions between a national and still growing xenophobic discourse on the one hand and the noticeably high degree of mutual recognition among Nørrebro residents of different origins are exacerbated by the policy of redistribution (Fraser 1992, 2000) and the positive selectivism (Titmuss 1974) of Copenhagen City Council. Added to this is the fact that of Copenhagen's twelve local district councils—the channel where immigrants can exercise political influence (Fraser 1992, 2000)—the largest representation of immigrants is found in Nørrebro, going by Council members' names.

We have shown that there is a high degree of mutual understanding between immigrants and their descendants and ethnic Danes in Nørrebro, while at the same time there are very large differences as far as their socio-economic living conditions are concerned. In the future, Nørrebro runs the risk of becoming even more divided, since many youngsters with migrant backgrounds, and especially men, are not getting an education. Will they end up forming a precariat (Standing 2011), with insecure work, low wages, and intensified competition from low-waged labour migrants from (East) European countries? The future for Nørrebro might be a highly segregated labour market, with well-paid jobs for the upper middle class and insecure, low-paid jobs for the unskilled workers.

All in all, Nørrebro's social sustainability is likely to be tested from several directions. Besides the large differences in socio-economic living conditions between immigrants and Danes, the national and media-driven xenophobic policy threatens not only Copenhagen City Council's policy of recognition, redistribution, and integration, but also the fabric of daily life, with its frequent interactions and high degree of mutual recognition between immigrants and Danes.

Conclusion

Nørrebro, a historical locus for immigration, and today one of Copenhagen's city districts with the highest proportion of immigrants from non-Western countries (mostly Muslims), was once a working class area, but starting in the 1970s regeneration programmes have transformed it into a multi-ethnic area where many of the residents are pensioners, belong to the industrial reserve army of labour, or are students, with a small group of middle-class people. Using the conceptual tools of recognition and redistribution, the analysis has addressed the discrepancies in living conditions between immigrants and ethnic Danes in the district. In spite of a strong policy of redistribution on the part of Copenhagen City Council, the data on income, poverty, health, education, and labour market participation show significant differences between immigrants and Danes, with the former at the lower end. However, and in spite of an increasingly xenophobic national integration policy egged on by the national media, the interviews with immigrants and Danes in Nørrebro show there is a markedly high degree of daily interaction and mutual recognition between the two groups.

There are questions hanging over the future of social sustainability in Nørrebro. Can local mutual recognition be maintained, or will it be overruled by the large differences in socio-economic living conditions, perhaps by an emerging precariat of young immigrant men without any education or labour market connections? The xenophobia of national policy shows no signs of abating—what will be the impact on the mutual recognition between immigrants and Danes? Can Copenhagen City Council's policy of redistribution and recognition continue if the national government continues to restrict the Council's immigrant-friendly policy and scupper its economic plans? Only time will tell.

References

AE (Arbejderbevægelsens Erhvervsråd) (2010), *Uligheden i sundhed skærer igennem Danmarks storbyer* (Copenhagen: Arbejderbevægelsens Erhvervsråd).
AE (2011a) *Fattigdommen rammer skævt i Danmark* (Copenhagen: Arbejderbevægelsens Erhvervsråd).

AE (2011b) *Mere end hver 3 Indvandrerdreng i Danmark får ingen uddannelse* (Copenhagen: Arbejderbevægelsens Erhvervsråd).
AE (2012) *Stigende indkomstforskelle i København* (Copenhagen: Arbejderbevægelsens Erhvervsråd).
Andersen, J., J. E. Larsen & I. H. Møller (2009) 'The exclusion and marginalisation of immigrants in the Danish welfare society', *International Journal of Sociology & Social Policy*, 29/5–6, 274–86.
At Home in Europe Project (2011) *Muslims in Copenhagen* (London: Open Society Foundation).
CASA (Center for Alternativ Samfundsanalyse) (2013) *Analyse af uddannelses- og beskæftigelsesindsatserne rettet mod unge på Nørrebro* (Copenhagen: CASA).
Danmarks Statistik (2014) *Indvandrere i Danmark 2014* (Copenhagen: Danmarks Statistik).
Ejrnæs, A. (2014) 'Det etnisk mangfoldige samfund', in B. Greve, A. Jørgensen & J. E. Larsen (eds.) *Det danske samfund* (Copenhagen: Hans Reitzels Forlag).
Fraser, N. (1992) 'Recognition and redistribution', *New Left Review*, 2, 68–93.
―― (2000) 'Rethinking recognition', *New Left Review*, 3, 107–120.
―― (2008) *Scales of justice: Reimagining political space in a globalizing world* (New York: Columbia University Press).
Honneth, A. (1995) *The struggle for recognition: The moral grammar for social conflict* (Cambridge: Polity Press).
Københavns Kommune (2007–2010) City of Copenhagen integration policy, <http://www.byensboern.dk/sitecore/content/Subsites/CityOfCopenhagen/SubsiteFrontpage/LivingInCopenhagen/-/media/Integration/Integrationspolitik/Integrations%20policy.aspx>, accessed 2011.
―― (2008) *Analyse af levevilkår og fattigdom i Københavns Kommune* (Copenhagen: Københavns Kommune, Socialforvaltningen, Projektkontoret).
―― (2011) *Integrations Barometer: Bland dig i byen* (Copenhagen: Københavns Kommune, Beskæftigelses- og Integrationsforvaltningen).
―― (2011–2014) *Bland dig i byen: Medborgerskab og inklusion* (Copenhagen: Københavns Kommune, Beskæftigelses- og Integrationsforvaltningen).
―― (2013a) *Boligbarometer 2013—Faktaark* (Copenhagen: Københavns Kommune).
―― (2013b) *BR-valget den 19 november 2013* (Copenhagen: Københavns Kommune).
Larsen, H. G., Hansen, A. L. (2012) 'Retten til byen', in J. Andersen et al. (eds.) *Byen i bevægelse: Mobilitet—Politik—Performativitet* (Frederiksberg: Roskilde Universitetsforlag).
Larsen, J. E. & I. H. Møller (2013) 'The increasing socioeconomic and spatial segregation and polarization of living conditions in the Copenhagen metropolitan area', paper given at the 2013 Annual Conference of Research Committee 19, ISA, 22–24 August, Budapest, Hungary.
Marx, K. (1971) *Kapitalen* (Copenhagen: Bibliotek Rhodos).
Mikkelsen, F. (2008) *Indvandring og integration* (Copenhagen: Akademisk Forlag).

Ministry of City, housing and rural districts (2012) *Liste over særligt udsatte boligområder pr. 1 oktober 2012* (Copenhagen: Ministeriet for By, Bolig og Landdistrikter).
Mouzelis, N. (1995) *Strategies for integration and socio-cultural differentiation* (Centre for Social Integration and Differentiation, CID studies, 11; Copenhagen: Copenhagen Business School).
Müller, M., M. A. Hussain, J. E. Larsen, H. Hansen, F. K. Hansen & M. Ejrnæs (2015) *Fattigdom, afsavn og coping* (Copenhagen: Hans Reitzels Forlag).
Møller, I. H., (2011) 'Liberalismens socialpolitik', in I. H Møller & J. E. Larsen (eds.) *Socialpolitik* (Copenhagen: Hans Reitzels Forlag).
Politiken (2008) 'Boys from inner Nørrebro: The truth behind the riots', 18 February.
Rafiqi, A. & J. P. Frølund Thomsen (2014) 'Når majoritetsmedlemmer og etniske minoritetsmedlemmer mødes', *Dansk Sociologi*, 1, 83–99.
Schmidt, G. (2012) 'Grounded politics: Manifesting Muslim identity as a political factor and localized identity in Copenhagen', *Ethnicities*, 12/5, 603–22.
Sen, A. (1992) *Inequality reexamined* (Oxford: Clarendon Press).
Standing, G. (2011) *The precariat: The new dangerous class* (New York: Bloomsbury Academic).
Thompson, S. & Hoggett, P. (1996) 'Universalism, selectivism and particularism. Towards a post-modern social policy', *Critical Social Policy*, 16/26, 21–43.
Titmuss, R. (1974) *Social policy* (London: Allen & Unwin).
Wacquant, L. J. D. (1996) 'The rise of advanced marginality: Notes on its nature and implications', *Acta Sociologica*, 39, 121–39.
—— (2008) *Urban outcasts: A comparative sociology of advanced marginality* (Cambridge: Polity).

CHAPTER 12

Conflicts and meaning-making in sustainable urban development

Magnus Johansson

In this essay, an urban development project with the overarching intention of meeting the effects of crises and supporting socially sustainable development in a specific area is analysed using the phronetic approach (Flyvbjerg 2001). The empirical material is a case study of a dialogue process, which was part of a large-scale urban regeneration project in a socio-economically exposed area of the city of Malmö in southern Sweden. The aim was to create a dialogue between a property development company and the municipality that would result in the construction of new homes, thus supporting the social transformation of the area. The starting point was an application from the property developer about a housing project, which the municipality first rejected. Instead, the planning office tried to convince the property developer to adjust its plans and build something that could support local, sustainable urban development. The dialogue was very far-ranging, but in the end the company withdrew its application and abandoned the whole project.

I will argue that this failure resulted from a failure to acknowledge central value conflicts, compounded by a lack of collective meaning-making about how to handle those conflicts in order to get the project done. Mainstream sustainable urban development is dominated by a growth-dependent planning approach (Rydin 2013). Most of it is also consensus-driven, taking the standpoint that everyone agrees on the need for sustainable urban development. Even if professional planners are aware of the conflicts, they avoid facing up to them in planning processes, mainly because urban development is dependent on market-driven actors, such as property developers. I would argue that public sector planners must find ways of both recognizing and handling those value conflicts in the public–private partnerships that seem to be the norm in contemporary urban planning. This must be done through collaborative meaning-making, which allows different perspectives and new ideas to revitalize established practices.

Planning as muddling through

Today, an increasing number of Western cities seem to work with sustainable urban development in one way or another as a means of supporting growth and meeting different urban challenges. However, there are multiple ways to understand—and work with—sustainable urban development. Dobson (1996) finds over 300 definitions of sustainable development alone. A majority of those definitions presume that the ecological, social, and economic dimensions of development must be combined to support one another. In reality, fundamental conflicts of principle between the three dimensions make it hard to combine them, let alone put the vision of sustainability into practice (Campell 2010). Such conflicts are often ignored in favour of an interpretation of sustainability as something everyone thinks is good, which favours an instrumental and consensus-driven process, run by experts. In the end, sustainable urban development becomes another variation on neo-liberal urban development, driven by public–private partnerships (Baeten 2012; Krueger & Buckingham 2012).

Without disagreeing with these analyses, I will try to understand this process from the professional planners' point of view. Professional planners are an active part of consensus- and expert-driven planning, but at the same time they are trapped in the dominant discourses of growth-dependent planning (Rydin 2013). On a daily basis, the business of urban planning—just like working with sustainable urban development—is as much about muddling through and coping with well-known problems as anything else. A new challenge sometimes presents itself, and others are solved or become obsolete. This is a process of framing and reframing, translation and adjusting (Czarniawska 2002): the naming and framing transforms unfamiliar and complex problems, such as how to develop a socially sustainable city, into working tasks that are familiar and graspable. Something complex and threatening is tamed and becomes possible to handle within established communities of practices.

Working with complex issues, such as planning for sustainable urban development, could therefore be seen as an ongoing process of meaning-making, by which professionals try to transform complex problems into manageable working tasks that can be solved in the course of an ordinary work process. New ideas and concepts need to be named and framed so they can fit into what is already there, and in so doing, new ideas and new knowledge creep slowly forward into existing practice, and change underway into something that is recognizable to those who work with it (Weiss 1980).

The process of translation takes the form of ongoing negations between the members of a specific practice. In those negations, some interpretations of the problems are highlighted and some are ignored (Wenger 1998). One reason is that there is always variation in the understanding of different working tasks among the members of a specific community of practice, if only about the purpose and meaning of those tasks. There are several ways to understand similar work assignments, which in turn affect how one chooses to carry them out in practice (Sandberg & Targama 2007). These negotiations could also be read as meetings between different organizational narratives; the organizing as a process of narration which determines the ends and means of specific ways of acting, such as a certain way of administering a city (Czarniawska 2002).

The phronetic approach to planning research

As my theoretical framework, I will use a phronetic approach (Flyvbjerg 2004) to planning research. A central task of phronetic research is to provide concrete examples and detailed narratives of the ways in which power and values work in planning, and with what consequences for whom, and to suggest how relations of power and values could be changed. The approach harks back to the more general approach of phronetic social science, originally launched by Flyvbjerg (2001; Flyvbjerg et al. 2012) in response to contemporary social science. The starting point for Flyvbjerg was the Aristotelian distinction between three intellectual virtues: *episteme*, or philosophical or scientific knowledge which is true and not context-dependent; *techné*, or technical knowledge and know-how; and, last but not at least, *phronesis*, or the knowledge of what it would be good to do in given circumstances. Phronetic social science strives for knowledge that has relevance to decisions about what can and should be done. The central question is not how things are, but what matters. The analytical tool is four phronetic questions, each designed to enhance practical wisdom about how we should understand a certain situation and what should be done: (*i*) Where are we going? (*ii*) Who gains and who loses, and by which mechanisms of power? (*iii*) Is it desirable? and (*iv*) What, if anything, should be done? This last question is impossible to answer without understanding the mechanisms of power that pertain in a specific situation (Flyvbjerg 2001).

In terms of planning research, the answers to those four questions explore the consequences when urban planners use a growth-dependent planning approach in order to tackle urban inequality and social segregation. In the analysis, I will put the greatest effort into answering the last question—What, if anything, should we do about it?—in relation to the working conditions of professional urban developers. If, as an employee in a municipal planning department, you are intent on planning for sustainable urban development, what could you possibly do? Is it a hopeless cause?

Seeking answers to these questions from a phronetic standpoint, I have followed one specific case very closely—shadowing it (Czarniawska 2007)—as an evaluator of the ongoing process, taking my empirical data from participatory observations of workshops and meetings, documents related to the process, and several interviews with the public sector planners who led the process. In the end, I obtained broad and dense descriptions of the dilemmas and tensions, not to mention the conflicting goals, roles, structures, and needs, which thus illustrate and give some suggestions as to why visions of sustainability seem to be so hard to put into practice. The ultimate failure of the process I followed could be traced back to the inability of the participants to handle those dilemmas through collaborative meaning-making and shared understanding in order to move the process forward.

A narrative of sustainable urban development

In Malmö there are local narratives that name and frame the work of sustainable urban development. The first is the norm of growth-dependent planning, which is the main narrative of all Western urban development: planning must support economic growth, and without economic growth there is no need for planning (Rydin 2013). Economic sustainability becomes the end and the means, because without economic growth, there will be no room for social and ecological sustainability.

This general narrative about contemporary urban development is then named and framed by a local story of how Malmö rose from the ashes of economic crisis and soaring unemployment to become a prosperous, post-industrial, creative city. In this transformation, 'sustainability' becomes a core concept, with Malmö known all over the world for its transformation of run-down urban areas, such as the former shipyard, into new, high-profile areas with ecological buildings. The siting of a new university and the bridge to Copenhagen are also symbols of the same transformation. This narrative is repeatedly told by the city's politicians and planners. At the same time, Malmö is a city with increasing segregation, high unemployment among immigrants, and a soaring benefits bill. The rise of post-industrial Malmö has not meant prosperity for all its inhabitants (Mukhtar-Landgren 2008; Holgersson 2014).

The narrative about a divided Malmö is also told by the city officials, who are well aware that its successful transformation to a more economically and ecologically sustainable city has not resulted in a socially sustainable city. Some of the poorest urban areas in Sweden are to be found in Malmö. Poverty and a growing sense of exclusion from the rest of the society feed people's resignation and frustration. From time to time, it explodes into violent confrontations between teenage gangs and the police and other representatives of society, such as firefighters (Hallin et al. 2010). There is also a growing feeling of insecurity among inhabitants in some parts of Malmö. One result is the growing number of gated housing estates, where the inhabitants of one block of flats try to protect themselves from vandalism and burglary. The majority of the gated areas were originally apartment buildings, where the inhabitants have converted council flats into privately owned flats (Herbert 2013): the result has been fragmentation and segregation on a micro level in an already segregated city. But there are also examples of neighbourhoods in these areas which are dominated by strong social networks, where people feel secure, and where there is less vandalism compared to similar areas (Gerell 2013). Malmö's development has resulted in a city with two faces, culturally, economically, and geographically.

The prosperous, post-industrial parts of Malmö have the new university, media companies, and well-known sustainable housing estates in the north-west of the city, close to the sea. Far away from the shore, in the south-east, is the other side of Malmö: large sink estates dominated by high unemployment and some of the poorest parts of Sweden. In Malmö as in Sweden, these areas have become a symbol of the social problems related to migration and poverty. Yet suggestions of how to support different forms of socially sustainable urban development are at the same time named and framed as different versions of growth-dependent, sustainable urban development. The story of the successful transformation of the former shipyard into an exclusive area of ecological housing—the Western Harbour—seems to be the accepted norm for how to develop other areas of Malmö. But what happens when that norm meets the reality of a less prosperous part of Malmö? Rosengård is just such an area, situated in the south-east of the city.

Fokus Rosengård, a stab at regeneration

Rosengård was built in the late 1960s as one of the last parts of Sweden's Million Programme. This ambitious housing programme was a national initiative launched by the social-democratic government in the mid-1960s in order to give Swedish citizens decent housing. Approximately 500,000 houses and 500,000 flats were built. Today, the Million Programme areas have become a symbol of socio-economic deprivation, dominated by huge, run-down blocks of flats and mostly housing immigrants. In many other cities, including Stockholm and Gothenburg, these areas are located on the outskirts, with a pronounced geographical and socio-economic separation from the more central and wealthier parts of the city. In Malmö, by contrast, they are far more central, mainly because the city is so geographically concentrated compared to Stockholm and Gothenburg.

The final parts of Rosengård were completed at the same time as Malmö was hit by the first economic downturn of the 1970s, and it almost immediately become a scapegoat for social problems and urban decline (Ristilammi 1994). Those who could afford their own homes moved out to the surrounding municipalities and commuted to Malmö, which resulted in a declining population and falling tax revenues for the city. During these years, some of the largest blocks in Rosengård had only a few inhabitants in buildings with hundreds of empty flats. At the same time, the immigration patterns changed from economic migrants to refugees.

During the 1980s and 1990s, those new immigrants moved to Rosengård and its hundreds of vacant flats. Those with a Swedish background who still lived in Rosengård started to move away, and were replaced by those new refugees who struggled to find work and make a decent living. Immigrants who had been in Sweden for a longer time and had jobs followed suit, and left the area. This process transformed several parts of Rosengård into transit areas, where success was measured by being able to leave the place. A narrative of Rosengård as a place of stigmatization, segregation, and unemployment sprang up, and has stuck to the area ever since (Ristilammi 1994).

Over the years, Malmö has launched several large-scale urban regeneration projects to stem the negative processes in the area. Even if the programmes differ in goals and aims, they share the idea that it is Rosengård and its inhabitants that must change, adjusting to the dominant narrative of Malmö as the entrepreneurial and sustainable city. Thus in January 2010 the City Council launched its latest attempt to change the area. The city received SEK 28 million (about EUR 2.7 million) from the European Regional Development Fund. The overall goal of this EU programme was to support economic growth: in Sweden, the fund was managed by the Swedish Authority for Economic Growth. The main goal for the project was to use the development of infrastructure in Rosengård as a way of supporting social change through collaboration and partnerships, which would ultimately bring prosperity to the area.

Fokus Rosengård, as it was called, was designed to develop three key elements: (*i*) structures for collaboration on local urban regeneration; (*ii*) local infrastructure along a central corridor, duly christened Rosengårdsstråket (lit. the Rosengård Strip); and (*iii*) a centre for sustainable urban development. The third part was never realized, because of a lack of political will and resources. That put the project team in a difficult position, because they needed this project—or something similar—in order to get the full funding for Fokus Rosengård in its entirety. The city was wholly dependent on external money for its investment in Rosengård.

Halfway through the project a new opportunity arose, more or less coincidently, when a property developer who owned a large plot in one part of Rosengård—Kryddgården—submitted an application for a change of use in the local area plan. The property developer wanted to build a new block on a greenfield site, adjacent to its other properties. The city's planning department turned down the application, but invited the company to discuss ongoing developments elsewhere in Rosengård. The project leader for Fokus Rosengård and the planning officer who was responsible for the other development project saw an opportunity to include this new project in Fokus Rosengård. But in order to do so, they would have to convince the property developer to amend its plans.

Their ambition was to use the property developer's interest to initiate a much broader development process where the physical change (a new building) could be used to support different kinds of social change in the area. By packaging two projects—the centre, which they had long since given up on, would be part of the negotiations—the municipality could use project funding that otherwise would have to be returned to the EU, and at the same time try new forms of value-based urban planning and development. This meant that they could use resources from the project for a much more ambitious and intensive dialogue. The change was duly approved by the Swedish Authority for Economic Growth.

The case of Kryddgården

The process was realized in six workshops, held in the autumn, winter, and spring of 2012–2013. The whole process was led by the project leader, seconded from the city's environmental department, and city planning officers. The core participants were the representatives from two property developers, the first having sent in the original application, and a second one that owned the land adjacent to the first company's plot. Other participants were invited to all workshops, including representatives from private companies, people who lived in the area, administrators from other city departments, and people who worked for local NGOs. The composition varied from workshop to workshop, with the exception of the administrators who led the process and the original property developer.

At the first meeting, the participants together identified six core values for the process, based on the value programme for Rosengård that had been developed by the city's urban planning department: mixed forms of living, a sustainable economy, attractive and equal meeting points, environmental friendliness, high accessibility, and increased social values. These core values were then used in a big matrix, which was used to structure the workshops: they were placed on the x-axis, while the y-axis had several steps for the discussion of each core value, which would result in an action plan for each value. At the end of the process, the action plans for the core values would be resolved into a general action plan for Kryddgården, as the development came to be known.

The first step was to identify critical issues for each core value and the obstacles to realizing each value. In the next step, concrete actions were to be formulated and strategic stakeholders identified. After that, having formulated strategic tools, the stakeholders who would be responsible for putting them into practice would be selected from those party to the process. After each workshop, the participants would agree on what would be done by whom in order to realize the core values that had been discussed during the meeting.

The whole process was tentative, which in turn meant the participants varied from workshop to workshop. The project leader, the planning officer, and one or several representatives from the property developer took part in all the workshops. Guests and specific stakeholders were invited to some of the workshops where they could contribute their knowledge and specific perspectives. The project leader justified this as a way of hearing a broad range of ideas, visions, and needs from different stakeholders, which would be important for the development of Kryddgården.

What, then, of the impact of global ideas and discourses on this specific local process? At first sight, the matrix and the related method of proceeding seemed to be an excellent way of structuring the processes of governance, where a municipality had to collaborate with different stakeholders in order to reach a common goal—in this case, to initiate social change that would take advantage of tangible investment in a low-income area. During the processes, no one disagreed about the core values. However, the turn of events shows there was heated disagreement about the best way to put those values into practice. The most obvious tension was over who should bear the financial cost of different investments in the development. When the discussions touched on the question of financing investments to realize core values, the property developers became very emphatic on the need for the municipality to support the development economically. Even if they agreed about the values, and that they as private companies would benefit from any investment, the discussions always ended up focusing on who should take the financial risk. Here, Rosengård's bad reputation scared the property developers into arguing that the City Council would have to provide subsidies, because the financial risk of building in an area like Rosengård was higher than in other parts of Malmö.

A similar kind of argument was raised by the representatives of a large national bank, who took part in the workshop on the second core value, the sustainable economy. The aim of the workshop was to discuss how local businesses could be developed as a way to raise income levels in the area. The bank representatives agreed that applications for loans for commercial start-ups would of course be assessed according to whether the idea was businesslike or not. However, they politely explained, prejudices about the area could be an obstacle, and could well affect assessments of a business idea, even if the local representatives from the bank would like to give it a try. These arguments affected how the project team organized the workshop on the third core value, attractive and equal meeting points. An expert on place-based marketing was invited to speak on the importance of changing Rosengård's 'trademark' in order to attract investors and resources.

The first two workshops were devoted to attempts by the city's representatives to convince the property developers that they should build housing with space for commercial enterprises, such as small cafes and corner shops. The picture that the municipality tried to paint was of an urban area with cool cafes, grocery stores with ecological products, and a young, urban middle class. Naturally, the property developers were far less convinced that it would be possible to create this environment in Rosengård, because of the area's reputation and population. They countered by asking the City Council for financial support and other forms of tangible assistance, because 'We're taking the financial risks'. The City Council responded that they could not favour specific private companies for several reasons, the main stumbling block being that the process had to follow the same economic rules throughout—and play 'the market game'. This was as far as the discussions got, because all parties became locked into their positions.

Halfway through the process, both property developers started to lose interest and failed to appear at planned workshops. One of the companies decided to withdraw from the whole process and said it was going to sell all its properties in the area. The other company, the original applicant, decided in the end to continue its participation. During the spring of 2013, the company's representative seemed to be more and more engaged in the project, apparently having grasped the area's potential. However, at the end of the spring, when the dialogue was almost finished, he decided to leave the company, and the whole process stopped dead. In the autumn of 2013, the property developer decided that it too would put all its property in Rosengård on the market, and all plans came to an abrupt end.

Taking a phronetic view

What can we learn from this? Was the idea quite impossible from the beginning, or could the dialogue have ended another way? Let us return to the four phronetic questions of where this development would have taken them, who stood to gain and who to lose as a result of whatever power relations pertained, whether the development was desirable, and what, if anything, could be done about it. The immediate answer to the first question is obvious: if private and public stakeholders cannot find alternative ways of developing urban areas that are less attractive to traditional growth-dependent planning, we must accept that some urban areas will be left behind. Therefore, we need new planning models as a complement to the established paradigms. If our ambition is to face the new global challenges outlined in this volume, planning and urban development are necessary tools (see Rydin 2013). In that sense, the Rosengård project was an ambitious attempt to develop and try out new methods for collaborative planning. Ultimately, the answer to the first question is therefore twofold: growth-dependent planning seems to not work in some areas, but those areas still need to be developed; and the only way forward is to try new ways, like the Rosengård project did. The risk of failure must not keep us from trying.

The answer to the second question is that no one seemed to win. True, the property developers would have profited from the sale of their land, but this could have been achieved without taking part in the dialogue process. Of course, it can be very profitable for property developers to buy and sell properties without maintaining them—slumlords have become a Swedish phenomenon as well (Lind & Blomé 2012)—but there are also plenty of property developers with greater scruples, and, in the end, Sweden's municipalities are still heavily dependent on private actors for all urban development. Therefore, municipalities must find new ways of governing urban development, if they are to fulfil the ambition of meeting social needs and creating good living conditions for all citizens. A good dialogue with private actors is key, as is engaging them in the development of different areas of the city.

However, as Flyvbjerg (2001) reminds us with the third phronetic question, all development is affected by power relations. In the present case, this is the most interesting and difficult to answer, because none of the actors had full power over the process, and no one could control the process of naming and framing. In the end, no solutions could be formulated because there were different ways of understanding the situation and what ought to be done. The process failed because the representatives from the city and the property developers failed to establish a process of collective meaning-making.

When it comes to complex concepts such as sustainable development, especially when framed on a detailed level—for example, in local construction projects—we should expect disagreements both about how to understand the concept, but also what it means to put it into practice. Such disagreements are something professionals must deal with as they try to adapt their working practices to the new set of challenges. In practice, this creates a great deal of tension between broad international or national aims for sustainable development and local, negotiated agreements on what a certain group of professionals, in this case urban planners, are being asked to deliver. In the end, sustainable urban development is to a large extent based on local interpretations, which are formed in established professional work contexts (Cooper & Symes 2009).

In the case of Rosengård, the local interpretations were initiated and controlled by the city's representatives. The six core values were never discussed or questioned. When conflicts arose, the city's representatives tried to resolve them by rational argument or references to the core values or sustainability as something that everyone could agree on as being for the common good. All the clashes between the three dimensions to sustainable development were ignored. The property developers' representatives were never given the opportunity to question the city's interpretation of sustainable development, or how such development should be realized in practice. There were no opportunities for renaming and reframing by reformulating its core values, say, or the purpose of the whole project.

The only way the property developers could intervene in the process was to resist, often by asking that simple question, 'Who is paying for this?' The process was deadlocked between two ways of naming and framing: planning for sustainable urban development or planning for property development. There were no opportunities for the participants from either side to rename and reframe the questions, and that obstructed new ideas from influencing the professional practices involved. And no change was achieved.

So, let us finish with the last question. Was this development desirable, and what, if anything, should we do about it? Of course, no one gains if commercial interests do not want to develop certain areas of a city. If our aim is new planning approaches that are not growth-dependent, then market-driven actors must be challenged and questioned. New ways of working with sustainable urban development to question the dominance of growth-dependent planning must question traditional professional territories and the division of labour between planners, citizens, the construction industry, and property developers. Established professions must be open to new ways of working (Cooper and Symes 2009).

Yet if we want to keep the established actors on board, we must give them enough time for the sea change. The processes of collective meaning-making that support the renaming and reframing of new ideas take time. If different actors strive for a shared understanding, even if they do not agree on everything, it is much easier to support processes where new ideas are adjusted to fit established practices. However, this is a time-consuming process, and in this case time was precious, because the project had to be finished and reported within six months. There simply was not enough time to recognize and accept conflicts, and then try to solve them. The project team could not allow disagreements and value conflicts about how to interpret sustainable urban development: they had to be sure that the project could be finished in time and reported back to the funders. With no time to resolve conflict, the whole process became bogged down in a fruitless discussion about who would foot the bills and who would profit in the end. The dialogue was reduced to a discussion of whether sustainable urban development was profitable or not.

Conclusion

Urban development is a form of management, and, like all kinds of management, it is to a large extent about muddling through. On the other hand, sustainable urban development is about groundbreaking changes and, because of the conflicts between the three dimensions of sustainability, about challenging established power relations. In the present case, the project leader and the city planning officer had to manage a project which aimed to do all that—groundbreaking change in urban planning, challenging established power relations—but had less than six months in which to do it. There was not time to discuss values or put the process on hold when a conflict arose in order to find new ways forward; no room for time-consuming processes of renaming and reframing the processes of urban regeneration. The time pressure made it necessary to ignore different opinions, different perspectives, and value conflicts, because the six workshops had to be done and dusted—and successful.

The project had to be successful so it could fit into the established narrative of Malmö as a creative, sustainable, and entrepreneurial city. Areas such as Rosengård, which do not easily slot into this narrative, must be tamed. The construction of new housing in such areas is the physical evidence the municipality needs to prove that the whole of Malmö is included in the transformation of the city, not only the fancy parts in the Western Harbour. The planners were therefore very eager to convince the property developers that they should build, but also to build in a way that materialized certain core values. They exerted themselves to control the meaning-making process, and left no room for the property developers to rename and reframe problems to suit their way of understanding and managing urban development.

Professional planners have a crucial role to play when cities try to meet the global challenges discussed in this volume. But in order to do so, they must also be aware of the importance of collaborative learning and meaning-making. If they fail in that, they will also fail to support a sustainable urban development that is transformative and results in significant changes to Scandinavia's cities. Being aware of the importance of shared understanding means that professional planners must question the idea that sustainable urban development should be a consensus- and expert-driven process. They must also accept that they may have the best tools for handling the planning process, but that others may have a better idea how those tool should be used, and what they should be used for. That said, professional planners who work for the municipalities also represent the public, and therefore have to put the public interest above all else. Perhaps, if our goal is sustainable urban development, one way forward might be a more phronetic approach to planning, involving all the parties to urban development in a dialogue about what would be best in the circumstances?

References

Baeten, G. (2012) 'Normalising neoliberal planning: The case of Malmö, Sweden', in T. Taşan-Kok & G. Baeten (eds.) *Contradictions of neoliberal planning: Cities, policies, and politics* (Dordrecht: Springer).

Campell, S. (2010) 'Green cities, growing cities, just cities? Urban planning and the contradictions of sustainable development', *Journal of the American Planning Association* 62/3, 296–312.

Cooper, I. and M. Symes (2009) (eds.) *Changing professional practice: Sustainable urban development*, iv (London: Routledge).

Czarniawska, B. (2002) *A tale of three cities, or the glocalization of city management* (Oxford: OUP).

—— (2007) *Shadowing: And other techniques for doing fieldwork in modern societies* (Malmö: Liber).

Dobson, A. (1996) 'Environment sustainabilities: An analysis and a typology', *Environmental Politics*, 5/3, 401–28.

Flyvbjerg, B. (2001) *Making social science matter: Why social inquiry fails and how it can succeed again* (Cambridge: CUP).

—— (2004) 'Phronetic planning research: Theoretical and methodological reflections', *Planning Theory & Practice*, 5/3, 283–306.

—— T. Landman & S. Schram (2012) (eds.) *Real social science: Applied phronesis* (Cambridge: CUP).

Gerell, M. (2013) *Bränder, skadegörelse, grannskap och socialt kapital* [Fires, damage, neighborhood, and social capital] (Malmö University Publications in Urban Studies, 11; Malmö: Malmö University).

Hallin, P.-O., A. Jashari, C. Listerborn & M. Popoola (2010) *Det är inte stenarna som gör ont: Röster från Herrgården, Rosengård—om konflikter och erkännande* [It's not the stones that hurt: Voices from Herrgården, Rosengård—about conflicts and recognitions] (Malmö University Publications in Urban Studies, 5; Malmö: Malmö University).

Herbert, M. (2013) *Stadens skavsår: Inhängnade flerbostadshus i den polariserade staden*. [The city's sore: Gated housings in the polarized city] (Malmö University Publications in Urban Studies, 12; Malmö: Malmö University).

Holgersson, S. (2014) *The rise (and fall?) of post-industrial Malmö: Investigation of city-crisis dialectics* (Ph.D. diss., Department of Human Geography; Lund: Lund University).

Krueger, R. & S. Buckingham (2012) 'Towards a "consensual" urban politics? Creative planning, urban sustainability and regional development', *International Journal of Urban & Regional Research*, 36/3, 486–503.

Lind, H. & G. Blomé (2012) 'Slumlords in the Swedish welfare state: how is it possible?' *International Journal of Housing Markets & Analysis*, 5/2, 196–210.

Mukhtar-Landgren, D. (2008) 'Postindustriella Malmö öppnas och stängs ner' [Post-industrial Malmö opens up and shuts down], in M. Thesfahuney, M. Dahlstedt & R. Ek (eds.) *Den bästa av världar? Betraktelser över en postpolitisk samtid* (Stockholm: Tankekraft).

Ristilammi, P.-M. (1994) *Rosengård och den svarta poesin—En studie i modern annorlundahet* [Rosengård and the black poetry—a study of modern alterity] (Stockholm/Stehag: Brutus Östlings Bokförlag Symposion).

Rydin, Y. (2013) *The future of planning: Beyond growth dependence* (Bristol: Policy).

Sandberg, J. & A. Targama (2007) *Managing understanding in organizations* (London: SAGE).

Weiss, C. H. (1980) 'Knowledge creep and decision accretion', *Science Communication* 1/3, 381–404.

Wenger, E. (1998) *Communities of Practice: Learning, meaning and identity* (Cambridge: CUP).

CHAPTER 13

Reflections on the right to health

Anna Lundberg & Emma Söderman

All human beings have a right to health, but what that means is vague. According to the World Health Organization, 'health is a state of complete physical, mental and social wellbeing and not merely the absence of disease or infirmity' (WHO 1946). The former UN Special Rapporteur on the right to health, Paul Hunt, defines it as access to an effective and integrated health system. Also included in the definition are underlying determinants of health that might influence a person's ability to live a healthy life (Hunt 2006).

The right to health is of central importance, of course, and we define it as having access to healthcare as well as aspects of everyday life of importance for a healthy life.[1] The latter means such things as friendship, support networks, and access to educational institutions. These were identified as central to our research because they are determinants of health, in the sense that the young people participating in our study referred to them as important. Furthermore, previous research shows that these are important aspects of coping and struggling in everyday life for children who are in a marginalized position (Andersson et al. 2010). Regarding healthcare, this is also an area that has recently been subject to a progressive political or legal development in Sweden and its third largest city, Malmö.

The undocumented youths in this study are those children and young people who have been forced to emigrate from their countries of permanent residence because of individual persecution, armed conflict or a massive denial of economic, social, and cultural rights, and who lack Swedish residence permits. There are several terms to describe people in this position—overstayers, refugees in hiding, clandestine refugees, irregular migrants—but we use the term 'undocumented' migrants, since it reflects the terminology used by young people themselves, being *papperslös*, literally without papers. The term *youths* or *children* in this text refers to children aged between 15 and 18 and in a few cases young adults between 18 and 20. The UN Convention on the Rights of the Child (CRC) states that children are persons below the age of 18 (Article 1); however, since it is often unclear to everyone involved in the situation of individual undocumented migrants exactly how old they are, people slightly over 18 have been included in this study. All the participants in the study were also subject to the Dublin II Regulation, requiring that every person seeking refuge should do so by filing an application in the first country of arrival.

Taking the experiences of undocumented, unaccompanied youths, this essay aims to analyse the human right to health as it has played out in the city arena of Malmö. Specifically, we describe discrepancies between the right to health in policy and in practice, and explore the tensions between human rights regulations on the one hand and migration control on the ground in Malmö on the other. We argue that the experiences of undocumented youths illustrate fundamental dimensions to these tensions. Neither convincing legislation at the national level, nor clear policies in the city or region, are a guarantee for access to one's rights. What is crucial, we would argue, are rather the strategies to cope with everyday hardships used by the undocumented persons themselves and their support networks, and a knowledge of human rights on the part of the service providers in their everyday work. The conclusion here is that practices of human rights in the city can contest state-level migration control policies.

Our analysis is based on empirical fieldwork carried out using participant observations in Malmö in January to December 2012, including ten in-depth interviews with undocumented youths. The interviews, which we conducted together, lasted one and a half to two and a half hours. We used a flexible interview guide to frame the conversation, structured in a manner where the interviewee was first asked to describe a normal day, followed by broad themes such as school, resources, health, and access to healthcare. We did two interviews in English and two interviews with interpreters (not official interpreters but a friend of ours in one case and a friend of the interviewee in the other case). They interpreted from Dari and Somali to Swedish. The rest of our interviews were conducted in Swedish.

Theoretical framework

In the terminology of the political philosopher Hannah Arendt, being excluded from the protection of nation-states also leaves a person excluded from the right to have rights. Having herself experienced statelessness in the aftermath of the Second World War, Arendt famously concluded that human beings, when losing political status such as citizenship, were also excluded from human rights (1951, 300). Starting from the situation of the stateless people of her day, Arendt claimed that there is one right necessary to get access to all other rights—the right to have rights. Without this, a person was nothing but a human being stripped of all rights, and the world found 'nothing sacred in the abstract nakedness of being human' (Arendt 1968, 299). In other words, when a person is merely human, he or she paradoxically loses all human rights.

The relationship between citizenship and rights brought up by Arendt is not as evident today. Various human rights documents, as well as expert committees within the UN, have gradually expanded the interpretation of who is included within the scope of human rights (Benhabib 2006). Yet even so, undocumented persons still do not have unconditional access to the inalienable human rights that supposedly afford much-needed protection. Legal scholars describe this in terms of an unstable relationship between entitlements and humanity (Noll 2010) or as a site of contestation for the meaning of the right to have rights (Kesby 2012, ch. 5). One aspect of the problem is the law, since, as Lindahl (2010) argues, it is the law that determines the concept of humanity for legal purposes and the legal order is therefore by definition exclusionary.

On a practical level, claims to human rights can be used as an instrument for inclusion in the regulatory frameworks of the nation-state. An example of this is when claims are made from organizations and other actors that people who lack residence permits should nevertheless be covered by the welfare system. At a theoretical level, the problem is more complex than this simple inclusion of all those who are formally excluded would imply. This has to do with the point made by Lindahl that inclusion always requires exclusion, and this is situated in the legal design. Specifically, this means that rights must be determined by someone, and this process of defining who is entitled to what human rights implies of necessity various forms of sorting and categorization: they may take different forms depending on the level of regulation.

What does it mean then to be categorized as an undocumented person? In several ways, yes, it is about losing those rights that every human being is entitled to. Yet it is also about losing the mastery of the language in which to claim rights. As an undocumented migrant, one does not have a voice that counts in the same way as a citizen's would, and this despite the multiple instruments adopted by the world community, the Universal Declaration of Human Rights and the European Convention on Human Rights being perhaps the best known. In these human rights instruments, each and every member of humanity is entitled to the protection of the law and should be subject to the principle of equality. To claim that everyone is entitled to equality before the law and access to basic human rights is thus uncontroversial—the rights are explicitly inalienable for all members of the human family—which makes them self-evident. However, to treat everyone as equal, independent of their legal status, seams to be a contradiction in terms. The widespread problems with racism and the marginalization and criminalization of migrants in the contemporary world are well-known illustrations of this (CRC Committee 2012). While the rights belong to one group, it is another actor that has the mandate to implement them. We will return to the problem of exclusion as part of legal design; our point here is that human rights legislation is embedded in superiority and dependency, in stark contrast to the idea of equality.

Inspired by Arendt and others, and applying the perspectives of rights-holders themselves, we understand human rights mainly as a political enactment (Ingram 2008; Squire & Darling 2013). In this sense, the invention and reinvention of human rights is a question of coming together in plurality and granting each other reciprocal conditions (Kesby 2012, 67)—rights are not a status but an activity. Such an activity (claims to rights), wherever it takes place, is a demonstration of how rights might occur (Ingram 2008, 413).

Furthermore, we draw on Kesby's argument (2012) that human rights have a double function in the position of undocumented persons: they provide for entitlements to rights, and they also 'realign national citizenship' with international norms (ibid. 369). It is relevant to explore how this might develop in the city, as the city is one social space for rights realization (Oomen & Baumgärtel 2012).

Thus undocumented persons constitute an anomaly to that full legal, political, and social presence within a state that a residence permit represents. This makes it relevant to explore the exercise of human rights from their standpoint, in local contexts, which, in combination with an investigation of different levels of regulation, we would argue is a suitable beginning when exploring the disputed meaning of human rights today.

A spectacle in Malmö

Over the years, youths arriving on their own to seek refuge in Sweden have greatly increased in number, from fewer than 500 in 2005 to more than 2,000 every year since 2009. At time of writing they constitute some 10 per cent of the total number of asylum seekers. In 2013, almost 4,000 unaccompanied children applied for asylum in Sweden—the highest number in Europe (Migrationsinfo 2013). The majority are boys from Afghanistan aged between 15 and 17, who have been forced to escape because of a massive denial of their human rights or direct threats from the Taliban (Migration Board 2011). Approximately 45 per cent of the children concerned arrive in Malmö, Sweden's third largest city with 300,000 inhabitants, situated near the Danish border. By the end of 2013 there were approximately 265 youths being sought in Malmö for deportation: youths whose asylum applications had been referred to another European state or who had had their claims for refuge rejected, in other words (Malmö Police Department 2013).

In the Malmö context, we are concerned with everyday life as an undocumented person and the role of international human rights at the city level. As noted by Jonathan Darling (2010), cities have a strong role in the realization of human rights, and this brings to the fore tensions between different levels of regulation—a point at which the invention and reinvention of human rights can be studied. It is no longer clear that human rights are a matter of state obligations towards the individual, or the individual's claims on the state. A recent development is the direct engagement of local communities in international human rights. Malmö, for example, has increasingly taken the initiative on human rights issues (Platform 2010–2014). This might also imply that human rights have a greater impact in terms of actual access for undocumented migrants to welfare services, as these are provided at the municipal level (Darling 2010).

In Malmö, as in other European cities, the idea of non-discrimination of irregular migrants has become one of the most politicized of our time and has called for increased attention in public debate. Gradually, the city has expanded the target groups of its welfare services to include undocumented children, partly due to initiatives by the Green Party and a vocal, broad-based refugee rights network in the city. There was controversy in Malmö about the dangers facing undocumented youths in Sweden, such as the risk of deportation when attempting to attend school. Despite national legislative changes intended to enshrine the right to an education for all living in Sweden (Skollag 2010:800), there was nothing to stop the police searching schools or the immediate area for persons they were to deport. Furthermore, in 2012 a EU-funded project was started in collaboration by the police, the Migration Board, and the Swedish Prison and Probation Service to promote 'Legally secure and efficient enforcement work' (REVA). This project made the situation for children and young people living in Sweden without residence permits even more insecure. The project started as a pilot in Malmö where the police adopted an intensified approach to searches. This lead to loud protests and much public debate about violent migration control (Sveriges Television 2013). The resultant demonstrations, media reports, and other local initiatives in Malmö serve to exemplify the attempts to rework and contest boundaries between 'us and them'. Rather than the question of who should be included, it was the city as a spatial unit that was the focus. A central and recurring question is what sort of city people want.

The tension between state migration control and the policymakers in Malmö was brought up by City Councillor Katrin Stjernfeldt Jammeh when she was asked to comment on the REVA project in Malmö (the Councillor had not been informed in advance by the police about their new tactics):

> If children in Malmö don't dare to go to school or seek medical care because they are afraid the police will take them, we won't reach the city's goal of all children having access to school. (Stjernfeldt Jammeh interview 2013)

At the heart of the Malmö context is an ongoing negotiation between the city, trying to provide for its inhabitants' interests and needs, and the nation-state's interest in upholding an effective migration control. Human rights are increasingly used in the struggle within institutions to counter the sorting of people based on legal status. This was the case when it was decided that undocumented children had a right to support from social services. It was clearly stated that social workers should treat all children equally, regardless of their legal status (Malmö stad 2013).

The children, and thus also the youths, we met in our study are afforded strong protection under the policies on human rights while they are particularly vulnerable because of their position as undocumented residents. There are several reasons for this. There are the tensions between the circulation of persons and the increased control of persons, and between their inclusion in welfare systems and the workings of streamlined migration management on the part of the state. These tensions may be understood as a spectacle, or, as De Genova describes it, a 'vertiginous spiral of inequalities that are deeply imbricated within the fabric of citizenship itself' (2013, 1194). Drawing on Balibar's proposition that the management of borders 'establish and maintain "a world apartheid", which institutes a "color bar"', De Genova argues that this 'runs through all societies' (ibid. 1192). In our study, there is the spectacle of youths excluded from much of the welfare state, and at the same time completely dependent on the kindness of these institutions to get access to those rights they are entitled to under international law.

They are subject to a conditional inclusion in a process where they have severely limited scope of influence.

Nevertheless, undocumented persons cannot hope to engage 'a state's welfare jurisdiction' without also 'triggering its immigration jurisdiction' (Noll 2010), or as Kesby puts it,

> Even though a person may be physically present, they are to be socially and legally absent through the denial of key rights or formal and practical impediments to their enjoyment—not least detection by the authorities and subsequent expulsion. (Kesby 2012, 110)

This brings us to the question of rights claims in what is, after all, an irregular context at the local level (see Strange & Lundberg 2014). What are rights claimants' strategies to cope with everyday life in Malmö?

The example of the right to healthcare

The right to healthcare for children without a residence permit is an absolute human right in policy, and there are clear guidelines stating that *all* children resident in Sweden should have full access to healthcare on equal terms. Referring to an agreement in June 2012 between the Green Party (which was in opposition at the time) and the Swedish government, undocumented children were included under the heading of people entitled to access to full healthcare and dental care. At the time of our field study, children whose application for asylum had been turned down were included in the regulations at the national level. However, until 2013, undocumented children who had not yet had their asylum claims assessed in a formal process were excluded from the right to healthcare. In Skåne County Council (in which Malmö is the largest city), the right to healthcare has extended to both children and adults since 2008; however, for adults, payment for care is still an issue, while by contrast all undocumented children receive subsidized care. The extension of the right to healthcare in Skåne predated the national level. Furthermore, according to Skåne County Council policy from 2011 on non-citizens and undocumented migrants, 'the medical care, as with other patient groups, shall be the first priority and ability to pay comes second' (Region Skåne 2011). A complementary policy states that whatever their legal status, migrants and refugees should be treated professionally and with respect, and with a certain understanding for their special living conditions and experiences (Region Skåne 2011). However, despite the formal obligations, it is still the case that undocumented people cannot access welfare services without also triggering the system of migration control (Noll 2010).

The fear of control and detection severely limited access to healthcare services among the youths in our study. As one of them puts it:

> Now I'm really scared, I hope I don't get sick. [Why?] I get scared because you never know if the police come and get you, or if a racist doctor may call the police. (Erfan)

Clearly, in practice the experience of access to rights is conditional—here, in the meeting with the individual doctor who should provide care, but where the young man is frightened that he might be confronted with a racist doctor. Naturally, worrying about being confronted by racism is not dependent on a lack of legal status, but evidently Erfan's situation as an undocumented person adds to the perceived insecurity. Even though the regulations do not require healthcare providers to inform the police of their patients' presence, the possibility that someone might call the police, for example due to lack of knowledge or racism, cannot be completely ruled out.

In our fieldwork we found among receptionists and other healthcare personnel that a lack of knowledge of undocumented persons' right to healthcare was indeed an obstacle to access to healthcare. On one occasion we accompanied 17-year-old Mohammad, who had violent stomach pains, to accident and emergency. We had a long argument with the receptionists before they would let us in to see the doctors. We were also billed EUR 350 instead of the usual highly subsidized sum. The issue of having to argue with medical receptionists for one's right to healthcare was a common theme in our informants' experiences. Receiving care, they emphasized, was dependent on someone helping them get access. In Arendt's words, the youths were stripped of all rights by dint of not being categorized as a member of the nation-state. However, our findings show that the meaning of the right to have rights is indeed contested. It seems that the right to have rights is connected to being recognized, and when it comes to access to welfare services this is not limited to being recognized by the state. Access to the right to healthcare is connected not only to formal regulations, but also to being recognized by the receptionist, doctor, or other staff as a person belonging to the community of rights-holders.

Turning to the underlying determinants of health, in our study a lack of legal status is also directly connected to a lack of other resources. All our respondents knew what it was to be poor, and in school and elsewhere were treated differently to their peers who had residence permits. This affected their sense of being part of the community in which they lived. Ostensibly 'small' things such as not being able to participate in school activities—going on trips, appearing in school photographs, or having a library card—all contributed to the feeling of subordination due to their lack of legal status. They were not fully part of the community, but had conditional access to it. In this situation, developing a sense of belonging and being recognized appeared as an example of the how the relation between entitlement and humanity is unstable.

It should also be emphasized that all our respondents suffered from severe health problems due to their insecure situation and earlier experiences of flight and abuse. Faced with poor physical and mental health, their friends and a sense of community were central to how they coped with everyday struggles. The youths described how their network of friends, helped by activists in the local refugee rights network, was not only crucial for accessing their rights in practice, but also for creating a sense of belonging and what Arendt called a 'place in the world'. Hence Alireza talked about the difference in the treatment he experienced in school due to his lack of legal status, and how this affected him not only practically but also emotionally:

> I did not get so good self-esteem. But my friends said you are very good. You are good at Swedish. I got the energy to continue. Otherwise it would have been difficult to go to school. (Alireza)

The recognition he was given by his friends transcended the label of undocumented person that the state had burdened him with, and this promoted his well-being. Relationships and recognition thus appear important when trying to understand accessing rights to health in a broad sense, as a state of 'complete physical, mental and social wellbeing' (WHO 1946). In the end, as our study indicates, human rights as formal commitments are precisely that—formal commitments devoid of all practical content. As long as the risk of deportation remains and no sanctuary is to be found in the city, the rights claims go no further than being a plea for compassion. Practical access to your rights requires your recognition by someone else—in other words, human rights are relational.

Concluding remarks

Every aspect of our interviewees' lives was permeated by their position as undocumented immigrants. Their fear of being deported, the structural discrimination that characterizes life as 'unfree', poor health—all cuts away at what it means to be human enough to be a rights-holder. Our study illustrates that having networks of friends and activists indeed can facilitate a conditional access to welfare services. Yet even so, the gap between human rights on paper and human rights in practice is a bleak reality as long as deportation is an alternative. This is an inevitable consequence of the nation-states' migration management, and as we have highlighted, in Malmö it most definitely makes a spectacle of people's lives.

Arendt raised the question of the risk of being stripped of all those categories that make a human sufficiently human to be considered a rights-holder, arguing that human rights are groundless in the sense that when a person is a mere human, he paradoxically loses his right to have rights. The phenomenon of undocumentedness thus illustrates a contradiction inherent in the very idea of human rights. The fact that none of the people we met and spent time with chose to express their claims in terms of rights also points in this direction.

Nonetheless, although undocumented status permeates the life of the youths in our study, there is more to it than that. The exclusion of migrants under contemporary migration policy also offers a basis for solidarity. We saw in the study that the young stick together—they have not had any other choice. In coping with everyday life, there is also an underlying reinvention of human rights as being a member of a political community. Their activities and strategies in collaboration with activists make it clear that, despite their subordination, they claim personhood in the sense of having a place in the world. To be viewed as a unique individual and not as someone who is merely undocumented can only strengthen one's self-esteem. Participation in social networks is a way to appear a person, someone who should be included in local contexts such as school, healthcare systems, and the like, despite still being excluded at a state level.

Despite being deprived of legal personhood, the youths we have talked to are very much active members of the city's population. In certain areas they are also under the eye of the public authorities. Access to the rights envisaged in official policy is always under contest; it does not end because there is an institution formally granting rights. Aware of their subordination, a conditional inclusion is reproduced over and over again, beyond and regardless of formal entitlements. In response to Arendt's injunction to think of the potentiality of the city as a 'nation-state without nationalism', a legal order that 'is open to all who happen to live on its territory', our study shows that a legal order with inclusive regulations at the city level alone is not enough.

Notes

1 This essay is based on the findings of a research project conducted in 2012, Irregular=Rightsless? An Investigation of Unaccompanied Undocumented Refugee Children's Entitlement and Access to Health in Malmö, with support from the research programme 'Challenges of Migration' [Migrationens utmaningar] and the Swedish Research Council.

References

Andersson, H. E., H. Ascher, U. Björnberg & M. Eastmond (2010) (eds.) *Mellan det förflutna och framtiden: Asylsökande barns välfärd, hälsa och välbefinnande*, <http://www.cergu.gu.se/digitalAssets/1319/1319551_mellan-det-forflutna-och-framtiden.pdf>, accessed 10 October 2015.
Arendt, H. (1951) *The Origins of totalitarianism* (San Diego: Harcourt Brace).

—— (1968) *The human condition* (Chicago: University of Chicago Press).
Benhabib, S. (2006) *Another cosmopolitanism* (New York: OUP).
CRC (Committee on the Rights of the Child) (2012) *Report of the 2012 day of general discussion: The rights of all children in the context of international migration*, <http://www2.ohchr.org/english/bodies/crc/docs/discussion2012/ReportDGD-ChildrenAndMigration2012.pdf>, accessed 10 October 2015.
De Genova, N. (2013) 'Spectacles of migrant "illegality": The scene of exclusion, the obscene of inclusion', *Ethnic & Racial Studies*, 36/7, 1180–98.
Darling, J. (2010) 'A city of sanctuary: The relational re-imagining of Sheffield's asylum politics', *Transactions of the Institute of British Geographers*, 35, 125–40, doi: 10.1111/j.1475-5661.2009.00371.x.
Hunt, P. (2006) 'Economic, social and cultural rights: Report of the special rapporteur on the right of everyone to the enjoyment of the highest attainable standard of physical and mental health, E/CN.4/2006/48' <http://daccess-dds-ny.un.org/doc/UNDOC/GEN/G06/114/69/PDF/G0611469.pdf?OpenElement>, accessed 10 October 2015.
Ingram, J. (2008) 'What is a "right to have rights"? Three images of the politics of human rights', *American Political Science Review*, 102/4, 401–16.
Kesby, A. (2012) *The right to have rights: Citizenship, humanity, and international law* (Oxford: OUP).
Lindahl, H. (2010) 'A-legality: Postnationalism and the question of legal boundaries', *Modern Law Review*, 73/1, 30–56.
Malmö Police Department (2013) Phone conversation with Police Department in Malmö, Sweden, autumn 2013.
Malmö stad (2013) 'Riktlinjer för handläggning av försörjningsstöd och ekonomiskt bistånd för livsföring i övrigt', 28 November <http://malmo.se/download/18.1d68919c1431f1e2a9636e7/1389365268757/Riktlinjer+för+handläggning+av+försörjningsstöd+och+ekonomiskt+bistånd_Malmö+stad.pdf>, accessed 10 April 2015.
Migration Board (2011) Årsredovisning [Annual Report], <http://www.migrationsverket.se/download/18.478d06a31358f98884580001427/Årsredovisning+2011.pdf>, accessed 3 May 2014.
Migrationsinfo (2013) 'Ensamkommande barn och ungdomar', Green and Liberal Research Institute, <www.migrationsinfo.se>, accessed 3 May 2013.
Noll, G. (2010) 'Why human rights fail to protect undocumented migrants', *European Journal of Migration & Law*, 12, 244.
Oomen, B. & M. Baumgärtel (2012) 'Human rights cities', overview for *The Sage Handbook on Human Rights*, <http://www.philodroit.be/IMG/pdf/human_rights_cities.pdf>, accessed 23 March 2015.
Platform (2010–2014) *Överenskommelse mellan Socialdemokraterna, Vänsterpartiet och Miljöpartiet de gröna: Riktlinjer för det politiska samarbetet i Malmö under mandatperioden 2010–2014* (Malmö: Malmö stad).

Region Skåne (2011) 'Region Skånes policy för vård av personer från andra lander', 22 March, <http://www.skane.se/sv/Webbplatser/ValkommentillVardgivarwebben/Patientadministration/Vard-for-personer-fran-andra-lander1/asylsokande-flyktingar/Lagar-tillampningar-och-forordningar/>, accessed 20 January 2015.

Stjernfeldt Jammeh, K. (2013) radio interview, Swedish Radio P1, available at <http://sverigesradio.se/sida/avsnitt/174166?programid=3071>, accessed May 2 2013.

Skollag (2010) SFS 2010:800 *Skollag* [Sweden's School Law].

Strange, M. & A. Lundberg (2014) 'Education as hospitality', *Peace Review. A Journal of Social Justice* (special issue L. A. Lorentzen (ed.) 'Migrants and Cultures of Hospitality), 26/2, 201–8.

Squire, V. & J. Darling (2013) 'The "minor" politics of rightful presence: Justice and relationality in city of sanctuary', *International Political Sociology*, 7/1, 59–74, doi: 10.1111/ips.12009.

Sveriges Television (SVT) (2013) 'Debatt REVA-projektet', <http://www.svt.se/search/?q=debatt+reva>, accessed 10 April 2015.

WHO (1946) 'Preamble to the Constitution of the World Health Organization as adopted by the International Health Conference', New York, 19–22 June 1946; signed on 22 July 1946 by the representatives of 61 States', entered into force on 7 April 1948 (Official Records of the WHO, 2), 100.

CHAPTER 14

Behind the line of disintegration
Practices of transborder citizenship among diasporan Kurds in Sweden

Khalid Khayati

This essay will argue that the formation and development of diaspora and the practice of transnational relationship among Swedish Kurds display a set of dynamic processes which derive their strength from (*a*) a politically, culturally, and socially heterogeneous and diversified population, and (*b*) a favourable Swedish political environment that creates opportunities for the Kurds to develop their transnational organizations and networks. Accordingly, this essay goes beyond the negative experiences of exclusion and discrimination among the Kurds to pick out a number of positive and dynamic aspects to diasporic performances, in Sweden and elsewhere, promoted—as mentioned above—by a highly heterogeneous and diversified population as well as a favourable Swedish context. What are these positive and dynamic diasporic trajectories and occurrences that should be included in the case of the Kurdish diaspora in Sweden? To what extent do the social and cultural diversity of the Kurdish diaspora, together with the Swedish political context, determine the distinctiveness of transnational organizations and networks that Kurds create in Sweden? However, this essay will acknowledge that—contrary to a number of popular discourses that advance the aspect of victimhood (see Khayati 2008)—diasporan populations in Western states, empowered equally by their current home contexts, appear today more and more to be transborder citizens; alluding to those groups and members of diasporic populations who occupy influential societal positions in both sending and receiving countries. Transborder citizenship, used here as the instructive concept of this essay, describes those individuals and groups who live their lives across the borders of two or more nation-states, participating in the legal and institutional systems and political practices of these various states and acting in response to more than one government (Glick Schiller & Fouron 2001; Glick Schiller 2005; see also Khayati 2008, 2011).

In recent years, various scholars have treated the issue of claiming membership of more than one state. In order to support the idea of so-called 'polyethnic rights', Will Kymlicka (1998), critical of the democratic process in Western society for its inability to represent ethnic and cultural differences, has conceived the notion of 'multicultural citizenship'. That inability is rooted in the inadequacies of the concept of citizenship—that is, the conditions under which the rights of marginalized groups in society are realized (Vali 2003, 71). Michel Laguerre (1998) speaks of 'diasporic citizenship', while Rainer Bauböck, who earlier presented the notion of transnational citizenship (1994), supports the idea of 'multiple citizenship', with its reference to overlapping membership of various political communities (Vertovec 2001). The concept of 'flexible citizenship' has been proposed by Aihwa Ong (1999) in order to provide an analysis of new transnational narratives of Asian modernity and valorize 'new heroes' of Asian capitalism as the adaptable subjects of transnational identity. Ong has argued that a new strategy of flexible accumulation, which challenges the 'hegemonic link between whiteness and capitalism', has promoted a similarly flexible attitude toward citizenship; a flexible citizenship that refers, however, to a set of 'flexible practices, strategies and disciplines associated with transnational capitalism', which create new 'modes of subject making and new kinds of valorized subjectivity' (Chakravartty 2001, 71 citing Ong 1999).

If we take into account the consequences of contemporary transnational movements that cross nation-states' territorial, cultural, and political boundaries, the concept of transborder citizenship seems to be relevant not only because of the continuous 'politics of difference' that are claimed by diasporan populations in Western democracies, but also because of the 'expression of identity', born of an experience of immigration, which in fact interconnects two national spaces

(Pries 1999) as well as a number of localities in various states. In this respect, the identity of diasporic populations that reflects the places where they live gives birth to a range of transnational arrangements that connect the immigrants' homelands to their new localities in the countries of settlement (Glick Schiller 2005, 66).

This essay will pay particular attention to Sweden. Considered to be a 'centre of gravity' (see Ahmadzadeh 2003; van Bruinessen 1999, 2000; Khayati 2011), Sweden offers diasporan Kurds a favourable socio-political environment that has enabled them to set up a broad range of cultural associations, social and professional institutions, and youth and women's organizations and networks over the course of the last thirty years.

Much of the essay's material is taken from wide-ranging fieldwork carried out among Kurds in Sweden in the second half of 2010, complemented by additional studies carried out in the course of 2011–2013 among a number of Kurdish cultural and political elites—celebrities, journalists, politicians and other public figures, association leaders, writers, artists, young activists, and association members. These people were chosen due to their prominent position in the Kurdish diaspora, from where they had the possibility of influencing the political and cultural life of both their former and their new homeland. Stockholm, which is considered one of the most important loci for Kurds in Sweden (van Bruinessen 1999; Khayati 2008), was the geographical focus of all these studies. Transnational activities among the Kurds in other Swedish cities such as Uppsala, Linköping, Gothenburg, and Örebro have also been incorporated into this work in proportion to the position they hold within the Kurdish diaspora. Online research, mostly visiting a range of different Kurdish websites and chat rooms, was used as a complementary method; a method that focuses on the ways in which computer-mediated communication enables geographically distant individuals to come together to occupy new social spaces online and to define their own realities (Carter 2005).

Diaspora formation among Kurds

The experience of exile has been part and parcel of the history of Kurdish nationalism. According to van Bruinessen (2000: 4), there is a close connection between exile and nationalism. Forced displacement and population movements in Kurdish societies have brought about the partial transformation of Kurdish political identity, as part of the Kurdish nationalist movement became deterritorialized and transnationalized (van Bruinessen 1999, 2000). A large number of diasporan Kurds have maintained or rediscovered a sense of Kurdish identity and have organized themselves into various institutions and networks. Along with their political mobilization, the Kurds have made use of effective means of communication, which have enabled them to (re-)orient themselves toward the politics of the Kurdish homeland as well as those states in the Middle East that discriminate against them (van Bruinessen 2000, 4). For instance, film productions and radio broadcasts in the Kurdish language are considered an effective way for Kurds in exile to preserve and develop their ethno-national identity. Many Kurdish authors and intellectuals have produced a substantial number of Kurdish books, journals, and other publications, published in Germany, France, Belgium, and the Netherlands, but above all in Sweden, where the enterprise has been generously supported by various state subsidies (van Bruinessen 1999, 9). The literature in Northern Kurdish (Kurmanji), the dialect spoken by the majority of Kurdish people in Turkey and Syria and many in Iraq and Iran, is even said to have experienced a renaissance in exile (van Bruinessen 2000; Ahmadzadeh 2003). The Kurdish Institute of Paris, which was founded with the support of France's Mitterrand government by Kurdish intellectuals from different European countries, has developed a standard for Northern Kurdish and organized a number of 'conferences and a journal that published lists of agreed upon terms for objects and concepts in various spheres of life' (van Bruinessen 1999, 9). In order to reinforce the Kurdish language, culture, and literature, similar institutes have been established by Kurdish intellectuals in Brussels (1989), Berlin (1994), Moscow (1996), and Washington DC (1997), as well as a well-endowed Kurdish library in Stockholm (1997), each serving a different clientele and promoting a distinct type of activity (van Bruinessen 1999, 9).

Sweden as a conducive political environment

Since the end of the Second World War, Sweden has received asylum seekers, refugees, and economic migrants from a staggering range of regions and countries, and in very large numbers relative to the size of its population. The arrival of hundreds of thousands of immigrants and refugees in Sweden has generated not only a new demography, but also a new social and cultural reality. In order to manage this new reality, an impressive body of immigration, immigrant, refugee, and integration policies and laws has taken shape. On several occasions they have been amended and reformulated, and the institutional framework adjusted, sometimes radically. With such a legal and institutional framework, the Swedish state was expected to give immigrants and refugees the same living standard as the rest of the population (see also Södergran 2000; Johansson 2005).

Like many of the non-European ethnic and cultural groups, however, diasporan Kurds in Sweden benefited from a number of policies designed to promote immigrant associations. In Sweden, the proportion of immigrants organized in associations is striking. At the start of 2000, there were more than 50 national immigrant organizations and more than 1,000 local associations throughout the country, which benefited from a relatively liberal immigrant policy (see Khayati 2008). The tradition of supporting immigrant associations stems from the grassroots social movements (*folkrörelser*) that characterized most of Sweden's social and political history in the nineteenth and twentieth centuries. As an essential feature of the nation-making process in Sweden, the social movements contributed much to the construction of the Swedish welfare state, or the People's Home (*Folkhemmet*) as it was christened. The standard social movement was the trades union, inspired by the ideology of Swedish social democracy. During the construction of the welfare state, these movements were an effective means of achieving ideological integration, political socialization, and popular mobilization.

Since 1975 they have proved useful tools for integrating immigrants into society (see Ålund & Schierup 1991). As for the Kurds, in Sweden they have found a favourable environment in which to develop their social, ethno-cultural, and professional associations. A wide variety of Kurdish groups have since the 1980s made use of this advantageous milieu to promote their particular interests.

The principal objectives of Swedish policy on immigrant associations are said to be preserving immigrants' culture and identity, organizing educational courses and activities for refugees and immigrants, and encouraging them to take part in the process of integration and political decision-making (see Berruti et al. 2002; Khayati 2008). However, it was state subsidies that made it possible for immigrants and refugees to develop a significant associational life in the country. Immigrant associations set up along cultural and ethnic lines receive various state and local authority subsidies; religious institutions, meanwhile, obtain their share of subsidies directly from the state. In addition to the official grants schemes, Islamic associations finance some of their activities from the support that they receive from various private donors and a number of Islamic states in the Middle East (see Khayati 2008).

A diversified diasporic group

Diasporan Kurds in Sweden—whose number is highly difficult to estimate—display a high level of cultural, political, and social diversity. They come from all parts of Kurdistan and highly differentiated social backgrounds, and engage in any number of skilled occupations in Swedish society. At present, Sweden is among those Western countries where the Kurds' transnational cultural and political activities are said to have come furthest (van Bruinessen 1999, 2000; Khayati 2011). A significant number of artists, political leaders, intellectuals, scholars, and journalists have arrived in Sweden since the 1970s—indeed, the number of Kurdish writers in Sweden has long surpassed the number who remained in Kurdistan (Ahmadzadeh 2003). In 1994, the Swedish journalist Stefan Hjertén noticed the dynamic aspects of the Kurdish population in Sweden. He believed that the presence of the Kurdish intelligentsia has created a specific situation where Sweden is willy-nilly an extension of Kurdistan (Hjertén 1994). If nothing else, it shows how the encouraging Swedish political context, together with the diversified social composition of the Kurdish population, enabled the Kurds to develop a considerable diaspora organization and a strong sense of diasporic belonging (Khayati & Dahlstedt 2014).

As part of the social, cultural, and political arrangements in a globalized and transnationalized world, diasporan Kurds throughout the West are becoming increasingly aware of the significance of their transnational organizations and networks. Today, diasporan Kurds living in Sweden have constructed considerable transnational structures that function not only as a substantial means of integration in Swedish society, but also as genuinely transnational institutions, designed to affect the politics of their former homelands, especially by promoting democracy, human rights, and peace settlements by non-violent means. These diasporic structures—which encompass a range of associations, radio and television stations, publishing houses, social networks, and websites, and the activities of a large number of political personalities and cultural celebrities—exist within a specific transnational social field that connects Sweden to Kurdistan and vice versa in a variety of ways.

This specific Swedish–Kurdish juxtaposition, which encompasses a multidimensional diasporic space and a range of transnational activities, makes it possible for diaspora populations to maintain their social and political commitments vis-à-vis two different but interrelated political contexts: their former homelands and the countries in which they currently reside.

Simultaneous political participation

Today, there are clear indications that the number of Kurds who interact with both their former and their new countries is continuing to increase. For instance, most Kurds show a great commitment to Kurdish politics. The Kurdish diaspora in Sweden maintains a strong political profile, continuously updated in political manifestations and a cycle of traditional holidays and commemorations: Newroz, or New Year, which is celebrated on 21 March, and is now the key date in the Kurdish political calendar; the commemoration of Anfal, the Iraqi regime's genocidal campaign against the Kurdish people in 1987–8; and Halabja, the scene of a brutal gas attack by the Iraqi regime in 1988, marked every year by Kurds across the world. Political manifestations have become something of a signature of the Kurdish diaspora in the West, with Stockholm, as one of the loci of the diaspora (see Khayati 2008), the stage for mass demonstrations and other forms of political manifestation designed to sway the politics of their land of origin. One major event was the mass protest that followed the arrest of the Kurdish leader Abdullah Öcalan in February 1999. Fifteen years later, in July 2014, the streets of Stockholm were once again the gathering place for a huge number of Kurds, demonstrating for the independence of Iraqi Kurdistan. Between these two major events, there have been innumerable political actions instigated by diasporan Kurds in Sweden.

The Kurds' political participation stretches far beyond general elections. For instance, the massive turnout of diasporan Kurds in the Iraqi elections at the end of 2005 is a further indication of how they will willingly 'politicize' the transnational social fields in several Western societies when the moment comes to vote for their preferred political platform, in this case the Kurdistan Alliance. On election day, thousands of Kurds living in Western countries descended on the polling stations, in order, as many voters put it, to 'enjoy their democratic rights in the European countries in order to exert influence on their own political destiny in Iraq' (Khayati 2011, 90). The unofficial results, which were communicated by the Independent Electoral Commission of Iraq, showed that in Sweden the Kurdistan Alliance had obtained more than 10,000 votes out of a total of 18,000 Iraqi voters (Khayati 2008). The general election in Iraqi Kurdistan held on 25 July 2009 was a further example of how diasporan Kurds in Sweden can exert influence over the political processes in Kurdistan. In many Western states, a range of communication platforms (associations, political networks, websites, online forums, and so on) were established to promote what many Kurds saw as an active and effective participation in the electoral process, and equally to support certain political forces in the election. Fieldwork and interview data indicate significant support in

Sweden for the oppositional group, Lîstî Goran (Change List), a reform-oriented political movement, which in its election manifesto sharply criticized the two dominant Kurdish parties, the PDK and the PUK, for what it described as their 'corrupt and non-democratic methods'. Lîstî Goran obtained 25 per cent of the vote, partly as a result of the support from Swedish Kurds (Khayati 2011).

The participation of diasporan Kurds in these elections is an example of how exiled Kurds mobilize themselves in Europe in order to influence the politics of their former homelands. In this context, the frequency of transnational contact between Sweden and Iraqi Kurdistan was considerable, as it was for other European states, because the polling stations were set up in only a few places. This did not deter the Kurds, who went to the ballot *en masse*, travelling in from remote areas and even neighbouring countries. In Scandinavia, Sweden was the only host country, with voters coming in from Finland, Denmark, and Norway (Khayati & Dahlstedt 2014, 2015).

Transnational organizations and networks

A favourable Swedish environment has enabled Kurds to develop a significant number of social, ethno-cultural, and professional associations. At the national level, there are two important Kurdish umbrella organizations. The Federation of Kurdish Associations in Sweden (Kurdiska Riksförbundet i Sverige), with its 42 affiliated associations, was created on the initiative of a number of associations and representatives of Kurdish political parties in 1981. It is the oldest and probably the largest Kurdish organization in the country, and sees itself as religiously and politically independent. Moreover, it considers itself unique, claiming to have 8,500 members of all shades of political opinion from all parts of Kurdistan. The other major umbrella institution is the Council of Kurdish Associations in Sweden (Kurdiska Rådet i Sverige), which was founded in 1994, and has more than 20 affiliated associations.

Young Kurds, who tend to dislike the legacy of the Kurdish political movement in the diaspora, have criticized the Kurdish umbrella organizations for paying them too little heed, and have gone on to set up their own organizations, as one young Kurdish leader puts it, to 'solve the problem of young people's under-representation by coming forward and managing our part of the societal duties in our way' (Khayati 2008, 233–4). It is interesting to note the growth of the national Kurdish Student and Academic Federation (Kurdiska student- och akademikerförbundet, KSAF), established in 2009 by Kurdish student and academic associations to organize intellectual and cultural activities focusing on the Kurds and Sweden; similarly, there is the Young Kurds' Network (Unga kurders nätverk), which is a common venue for Kurdish youth, and the Kurdistan Student Federation in Sweden (KSF), which was founded in 2004 on the initiative of a number of students, almost exclusively from Iraqi Kurdistan. In the 2000s, the KSF worked together with the Social Democratic Students of Sweden (Svenska socialdemokratiska studentförbundet, SSF) on a project called 'Baba Gurgur' to build a youth centre in Iraqi Kurdistan. WeKurd is another Swedish organization that was created by second-generation youths from all parts of Kurdistan. Primarily active in 2004–2008, it was said to be a reaction to the Kurdistan's Worker Party (Partiya Karkerên Kurdistan, PKK) and its 'less progressive, passive and distorted' nationalistic line on the Turkish state. The organization played a key role in the Swedish elections of 17 September 2006 by drawing up a ballot paper of all the Kurdish candidates who were standing in the Swedish local, regional, and national elections. During the same election, WeKurd sent questionnaires to all the Swedish political parties, asking them for their views on the Kurdish question.

A further example of a Kurdish diasporic, transnational organization is the Swedish-Kurdish football team Dalkurd FF, started in 2004. At a well-attended Swedish-Kurdish gala held in Stockholm in 2009, the team was hailed as 'Kurd of the Year' for 'breaking records in the Swedish football league', since they had climbed from the sixth to the second division in only four years. These youth associations also include an anti-racist and integrationist discourse in their programmes, urging both Kurds and Swedes to work for integration.

In response to the brutal attacks of the terrorist group the Islamic State of Iraq and Syria (ISIS) on Kurdish towns and villages in 2014 and 2015, Swedish Kurds—as my field observations show—have mobilized extensively, both in political demonstrations held in several larger cities and in the creation of a number of initiatives to deliver humanitarian aid to the victims of ISIS attacks. Kurdish Diaspora and Kurdish Doctor Companionship are among the transnational NGOs to be founded by Swedish Kurds.

Generally speaking, it is common for Kurdish transnational associations and networks to operate simultaneously in two different but related loci. They follow events in different parts of Kurdistan and endeavour to reach a level of political mobilization that enables them to promote the so-called 'politics of homeland', whether by celebrating Newroz and other Kurdish cultural events, promoting Kurdish publishing and broadcasting, organizing political demonstrations, creating mixed (Swedish–Kurdish) political and social networks, carrying out diplomatic visits, or attracting the attention of the national and local media. At the same time, they claim to participate in the political and social processes of the host country, a claim that they invariably legitimate by maintaining an anti-racist and integrationist discourse and working for the good of the Kurdish people in Sweden. This 'dual agenda' (Østergaard-Nielsen 2000) is a manifestation of the far-reaching transborder performances that the Kurdish population undertake in Sweden. Many diasporan Kurds consider the practice of 'long distance nationalism' (Anderson 1998) and participation in the receiving country's political and social processes as necessary if they are to instil a sense of togetherness and diasporic identity.

On-air and online activities

Today, the Kurds have access to a large number of radio and television stations, whose existence, according to the Canadian-Kurdish scholar Amir Hassanpoor (1998), is a reaction to censorship in the states where Kurds are subjected to discrimination. Sweden is currently home to three Kurdish television stations (Asosat, Komalah TV, and Newroz TV) and a number of production offices for other Kurdish television stations that broadcast a variety of different programmes to the diaspora and Kurdistan. Together with Kurdish websites and internet forums, they serve as cross-border instruments of identity-making and nation-formation (van Bruinessen 2000, 12; see also Khayati & Dahlstedt 2014).

Online and on-air activities among diasporan populations, as correctly evoked by the collective term 'diasporic media' (Karim 2003), commonly answer for the media production and consumption of transnational communities. These transnational communities make use of the internet, television, and radio in the (re)construction of their identities. Due to its extensive and expansive reach, electronic media such as radio, television, and the internet are more compatible with diaspora needs, as they are unaffected by large diasporic spaces or shifts between various 'topics of interest, languages, and locations of broadcasting and narrowcasting' (Georgiou 2005, 11). Consequently, the diasporic media are plainly useful in helping diasporic groups rediscover their affinity with localities and communities that transcend their physical and geographical limitations (ibid. 12). A significant feature of globalization, the diasporic media hinges on the transfer of media programmes designed in a number of transnational spaces. Depending on the strategy adopted by each group, media activities among diasporan populations can appear as 'fragmented', 'resistive', or 'constitutive' (see Karim 2003; Georgiou 2005).

However, diasporan Kurds' linguistic and cultural activities, sustained to a great extent by the Kurdish media's activities, are thought a compensatory alternative to the literary and cultural deprivation caused by the policies of denial and majority censorship, inflicted on the Kurds in their countries of origin. Thus, the Kurdish cultural revival in Sweden follows the same dialectical pattern of exclusion–inclusion in the world of broadcasting seen in the exercise of linguistic, political, and cultural power in Turkey, Iran, Syria, and Iraq prior to the establishment of the autonomous Kurdish administration in 1992 (Hassanpour 1998).

Influential elites

Besides its well-established organizations, the Kurdish diaspora in Sweden is also shaped by a Kurdish elite who are the embodiment of successful transborder citizens. People who in their everyday lives depend on unbroken, multiple interconnections across various national borders, their identities as public figures are configured in relation to more than one nation-state. But it should not be thought that they are sojourners in their new countries. They are settled and integrated in the economy and political institutions, localities, and patterns of daily life where they live, while all the while they maintain connections, build institutions, carry out transactions, and influence local and national events in the countries from which they have emigrated (see Glick Schiller et al. 1995).

Swedish cultural and political life has welcomed a large number of Kurdish celebrities, who regularly figure nationally. For instance, the broadsheet *Dagens Nyheter* (Forsström & Runarsdotter 2006) carried a long feature on the number of Kurdish celebrities of the stage and screen, politics, and the press. Under the front-page headline 'Kurd in the City', the reporters Anders Forsström and Sofia Runarsdotter (2006) went through a long list of Kurdish personalities, while asking why so many Kurds were in the limelight. According to Forsström and Runarsdotter their Kurdish background, their memories of oppression, played a considerable role in the 'successes they achieved in Sweden', and he repeatedly used the appellation Swedish Kurd (*svenskkurd*), presumably to express their dual identity or 'translocational positionality', as Floya Anthias has it (2002). It is worth noting that the vast majority of the Swedish Kurds named in the article had arrived in Sweden at a very young age, together with their asylum- or job-seeking parents.

As for the presence of diasporan Kurds in Swedish political life, in the 2006 Swedish elections, about 33 Kurdish candidates stood for Parliament, as many for the county councils, and more than 70 for the municipal councils. In the Swedish general election of 2014, six MPs with Kurdish backgrounds were elected to Parliament.

Conclusion

Diasporic and transnational performances among Kurds in Sweden show that migration movements 'are not like one-way streets' (Pries 2006), starting from countries of origin and ending in countries of settlement. This has never been more true than in our present era of globalization, where the changing dynamics of migration and global communications, and the declining hegemony of the nation-state, have led to the growth of an increasing variety of transnational identities and practices (Pries 2006; Faist 2000). Equally, diasporas and diaspora communities, with their dual orientation towards countries of origin and residence, encompass a range of transnational organizations and networks of influential individuals, which to a certain extent appear as alternative spaces of integration—alternative to the (inadequate) national integration project, that is. The Kurdish case shows that these transnational networks and institutions enable diaspora populations to counteract the negative consequences of discrimination and disintegration where they live. At the same time, the commitment of diaspora Kurds in Sweden to their Kurdish homelands highlights the functioning of transnational social movements and the expansion of NGOs and networks aimed to strengthen democracy and nation-building in Kurdish life.

The case of the Swedish Kurds also illustrates a specific case of juxtaposition, where the particularity of the Swedish political context and the dynamic social composition of the Kurdish population not only enable the Kurds to develop a strong sense of diasporic identity and diasporic belongingness, but also to maintain what Eva Østergaard-Nielsen (2000) calls the 'dual political agenda' and what Glick Schiller (2005) describes as 'transborder citizenship'. Of course, the latter refers to people participating in the institutional systems and political practices of various states, and developing relationships with more than one government. Here, the diasporic and transnational performances by Kurds in Sweden show that there is a multidimensional transnational social field with a broad repertoire of ethnic and cultural associations, social and professional institutions, online and on-air arrangements, and networks of influential people in various political and cultural fields, not only connecting Sweden and Kurdistan, but crossing the boundaries of several nation-states.

References

Ahmadzadeh, H. (2003) *Nation and novel: A study of Persian and Kurdish narrative discourse* (Ph.D. diss., Uppsala: Acta Universitatis Upsaliensis).

Ålund, A. & C.-U. Schierup (1991) *Paradoxes of multiculturalism: Essays on Swedish society* (Aldershot: Avebury).

Anderson, B. (1998) *The spectre of comparisons: Nationalism, Southeast Asia and the world* (London: Verso).

Anthias, F. (2002) 'Where do I belong? Narrating collective identity and translocational positionality', *Ethnicities*, 2/4, 491–514.

Bauböck, R. (1994) *Transnational citizenship* (Aldershot: Edward Elgar). F

Berruti, D., E. Doru, E. Erle, F. Gianfelici & K. Khayati (2002) *Kurds in Europe: From asylum right to social rights* (Naples: Marsico).

van Bruinessen, M. (1999) 'Migrations, mobilizations, communications and the globalization of the Kurdish question' (Working Paper, 14; Islamic Area Studies Project, Tokyo).

—— (2000) 'Transnational aspects of the Kurdish question' (Working paper, Robert Schuman Centre for Advanced Studies, European University Institute, Florence).

Carter, D. (2005) 'Living in virtual communities: An ethnography of human relationships in cyberspace', *Information, Communication & Society*, 8/2, 148–67.

Chakravartty, P. (2001) 'Flexible citizens and the internet: The global politics of local high-tech development in India', *Emergences: Journal for the Study of Media & Composite Cultures*, 11/1, 69–88.

Faist, T. (2000) 'Transnationalization in international migration: Implications for the study of citizenship and culture', *Ethnic & Racial Studies*, 23, 189–222.

Forsström, A. & S. Runarsdotter (2006) 'In town: The Kurds in town', *Dagens Nyheter*, 27 April.

Georgiou, M. (2005) 'Diasporic media across Europe: Multicultural societies and the universalism–particularism continuum', *Journal of Ethnic & Migration Studies*, 31/3, 481–98.

Glick Schiller, N., L. Basch & C. Szanton Blanc (1995) 'From immigrant to transmigrant: theorizing transnational migration', *Anthropological Quarterly*, 68/1, 48–63.

—— & G. E. Fouron (2001) *George woke up laughing: Long distance nationalism and the search for home* (Durham, NC: Duke University Press).

—— (2005) 'Transborder citizenship: an outcome of legal pluralism within transnational social fields', (Department of Sociology, UCLA, Paper 25) <http://www.sscnet.ucla.edu/soc/soc237/papers/ninatransborder.pdf>, accessed 12 March 2014.

Hassanpour, A. (1998) 'Satellite footprints as national borders: Med-TV and the extraterritoriality of state sovereignty', *Journal of Muslim Minority Affairs*, 18/1, 53–72.

Hjertén, S. (1994) *Kurds* (Stockholm: Rubicon).

Johansson, C. (2005) *Welcome to Sweden?: Discourses of the Swedish migration politics during the second half of the 20th century* (Malmö: Bokbox).

Karim, H. K. (2003) 'Mapping diasporic mediascapes', in H. K. Karim (ed.) *The media of diaspora* (London: Routledge).

—— & M. Dahlstedt (2014) 'Diaspora formation among Kurds in Sweden: Social transformations in Scandinavian cities transborder citizenship and politics of belonging', *Nordic Journal of Migration Research*, 4/2, 57–64.

—— —— (2015) 'Diaspora: Relationships and community across borders', in

Magnus Dahlstedt & Anders Neergaard (eds.) *International migration and ethnic relations: Critical perspectives* (London: Routledge).
Khayati, K. (2008) *From victim diaspora to transborder citizenship? Diaspora formation and transnational relations among Kurds in France and Sweden* (Linköping: Department of Social and Welfare Studies, Linköping University).
—— (2011) 'Diaspora and transborder citizenship', in P. Bevelander, C. Fernandéz & A. Hellström (eds.) *Vägar till medborgarskap* (Lund: Arkiv).
—— & M. Dahlstedt (2014) 'Diaspora formation among Kurds in Sweden: Transborder citizenship and politics of belonging', *Nordic Journal of Migration Research*, 4/2, 57–64.
—— —— (2015) 'Diaspora: Relationships and community across borders', in Magnus Dahlstedt & Anders Neergaard (eds.) *International Migration and Ethnic Relations: Critical Perspectives* (London: Routledge).
Kymlicka, W. (1998) 'Multicultural citizenship', in G. Shafir (ed.) *The citizenship debates: A reader* (Minneapolis: University of Minnesota Press).
Laguerre, M. S. (1998) *Diasporic citizenship: Haitian Americans in transnational America* (New York: St Martin's Press).
Ong, A. (1999) *Flexible citizenship: The cultural logics of transnationality* (Durham: Duke University Press).
Østergaard-Nielsen, E. (2000) 'Trans-state loyalties and politics of Turks and Kurds in Western Europe', *SAIS Review*, 20/1, 23–38.
Pries, L. (1999) (ed.) *Migration and transnational social spaces* (Aldershot: Ashgate).
—— (2006) 'Transnational migration: New challenges for nation-states and new opportunities for regional and global development, <http://pdc.ceu.hu/archive/00004803/01/rap_i_an_0106a. pdf>, accessed 13 March 2014.
Södergran, L. (2000) *Svensk invandrar- och integrationspolitik: En fråga om jämlikhet, demokrati och mänskliga rättigheter* (Umeå: Department of Sociology, Umeå University).
Vali, A. (2003) 'Genealogies of the Kurds: Constructions of nation and national identity in Kurdish historical writing', in A. Vali (ed.) *Essays on the origins of Kurdish nationalism* (Costa Mesa: Mazda Publishers).
Vertovec, S. (2001) 'Transnationalism and identity', *Journal of Ethnic & Migration Studies*, 27/4, 573–82.
Werbner, P. (2002) 'The place which is diaspora: Citizenship, religion and gender in the making of chaordic transnationalism', *Journal of Ethnic & Migration Studies*, 28/1, 119–33.

Urban marginalization in Scandinavian cities
Conclusions and ways forward

Magnus Johansson, Tapio Salonen & Erica Righard

In this volume we have scrutinized urban marginalization and social sustainability from a Scandinavian perspective. With a detailed investigation of urban development in Denmark, Sweden, and Norway, we have sought to capture the characteristics of urban marginalization. For that reason, it is a worthwhile exercise to distinguish the similarities and differences of Scandinavia's urban transformation compared to Europe and the US. In our introduction we suggested that urban marginality must be understood in its societal context. The role of the state and its policies, not least its social policies, must be considered in the process. Mustafa Dikeç (2007) argues that urban transformations in France can only be understood in relation to the republic, and in the same way, we must view this process against the background of the Scandinavian welfare regimes. The crucial change has been seen in the national welfare systems, which, once based on a universal view, have now taken an increasingly particularistic line on who should benefit, and from which part of the system (for example, Morel et al. 2012; Hort 2014a, 2014b). The slow but consistent withdrawal of universal welfare is both a consequence and a cause of urban marginalization and segregation.

New forms of urban transformation

Wacquant (2008) claims that contemporary urban change is driven by four structural logics: increasing inequality, which follows on the heels of the increasing gap between high-paid and low-paid jobs; the retreat of the welfare state, and the growth of the gap between those who benefit from globalization and those who do not. Further, the spatial dynamics of the city result in geographies of inequality, as some parts of the city become territorially stigmatized. In European countries such as France and the UK, stigmatized areas have been transformed into new forms of urban space—witness the suburban areas surrounding Paris (Dikeç 2007) or the 'hyper ghettos' that Wacquant (2008) identifies in Europe and the US, which amount to new forms of urban space, floating as it were in a different universe, cut off from established societal structures. The hyper ghetto could be a symbol of the rise of postmodern society, where it again matters who your parents are and where they live.

In an American context, the discussion about inequality often conflates related but distinct issues: equality of income and wealth, and equality of opportunity and social mobility. These two forms of equality are linked, since the distribution of income in one generation to some extent affects the opportunities open to the next. Today, class matters in new ways, and people born poor seem to stay poor. The most import factor is the failure of the educational system. The segregation of American schools follows much the same pattern as economic segregation, and literally traps people with the 'wrong' parents in poverty (Putnam 2015).

The Scandinavian countries, thus far, have been characterized by equality of income and wealth, and high equality of opportunity and social mobility. There are several reasons for this, the most important being the best known: tax-funded, universal welfare. Yet, the same development Putnam describes in America, with increasing segregation in the education system, both economic and ethnic, can also be seen in Scandinavia. Putnam recalls the neighbourhood where he grew up, where wealthy and not-so-wealthy families lived along the same street, and people from different socio-economic backgrounds mingled with one another and went to the same schools. Today, a combination of migration, unemployment, and changes in the housing markets have co-produced urban marginalization, which mirrors the increasing economic dislocation. In the last two decades, social differentiation between neighbourhoods in Scandinavian cities such as Malmö has mirrored the broader social changes in the region as a whole. Residential segregation can be seen as the spatial manifestation of growing income inequality. Political reforms—the freedom to choose schools in Sweden (Bunar & Sernhede 2013), for example—increase the difference between different parts of the city. Instead of Putnam's mixed neighbourhoods, we now have divided cities, and the rifts are spatial and economic.

However, we must not be blinded by nostalgia—always a danger in political debate. Putnam agrees that his 1950s city was not a paradise, as it was racked by ethnic and gender inequality. Spatial dynamics in Scandinavian cities that today have resulted in geographies of inequality can often be traced back to processes which started long before globalization became an issue. The fourth structural logic pinpointed by Wacquant often adduces the historically well-established patterns in the segregation of cities. In Oslo, for example, the contemporary division between the affluent west and the disadvantaged east of the city has historical roots going back at least four centuries. The differences are still being nurtured, these days in media discourses and property developers' strategies, and reproduced by its inhabitants in their everyday practices. The same patterns can be seen in other Scandinavians cites, such as Malmö or Copenhagen. Frequently, the areas that have acquired the 'ghetto' label were originally part of some ambitious scheme by the welfare state to provide citizens with affordable housing, now overtaken by the wholesale transformation of the labour market and new migration patterns as the blue-collar workers who once lived there were replaced by groups of immigrants. Here, the small scale of Scandinavian cities adds to the spatial stigmatization of some urban areas, because they become places filled with 'others', standing out next to the wealthier areas. They are, of course, not 'hyper ghettos' in Wacquant's sense (2008); rather, in the Scandinavian discourse, they have become rhetorical symbols for social problems and segregation, occupied by 'others'.

Urban transformations in Scandinavia

Several of the examples of urban marginalization described in this volume are also stories about contemporary Scandinavia's abrupt reversals, by turns including and excluding 'others' who were not born and bred there. Those others are sometimes described as a faceless crowd, like the beggars in the street, who disturb the Scandinavian self-understanding as a clean and wealthy part of the world. Sometimes they are invisible, like the asylum seekers and irregular migrants working in the grey economy in Scandinavian cities such as Gothenburg. This informal labour market has become essential to the parts of the urban economy in Scandinavian cities that are dependent on low-paid work. Other times, the others appear as single individuals, who need to be remade before they can become part of Scandinavian society. One example of this is the politics of activation, where the others must be activated in order to become a full citizen. The idea of active citizenship harks back to the hardening tone when talking about the causes of inequality of opportunity and social mobility, when urban marginalization went from being a structural to an individual problem. That and the lack of opportunities would fuel frustrations and tensions between different groups in the cities.

When increasingly large groups of immigrants are forced to work under the threat of deportation, all the bold talk of 'employability' and 'active citizenship' takes on an unintentionally coercive twist. For informal workers, 'deportability' is what it is all about. To be 'deportable' means losing one's access to the rights and services enjoyed by other people living in the same space. Another example of spatial inequality with the same coercive twist is the slew of stories about undocumented young men who arrived in Sweden as unaccompanied minors. Lacking official documents, they became citizens without citizenship, locking them out from basic welfare systems, such as healthcare. Their situation begs the question of whose needs are being recognized here, and when. The undocumented youths and beggars are two examples of new groups of citizens who have clear and pressing needs, but are not included in national welfare systems. On a more positive note, their existence has also spurred into action the networks of activists who help undocumented young people to gain access to healthcare. From their resistance, a very different set of stories about Scandinavia's 'others' has evolved, which ultimately become alternative narratives.

A further example of tension between local and national narratives about 'the other' is the example of how public discourses of 'ghettoization' and 'parallel lives' in Denmark contrast with the narratives and practices of those who actually live in mixed neighbourhoods in Copenhagen. Citizens' everyday experiences do not fit the national narratives about 'problematic' and 'dangerous' parts of the city. This is an important difference between urban marginality in Scandinavian cities and in, say, France or America. It is still not uncommon for Scandinavian cities to have mixed neighbourhoods, which again opens the way for alternative narratives, based on the actual experiences of those living there, and is only possible in a Scandinavian setting because cities such as Copenhagen can set their own policies, which are more inclusive and less detrimental to ethnic and religious pluralism in the city. This is a prime example of how cities can pursue alternatives to national policies, in something amounting to a new form of urban governance.

Yet those same new forms of urban governance can also increase urban marginalization. Witness the dislocation between the concept of social sustainability in Swedish urban governance and Malmö's actual urban strategy. In Malmö, 'the whole city' seems to drift perilously close to being 'the city as whole', a shift that invokes one future for the city as the unifying notion of a single entity. This is not a process unique to Scandinavian cities. The global idea of sustainable urban development often seems to lose its critical momentum as soon as it is put into practice. In Scandinavia, there are all too many examples of 'sustainable urban development' going hand in hand with increasing inequalities in income, wealth, opportunity, and social mobility, which is arguably the consequence of the rifts between social and economic sustainability (Kreuger & Gibbs 2007). If diverging representations of the city and conflicting policy goals are neglected, the strategic framing of social sustainability risks reproducing the status quo, fuelling the further marginalization of targeted populations.

Transborder citizenship and global welfare systems

When Robert Putnam looks for solutions to the increasing inequality in opportunities and social mobility, he suggests investment in poor neighbourhoods; affordable housing and, of course, large-scale investment in the education system. Ironically, this is similar to what countries such as Sweden did when they established the Scandinavian welfare regimes. One question for further inquiry is whether the Scandinavian countries need to look abroad for new solutions to old problems. One way forward might be to view urban sustainability as a matter of striking a balance between security, development, and justice. But in order to pursue this idea, cities must also take greater responsibility for welfare and equality, and for creating equality of opportunity and social mobility, and that will call for new forms of urban governance, as cities increasingly become nodes in global networks. Today's city leaders form global alliances which may well have a growing political impact at a global level. One example is the global network of cities that agreed to reduce their carbon footprint in response to the failure of national governments to agree on a reduction of greenhouse gases. Perhaps we need similar global alliances to address social issues, which could be the first step in a welfare system that transcends the borders of the nation-state. It cannot be denied that today's marginalization can be traced back to yesterday's global changes. Does that call for new forms of global welfare systems, however utopian that may seem? Certainly, once upon a time, national welfare systems were also seen as utopian. The idea that urban marginalization must be understood in relation to its societal context leads us to the conclusion that urban marginalization can only be overcome if we step beyond the national context. One of the last essays in this volume concerns the dynamics of transborder citizenship among Swedish Kurds. Transborder citizenship refers to identities and practices of belonging that are simultaneously anchored in one's country of choice and one's country of origin; in this case, Sweden and Kurdistan. Let us conclude with this, with the opening offered by transborder welfare systems, utopian or not.

References

Bunar, N. & O. Sernhede (2013) *Skolan och ojämnlikhetens urbana geografi: Om skolan, staden och valfriheten* [School and the geography of inequality: On schools, cities, and freedom of choice] (Gothenburg: Daidalos).

Dikeç, M. (2007) *Badlands of the republic: Space, politics, and urban policy* (Oxford: Blackwell).

Hort, S. (2014a) *Social policy, welfare state and civil society in Sweden*, i: *History, policies and institutions, 1984–1998* (Lund: Arkiv).

—— (2014b) *Social policy, welfare state and civil society in Sweden*, ii: *The lost world of social democracy, 1998–2015* (Lund: Arkiv).

Kreuger, R. & D. Gibbs (2007) (eds.) *The sustainable development paradox: Urban political economy in the United states and Europe* (New York: Guilford Press).

Morel, N., B. Plaier & J. Plame (2012) (eds.) *Towards a social investment welfare state? Ideas, policies and challenges* (Bristol: Policy Press).

Putnam, R. (2015) *Our Kids: The American dream in crisis* (New York: Simon & Schuster).

Wacquant, L. (2008) *Urban outcasts: A comparative sociology of advanced marginality* (Cambridge: Polity Press).

Acknowledgements

This volume is the product of the research network Social Sustainability and Social Disintegration in Scandinavian Cities, which brings together researchers from various disciplines in Denmark, Norway, and Sweden. The network grew organically from a local workshop at Malmö University on the theme 'Local Footprints of Globalization' in May 2011, which in six months expanded to include researchers from Denmark, Norway, and elsewhere in Sweden, and has gone on to hold a substantial number of network meetings. We would like to thank all those who have contributed to the network for their continued dedication and participation in a fruitful intellectual exchange that transcends disciplinary and national boundaries. We would like to single out for acknowledgement Hans Abrahamsson (University of Gothenburg), who has been co-organiser of several of the workshops, and Mikael Klingberg and Anna Floren (Voksenåsen, Oslo), who initiated the first meeting.

We would like to extend our thanks to the Swedish Research Council for Health, Working Life and Welfare (Forskningsrådet för hälsa, arbetsliv och välfärd, FORTE) for funding the network funding for a three-year period (2012–2014) and to Riksbankens Jubileumsfond (RJ) for financing the first network meeting (December 2011). We would like to thank Ingrid Forfang for kindly giving us permission to use her painting *Something Rotten in Oslo* for the book jacket. And last but not least, we wish to thank our publisher Annika Olsson and all the team at Nordic Academic Press for their support and encouragement.

Erica Righard, Magnus Johansson & Tapio Salonen

About the authors

Hans Abrahamsson is Associate Professor of Peace and Development Studies at the School of Global Studies, University of Gothenburg, Sweden. His research interests include the global political economy and its implications for local social sustainability. At present he is co-leader of a transdisciplinary research project on fair and socially sustainable cities within the Mistra Urban Studies framework.

Bengt Andersen, Ph.D., is a social anthropologist and urban researcher at the Work Research Institute (AFI) at Oslo and Akershus University College of Applied Sciences, Norway. He is generally concerned with urban development, particularly the relationship between social relations and architecture or the built environment, along with segregation, urban mobility, urban planning, urban history, youth, area stigmas, marginality, and exclusion, as well as immigration and integration. Andersen has conducted ethnographic fieldwork in Oslo, Norway, and Gaithersburg, MD, USA.

Pieter Bevelander is Professor of International Migration and Ethnic Relations at MIM (the Malmö Institute for Studies of Migration, Diversity, and Welfare) and a senior lecturer at the Department of Global Political Studies, Malmö University, Sweden. His main research field is international migration and different aspects of immigrant integration, and the reactions of natives towards immigrants and minorities. His latest research publications include articles in the *European Journal of Population*, *Ethnic & Racial Studies*, and the *Journal of International Migration & Integration*.

Magnus Dahlstedt is Professor of Social Work at the Department of Social and Welfare Studies, Linköping University, Sweden. He has an academic background in political science and cultural studies. His primary research interests are citizenship, democracy, and the politics of inclusion and exclusion. Currently, he is investigating the formation of citizenship and the struggle to define citizenship, specifically in the context of the multi-ethnic city. Dahlstedt has published several books, including, with Andreas Fejes, *The confessing society: Foucault, confession and practices of lifelong learning* (Routledge 2013) and, co-edited with Anders Neergaard, *International Migration and Ethnic Relations: Critical Perspectives* (Routledge, 2015).

Jørgen Elm Larsen is Professor of Sociology at the Department of Sociology, University of Copenhagen, Denmark. He has especially published books and articles on the welfare state, social policy, marginalization, poverty, and social exclusion. He has led several externally funded research projects. Among his current fields of research are the politics of marginal space, housing biographies, and poverty and coping strategies.

Ada I. Engebrigtsen is an anthropologist and research professor at the Norwegian Institute for Social Research (NOVA)—Centre for Welfare and Labour Research (SVA) at the Oslo and Akershus University College of Applied Sciences, Norway. Her main research areas are migration (focused on adaptation processes), interethnic relations, and childhood studies. Romanian and Norwegian Roma, and Somali refugees in Norway have been central to her research. In recent years she has worked with poor Roma migrants in Norway and their encounters with the Norwegian public.

Randi Gressgård is Professor at the Centre for Women's and Gender Research (SKOK), and is affiliated with the International Migration and Ethnic Relations (IMER) research unit at University of Bergen, Norway. Her research interests include migration and minorities, gender and sexuality, and urban studies. Among her recent publications are *Multicultural Dialogue: Dilemmas, Paradoxes, Conflicts* (Berghahn, 2010/2012) and 'The power of (re)attachment in urban strategy: Interrogating the framing of social sustainability in Malmö' (*Environment & Planning A* 46, 2015).

ABOUT THE AUTHORS

Anne Harju has a Ph.D. in Social Work and is today a senior lecturer at the Faculty of Education and Society, Malmö University, Sweden. Her research is mainly oriented towards childhood sociology and the understanding of children's everyday lives. She has also conducted studies within the field of urban studies and studies in higher education.

Iver Hornemann Møller is Professor of Social Work at Linnæus University, Sweden. He has also held chairs in labour market studies in Portugal and Austria. His main research interests include social policy, labour market marginality, concepts of inclusion and exclusion, immigrants, and welfare states. He has led a number of international research projects and has been an advisor to several European governments.

Tina Gudrun Jensen, Ph.D., is a guest researcher at the Centre for Advanced Migration Studies at University of Copenhagen, Denmark. Her research interests include migration, cultural complexity, social integration, and urban spaces. She is currently working on interethnic relations and coexistence-comprising processes of inclusion and exclusion, tolerance, and discrimination.

Magnus Johansson is Assistant Professor of Environmental Studies at the Department of Urban Studies, Malmö University, Sweden. He has a Ph.D. in pedagogy from Lund University. His current research concerns professional urban planners and administrators learning to work with difficult issues such as sustainable urban development, and how universities can support professionals in their work with these issues. He has long experience of various forms of collaborative research with professional planners and urban managers on such issues as urban planning and community work.

Khalid Khayati is a political scientist and has a Ph.D. in Ethnicity. His research is centred on diasporas, transnational relations, and the notion of transborder citizenship, where the Kurdish populations in Western Europe, and especially those in France and Sweden, constitute the principal empirical focus. Khayati received a DEA (Diplôme d'études approfondies) in Political Science on the Arab and Islamic world at the Institut d'Études Politiques, Aix-en-Provence, France in 1998. Currently, he holds a lectureship in Tourism Studies at the Department for Studies of Social Change and Culture (ISAK), Linköping University, Sweden, while collaborating with the Institute for Research on Migration, Ethnicity and Society (REMESO) at the same university.

Anna Lundberg is Associate Professor in Human Rights at Malmö University, Sweden, specializing in global political studies, and a member of the Malmö Institute for Studies of Migration, Diversity and Welfare (MIM), both at Malmö University, Sweden. She has a Ph.D. in Ethnicity and a Master's in Public International Law. At present Anna is managing a four-year research project 'Undocumented children's rights claims: A multidisciplinary project on agency and contradictions between different levels of regulations and practice that reveals undocumented children's human rights' (http://blogg.mah.se/undocumentedmigrants), funded by the Swedish Research Council. In this project, as in her earlier research, Anna has an activist critical approach, working in close collaboration with practitioners and rights-holders.

Klara Öberg has a Ph.D. in Anthropology and Ethnology. She is affiliated to the Institut de recherche interdisciplinaire sur les enjeux sociaux (IRIS) at the École des hautes études en sciences sociales (EHESS) in Paris, and is currently a lecturer at the Department of Global Studies at University of Gothenburg, Sweden. Her research interests include migration, border politics, mobility, the transformation of the nation-state, the informal economy, labour and class formation, global systemic anthropology, and urban social and economic inequality.

Erica Righard, Ph.D., is the Willy Brandt Research Fellow at the Malmö Institute for Studies of Migration, Diversity and Welfare (MIM), and a senior lecturer at the Department of Social Work, both at Malmö University, Sweden. Her research is multidisciplinary and considers different aspects of social justice and international migration, and in particular how formal and informal social protection intersects with geographical mobility and cultural diversity.

Per Gunnar Røe is Professor and Head of the Department of Sociology and Human Geography at the University of Oslo, Norway. His current research interests are suburbanism, housing, culture and place, place-making and architecture, and the social implications of smart city strategies. Among his recent international publications are the anthology *Green Oslo: Visions, Planning and Discourse* (Ashgate, 2012), and 'Analysing place and place-making: Urbanization in Suburban Oslo' (*International Journal of Urban and Regional Research*, 2014). He has published extensively on suburbanism, place-making, and urban travel mobility, and has conducted several research projects funded by the Norwegian Research Council and other public bodies.

Tapio Salonen is Professor of Social Work at Malmö University, Sweden. His main research interests include poverty, marginality, participatory strategies, and social policy. He has led a number of externally funded research projects at both national and international levels, and has been frequently called on as an expert by public inquiries, official commissions, and government committees.

Oddrun Sæter trained as a sociologist and at present she is Professor and Research Director of the Urban Research Program at Oslo and Akershus University College of Applied Sciences, Norway. Over her long career she has published widely on place studies and place philosophy; art in public spaces; urban neighbourhood studies; urban development and urbanity; youth and the city; and gentrification studies. She has been a member of several committees, and is a member of research boards in Norway and other Nordic countries.

Emma Söderman is a doctoral student at the School of Social Work at Lund University and a member of the Malmö Institute for Studies of Migration, Diversity and Welfare (MIM) at Malmö University, Sweden. She holds a B.A. in Human Rights and a Master's in Global Political Studies. Since 2005, Söderman has been an active member of the local refugee rights group in Malmö. In her work she draws on her experiences as an activist, leading to her focus on the rights of refugee children in Sweden and Europe. Her Master's dissertation attracted attention as it considered the politically inflammatory issue of the treatment of unaccompanied refugee children under the Dublin II Regulation. Her publications include 'I am Dublin' in *Immigrants & Minorities* (2010).